STUDY GUIDE

ABEL/BERNANKE

MACROECONOMICS

STUDY GUIDE

ABEL/BERNANKE

MACROECONOMICS

Charles W. Johnston
University of Michigan-Flint

▲▼▼ **ADDISON-WESLEY PUBLISHING COMPANY**

Reading, Massachusetts • Menlo Park, California • New York
Don Mills, Ontario • Wokingham, England • Amsterdam • Bonn • Sydney • Singapore
Tokyo • Madrid • San Juan • Milan • Paris

Copyright © 1992 by Addison-Wesley Publishing Company, Inc.

All rights reserved. No part of this publication may be reproduced, stored in a retrieval system or transmitted, in any form or by any means, electronic, mechanical, photocopying, recording, or otherwise, without the prior written permission of the publisher. Printed in the United States of America.

ISBN 0-201-50429-4
1 2 3 4 5 6 7 8 9 10-BA-95949392

PREFACE

Abel and Bernanke clearly, concisely, and carefully present contemporary economic theories and research. They use these economic theories and research to describe, explain, analyze, predict, and evaluate macroeconomic events, including changes in government policies. The textbook uses a unified model to teach intermediate macroeconomics; within that model, it presents most of the contemporary beliefs of the major macroeconomic schools of thought. It is an exceptional textbook.

Each chapter of the *Study Guide* has four sections: a review of chapter highlights; 15-20 multiple choice questions; 5-10 short-answer essay questions, with each essay question having 3-5 parts; and answers to all questions. The Study Guide questions test your understanding of the economic theories, policies, events, analysis, and research presented in the textbook. By studying Abel and Bernanke's *Macroeconomics*, you will learn how to answer the Study Guide questions. When you can answer the Study Guide questions correctly, you will have a good understanding of the main points taught in the textbook. I suggest that you also study the end-of-chapter questions in the textbook. You will also need to study any additional information introduced by your instructor and to highlight the information within the text and Study Guide that your instructor has emphasized.

In the Study Guide, I have highlighted the economic theories, policies, events, analysis, and research that I think instructors are most likely to emphasize in lectures and exams. The Study Guide can help improve your understanding of the text and your exam grades. To increase your learning, the Study Guide questions cover the entire range of instructional questions. I ask you to identify, define, state, describe, explain, analyze, compare and contrast, show by using a graph or equation, discuss, and evaluate.

While using the Study Guide, remember that what you learn by answering one type of question (e.g., multiple choice questions) can be used to answer other types of questions (e.g., essay or problem-solving questions).

Although many questions are rather narrowly focused and specific, it is thought-provoking to step back and consider larger sets of questions simultaneously. Some questions are quite general, focusing on the "big picture." For example: What causes recessions? Are Americans saving too little? Are budget deficits bad for the economy? How can we increase the rate of economic growth?

Ask yourself, what are the principal, useful ideas that I can learn from these questions and answers? It can also be fun and educational to make up some questions yourself, try to answer them, and ask some of them in class.

One way to increase your interest in the course is to place yourself into the analysis by viewing yourself as the economic actor being discussed. Picture yourself as a worker and entrepreneur, consumer and saver, borrower and investor, importer and exporter, fiscal policy maker and monetary policymaker. You and people like you are the market participants discussed in the text. Your behavior and the behavior of people like you create the economic events analyzed, explained, and predicted by economists in the textbook. While your decisions and actions affect the performance of the macroeconomy, the performance of the macroeconomy affects your decisions and actions. The textbook and Study Guide can help you to become a better economic decision maker and to better understand and appreciate the economic decisions made by others.

Economics teaches us how to describe, explain, analyze, predict, and evaluate economic events. Economic events are also social events, political events, business events, historical events, and so on. In many fields of study, economics is used to describe, explain, analyze, predict, and evaluate events that affect how time, factors of production, goods and services, money and other financial assets are allocated to alternative uses to achieve the goals of households, firms, and governments, nationally and internationally. This suggests that learning economics will help you in many academic fields of study, and will help you in life in general.

I wish you the best in this class and in life. If you have any comments or suggestions concerning the Study Guide, I would be happy to hear from you.

ACKNOWLEDGMENTS

I especially wish to thank Andrew Abel and Ben Bernanke for their careful review of the complete Study Guide and for their helpful corrections and suggestions. I wish to thank the anonymous outside reviewers of the early chapters of the Study Guide, including reviewers from Cornell, North Carolina State University, and Claremont McKenna College. I wish to thank Addison-Wesley Publishing Company, especially Kari Heen and Barbara Rifkind, for their excellent guidance, assistance, and patience throughout the preparation of the Study Guide. I accept full responsibility for any errors or omissions.

Charles W. Johnston
Department of Economics
University of Michigan-Flint
Flint, MI   48502

Note: All tables mentioned in this Study Guide refer to those found in the parent text *Macroeconomics*.

STUDY GUIDE

ABEL/BERNANKE

MACROECONOMICS

CHAPTER 1

INTRODUCTION TO MACROECONOMICS

A Review of Chapter Highlights

Macroeconomics is the scientific study of the structure and performance of national markets and of government policies that affect market conditions. The principal issues of macroeconomics include: long-run economic growth, business cycles, unemployment, inflation, the international economy, and macroeconomic policies. Macroeconomists use economic theories within economic models to analyze the economic events and economic policies related to these issues.

    Average labor productivity, the output produced per unit of labor in the macroeconomy, is a principal determinant of the long-run economic growth rate. Deviations in the national output from the long-run economic growth path are called **business cycles**: A period of slower than normal growth, known as a contractionary period, is usually followed by a period of faster than normal growth, known as an expansionary period. During a business cycle contraction, the economy is in a **recession**; national output declines or grows very slowly. Recessions create **unemployment**, called cyclical unemployment, but some unemployment persists even during sustained periods of economic expansion.

    Inflation is an increase in the average price of goods. **Deflation** is a decrease in the average price of goods. Inflation may occur during either phase of the business cycle as well as when the economy is on its long-run economic growth path; the same is true for deflation.

    The international economy highlights the interdependence of national economies in global markets. National economies that participate in international markets are called **open economies**. National economies that do not participate in international markets are called **closed economies**. A nation that increases its participation in international markets is becoming more open.

    Government policymakers attempt to improve the performance of the macroeconomy by implementing fiscal policies and monetary policies. **Fiscal policies** attempt to improve economic conditions by changing government spending and taxes. **Monetary**

policies attempt to improve economic conditions by changing the money supply.

To analyze the collective behaviors of all people in a nation, macroeconomists add together the data for each particular kind of economic behavior for the entire economy. This **aggregation** provides data on macroeconomic variables, such as aggregate consumption, aggregate investment, and aggregate output.

Macroeconomic researchers employ the scientific method of research investigation to develop economic theories and economic models that attempt to explain and predict the performance of the national economy. An **economic theory** is a scientifically testable hypothesis or statement of belief about some cause-effect relationship among economic variables that is supported by the empirical evidence. An **economic model** is a set of economic theories that are combined to investigate one or more macroeconomic issues. Although economic theories and economic models are simplifications of reality (in that they identify only the principal determinants of economic events), it is the ability of these theories and models, confirmed by **empirical analysis**, to explain and predict repeatedly and accurately real economic events (i.e., their reliability and validity) that determines their widespread acceptance.

All economists agree on the need for the rigorous, scientific investigation of economic events. Economic analysis based solely on the scientific method of research is called **positive analysis**; it attempts to explain reality—to tell us "what is." Positive analysis has provided a high degree of agreement among economists on which theories best explain economic events, although it has not provided complete agreement. Positive analysis of macroeconomic policies is strictly scientific analysis of their expected effects. Scientific investigation predicts these effects will occur, regardless of whether we want these to be the effects.

Normative analysis of macroeconomic policies is not strictly scientific, even though it may partially rely on positive economic analysis, because the normative analyst imposes her personal value judgments about what is good for society to determine which policy "ought to" be adopted or to determine what effects a policy "ought to" have. Normative analysis may lead to disagreements among economists whenever their personal value judgments differ. There is significantly more agreement among economists on positive analysis of economic policy than for normative analysis; the media, nevertheless, tends to highlight the disagreements.

Questions

These questions test your understanding of the **key terms**, **key relationships**, and **key diagrams** highlighted in your text.

Multiple Choice Questions: Circle the letter corresponding to the correct answer to each question.

1.   Which of the following is not a principal issue of macroeconomics?

     a.   business cycles.
     b.   inflation.
     c.   fiscal policies.
     d.   competitiveness of firms in the steel industry.
     e.   the international economy.

2.   The most direct effect of an increase in the growth rate of average labor productivity would be:

     a.   an increase in the inflation rate.
     b.   an increase in the unemployment rate.
     c.   an increase in the long-run economic growth rate.
     d.   an increase in imported goods.
     e.   an increase in investment.

3.   Which of the following best describes a typical business cycle:

     a.   economic expansions are followed by economic contractions.
     b.   inflation is followed by unemployment.
     c.   trade surpluses are followed by trade deficits.
     d.   stagflation is followed by inflationary economic growth.
     e.   government budget deficits are followed by government surpluses.

4.   Recessions:

     a.   don't occur in developed countries, like the United States.
     b.   cause the unemployment rate to increase.
     c.   never last more than two consecutive quarters.
     d.   are always followed by long periods of high rates of real economic growth.
     e.   always cause the inflation rate to decline.

5.   Deflation and stagflation:

     a.   always occur at the same time.
     b.   often but not always occur at the same time.
     c.   cannot occur at the same time.
     d.   are both causes of economic growth.
     e.   are both intended effects of macroeconomic policies.

6.   A nation that exports and imports goods has:

    a.   significantly reduced its national security.
    b.   severe trade deficits.
    c.   an open economy.
    d.   high rates of unemployment.
    e.   high interest rates.

7.   Critics of the large government budget deficits of the 1980s contend that these deficits:

    a.   create recessions.
    b.   are disinflationary.
    c.   reduce interest rates.
    d.   reduce imports.
    e.   reduce investment spending.

8.   Which of the following fiscal policies do Keynesians recommend to help the economy recover from a recession?

    a.   an increase in government spending.
    b.   an increase in taxes.
    c.   an increase in the money supply.
    d.   an increase in saving.
    e.   an increase in government regulation.

9.   In the United States, monetary policy is directly controlled by:

    a.   the President of the United States.
    b.   the Federal Reserve.
    c.   foreign central banks.
    d.   the U.S. Congress.
    e.   both the President and the U.S. Congress.

10. Economic theories:

    a.   are always correct.
    b.   are generally supported by the empirical evidence.
    c.   identify the personal value judgments of economists.
    d.   are the only basis for designing economic policies.
    e.   are not used in macroeconomic forecasting.

11. The two most comprehensive, widely accepted macroeconomic economic models are:

    a.   the classical model and the supply-side model.
    b.   the supply-side model and the real business cycle model.
    c.   the classical model and the Keynesian model.
    d.   the real business cycle model and the Keynesian model.
    e.   the Keynesian model and the monetarist model.

12. Which of the following best describes empirical analysis?

   a. flipping a coin to decide which of two competing
       theories will be presented as the accepted economic
       dogma for this year.
   b. asking leading economic authorities their opinion on
       which economic theories they prefer.
   c. using advanced, standardized, scientific research
       techniques to determine whether a theory is consistent
       with the available data.
   d. using logical reasoning based on social norms to show
       that the relationship expressed in the hypothesis is
       morally superior to other theoretical relationships.
   e. conducting informal discussions with business leaders
       to determine which of the competing theories they would
       like to see popularized by academia.

13. The principal distinction between positive analysis and
     normative analysis is that:

   a. positive analysis is useful and normative analysis is
       not useful.
   b. positive analysis is optimistic and normative
       analysis is neutral.
   c. economists always agree on the conclusions of positive
       analysis but could disagree on the conclusions of
       normative analysis.
   d. positive analysis tells us "what is," but
       normative analysis tells us "what ought to be."
   e. positive analysis always supports economic theory,
       regardless of the empirical evidence; normative
       analysis supports economic theory only when it is
       consistent with the empirical evidence.

14. Real economic growth in the United States, over the
     1890-1990 period, has:

   a. increased at a stable, average rate of about 10%.
   b. increased the real value of GNP in 1990 to
       approximately 24 times as large as its value in 1890.
   c. been more unstable after World War II than in the
       1920-1945 period.
   d. increased at too low a rate to significantly improve
       the standard of living of the average American.
   e. far exceeded the growth rate of all other nations.

15. Average labor productivity growth in the United States:

   a. increased at a stable, average rate of about 10%
       over the 1900-1980 period.

      b.   increased at too low a rate to significantly improve the standard of living of the average American over the 1900-1990 period.

      c.   was higher in the 1950-1969 period than in the 1970-1990 period.

      d.   explains why the average real economic growth rate for the 1980s was unusually high for the United States.

      e.   is not an important determinant of long-run real economic growth.

16.   During the Great Depression, the unemployment rate for the United States peaked at approximately:

      a.   10%.
      b.   70%.
      c.   45%.
      d.   25%.
      e.   5%.

17.   The average price of goods in the United States:

      a.   was relatively constant over the 1800-1945 period.
      b.   was relatively constant over the decade of the 1980s.
      c.   declined over the decade of the 1970s.
      d.   is always constant in the long run.
      e.   always increases in any five-year period or longer.

18.   Data on exports and imports for the United States over the 1890-1990 period show that:

      a.   the U.S. has had large trade deficits throughout this entire period.

      b.   the U.S. has had large trade surpluses throughout this entire period.

      c.   the percentage of total output exported by U.S. firms increased dramatically during the first world war and the second world war.

      d.   a much higher percentage of U.S. goods were exported in 1990 than in any previous year of its history.

      e.   the value of exports normally equals the value of imports, so that the trade account normally balances each year.

19.   Since the Great Depression, the share of national income collected in taxes and spent by the federal government in the United States has:

      a.   increased from less than 10% to more than 20%.
      b.   remained relatively stable at 15%.
      c.   remained relatively stable at 35%.
      d.   declined from about 35% to less than 15%.
      e.   increased until 1945, then declined dramatically.

Short-Answer Essay Questions

1. **What macroeconomics is about**: Identify and briefly describe five major issues studied by macroeconomists.

2. **Business cycles and government intervention**: a) Define recession. b) Briefly state the effect, if any, of recessions on the unemployment rate. c) Are recessions always accompanied by deflation? Briefly explain. d) Identify and briefly describe two macroeconomic policies that might be used to help pull the macroeconomy out of a recession. e) In the absence of government intervention do classical or Keynesian economists believe a macroeconomy would recover from a recession? Briefly explain.

3. **What macroeconomists do**: Briefly describe the following tasks of macroeconomists: a) forecasting; b) analysis; c) research; d) data development. e) Briefly evaluate the following comment: "The only useful task macroeconomists perform is macroeconomic forecasting and they're not even very good at that."

4. **Classical and Keynesian debate**: Compare and contrast the classical and Keynesian schools of thought for the following economic issues: a) causes of long-run economic growth; b) wage-price flexibility; c) length of economic recessions; d) importance of macroeconomic policies. e) How does the "unified model" of the text deal with the debate among classical and Keynesian economists?

5. **Models that fit the data**: a) With its long-run focus on full employment, economic growth, and price level stability, was the classical model consistent with the macroeconomic data for the United States over the 1800–1928 period? Briefly explain. b) Did the classical economists accurately predict the Great Depression, convincingly explain it, and propose efficient policy solutions to overcome it? Briefly explain. c) With its short-run focus on cyclical unemployment and effective macroeconomic policy intervention, was the Keynesian model consistent with the macroeconomic data for the United States over the 1929–1970 period? Briefly explain. d) Did the Keynesian model accurately predict the occurrence of stagflation in the U.S. in the 1970s, convincingly explain it, and propose efficient policy solutions to overcome it? Briefly explain. e) Is it important that economic models fit the data? Briefly explain.

Answers to Multiple Choice Questions

| 1. | d | 8. | a | 15. | c |
| 2. | c | 9. | b | 16. | d |

3.	a	10.	b	17.	a
4.	b	11.	c	18.	c
5.	c	12.	c	19.	a
6.	c	13.	d		
7.	e	14.	b		

Answers to Short-Answer Essay Questions

1.   What macroeconomics is about

Macroeconomists study the causes and effects of the following macroeconomic events to explain and predict these events.

1) Long-run economic growth: increases in real GNP over extended periods of time. Real GNP is a measure of national output.

2) Business cycles: periods of economic contraction, when real GNP grows more slowly than its potential rate, are usually followed by periods of economic expansion, when real GNP grows faster than its potential rate.

3) Unemployment and inflation: unemployment is the inability of some people to find jobs, even though they are willing to work at market wages. Inflation is the rate of growth in the macroeconomic price level (i.e., the average price of goods).

4) The international economy: the values and patterns of international trade, international aid, direct foreign investment, and borrowing among nations.

5) Macroeconomic policy: includes both fiscal policies and monetary policies. Fiscal policies attempt to improve the performance of the macroeconomy by changing government spending and taxation. Monetary policies attempt to improve the performance of the macroeconomy by changing the money supply.

2.   Business cycles and government intervention

a) A recession is a contraction in the business cycle. The contraction phase of the business cycle is sometimes called the recession phase. A recession is characterized as a slowdown in the growth rate of aggregate output, which may become negative.

b)   The unemployment rate increases during recessions. For
     example, Figure 1.3 in the parent text shows that the
     unemployment rate increased during the 1973-1975 recession
     and during the 1981-1982 recession.

c)   No, recessions are not always accompanied by deflation.
     For example, Figure 1.4 in the parent text shows that the
     recent recessions of 1973-1975 and 1981-1982 were
     accompanied by inflation (i.e., increases in the CPI).

d)   The two macroeconomic policies that might be used to help
     pull the macroeconomy out of a recession are:

     1)   fiscal policy: increases in government spending or
          reductions in taxes.

     2)   monetary policy: increases in the money supply.

e)   Yes, both classical and Keynesian economists believe the
     economy will recover from a recession, in the absence of
     government intervention. However, classical economists
     believe the recovery will occur quickly, and Keynesians
     believe the recovery will occur slowly.

3.   **What macroeconomists do**

a)   Forecasting: Macroeconomists develop macroeconomic models
     to predict the future values of macroeconomic variables in
     one or more markets. These models are usually mathematical
     in form, use macroeconomic data, and are based on economic
     theory.

b)   Analysis: Macroeconomists analyze changes in macroeconomic
     policies as well as other changes in macroeconomic market
     conditions. This analysis is based on economic theory, uses
     analytic reasoning techniques, and may rely on forecasting
     models.

c)   Research: Macroeconomic research is the scientific testing
     of hypotheses to develop, improve, and test economic
     theories and economic models that employ these theories.

d)   Data development: Macroeconomic data development provides
     the data needed in macroeconomic research, analysis, and
     forecasting. Macroeconomic data is developed by adding
     together the local market data for the entire national
     economy for each specific variable, using standardized
     aggregation techniques. Governments and international
     development organizations provide economists with the
     majority of their data, although some large private research
     organizations, such as the National Bureau of Economic

Research and the Brookings Institute are important data developers.

e)   Evaluation of the statement: "The only useful task macroeconomists perform is forecasting and they're not even very good at that.

This is a statement by someone who has a narrow view of what macroeconomists do and is not impressed with the forecasting performance of economists. Macroeconomic forecasters are, themselves, somewhat discontented with their inability to forecast the future path of the macroeconomy accurately. Yet such high expectations set an unreasonable standard. Forecasting is a relatively new aspect of economics; since its early development in the 1950s, the predictive validity of macroeconomic forecasts has significantly improved. However, forecasting is only a small part of what macroeconomists do; macroeconomic data development, research, and analysis are their other principal, useful tasks. Only a small share of macroeconomists are forecasters. Economists like to employ a "market test" of the social value of any task. Given the high and increasing market demand by both the private sector and public sector for what economists do, it appears that the market highly values macroeconomists.

4.   Classical and Keynesian debate

a)   Causes of long-run economic growth: There is no substantial disagreement between classical economists and Keynesians over the principal causes of long-run economic growth. Both schools of macroeconomists would agree that increases in the supplies of the factors of production, such as labor and capital, as well as increases in their productivities, such as those provided by technological progress and human capital investments, increase the rate of long-run economic growth.

b)   Wage-price flexibility: is a principal point of disagreement between classical economists and Keynesians. Classical economists believe that wages and prices are perfectly flexible; in response to some change in market conditions, wages and prices adjust quickly to their new market-clearing levels. Keynesians believe that wages and prices are rigid or, at least, sticky in a downward direction; in response to deflationary pressures, wages and prices adjust slowly to their new market-clearing levels.

c)   Length of economic recessions: is another principal point of disagreement between classical economists and Keynesians. Because classical economists believe wage-price flexibility will return markets to their long-run equilibrium levels quickly, they believe that economic recessions do not occur or, at least, have very short durations (e.g., six months). Because Keynesians believe wages and prices are inflexible in a downward direction, they believe that economic recessions could continue for long durations (e.g., five years).

d)   Importance of macroeconomic policies: classical and Keynesians also disagree about the use of macroeconomic policies. Given wage-price flexibility, classical economists believe that the market economy normally provides for full employment. They believe that government intervention, in the form of macroeconomic fiscal and monetary policies, is not needed to prevent recessions and cyclical unemployment. Given slow adjustments in wages and prices, Keynesians believe that economic recessions and substantial cyclical unemployment could plague the economy for a several years. They believe that efficient use of macroeconomic policies could return the economy to the full-employment level of output more quickly.

e)   Debate within a unified model: Professors Abel and Bernanke provide a model that highlights both the agreement of classical economists and Keynesians on the macroeconomic issues for the long run and disagreement on these issues for the short run. The debate between classical economists and Keynesians on the length of economic recessions and the effectiveness of macroeconomic policies stems from their disagreement about whether wages and prices adjust quickly or slowly; the unified model enables us to analyze macroeconomic events, assuming rapid wage-price adjustment, then assuming slow wage-price adjustment.

5.   **Models that fit the data**

a)   Yes. From a long-run perspective, the U.S. economy, for the 1800-1929 period, provided for full employment, high rates of economic growth, and price-level stability.

b)   No. The classical model predicts full employment over the long run; its long-run focus prevents it from predicting short-run business cycle fluctuations in output and unemployment. The Great Depression was a short-run economic contraction, although longer and more severe than the classical economists could explain. Classical economists opposed macroeconomic policy intervention to help the economy recover because they believed that the macroeconomy would recover more efficiently on its own. Given an unemployment rate approaching 25% by 1933, policymakers wanted a policy solution that would help the economy to recover more quickly .

c)   Yes. The Keynesian model, with its focus on sustained economic recessions and its endorsement of macroeconomic policy intervention to speed recovery, was consistent with the data for the U.S. economy over the 1929–1970 period. Increases in government spending, as suggested by Keynes, appeared to help pull the economy out of the Great Depression of the 1930s. Given the government's use of macroeconomic policies thereafter—whenever recessions appeared—the macroeconomy became more stable and achieved acceptable economic growth until 1970.

d)   No. The Keynesian model highlights the importance of changes in the macroeconomic demand for goods (i.e., shifts in aggregate demand); it fails to highlight the importance of changes in the macroeconomic supply of goods (i.e., shifts in aggregate supply) largely because the classical economists had already done that. The stagflation of the 1970s, however, was initially caused by a decline in aggregate supply—a change in market conditions that was outside the focus of the Keynesian model. The Keynesians failed to explain the period of stagflation because they were looking for a demand-side explanation. They failed to offer an efficient policy solution to the problem of stagflation because they were using demand-side macroeconomic policies.

e)   Models that fit the data: The ultimate test of macroeconomic models is whether they can explain macroeconomic events, predict their occurrence, and offer policy solutions, if needed, to help reduce these problems. To achieve all this, the models must fit the data (i.e., be consistent with the data and be supported by the data). The classical model dominated economic thought until the Great Depression because it best fit the data. After the Great Depression, the Keynesian model dominated economic thought until around 1970, because it best fit the data. After 1970, economists recognized the need for a model that would highlight the importance of changes in both aggregate supply and aggregate demand. In each period, economists and market actors, relying on economic research, analysis, and forecasting, have demanded a model that fits the data.

CHAPTER 2

THE MEASUREMENT AND STRUCTURE OF THE NATIONAL ECONOMY

A Review of Chapter Highlights

During the first half of this century, economists gathered and organized macroeconomic data into **national income accounts**. These accounts include three approaches to measuring the value of national output—a product approach, an expenditure approach, and an income approach. The **product approach** adds together the market values of final goods and services produced at home and abroad by the domestic factors of production during a specified time period (e.g., a quarter or year). For the same time period, the **income approach** adds together the before-tax income paid to the domestic factors of production, including profits. The **expenditure approach** to calculating GNP adds together the domestic and foreign consumption, investment, government, and net export spending on final goods and services produced by domestic factors of production for that particular time period. All three approaches, once adjusted for statistical errors, provide the same calculated value of national output.

Gross national product (GNP) is the largest measure of national output in the national income accounts. Although the value of GNP excludes the value of nonmarketed outputs, it does include an estimated value for goods and services produced in the **underground economy**. To avoid double counting, GNP figures exclude the value of **intermediate goods and services**, because their value is already included in the value of **final goods and services** that they helped to produce. A **capital good** is a final good that is purchased by investors to be used as a factor of production in a later time period. Those products that are produced but not sold in the same time period are added to the inventory of the firms that produced them; the net addition to the **inventories** of all firms is the nation's inventory investment. **Gross domestic product** (GDP) measures the final market value of national output produced within a nation's borders, including the domestic output produced by foreign-owned factors of production.

Household spending on final goods and services, called **consumption**, makes up approximately two-thirds of all expenditures. Business **Investment** is the purchase of new fixed capital equipment and structures, residential structures, and inventories. **Government purchases** of final goods and services include the purchases made by all levels of government—federal, state, and local. Social security payments and welfare payments are examples of government **transfers**. Government transfers and interest payments are not added as government expenditures in the expenditure approach to calculating GNP, because they are already included in the private disposable income used to finance private sector expenditures. **Net exports** measures the difference between exports and imports; if foreign expenditures on the exports produced by domestic factors exceeds domestic expenditures on the imports produced by foreign factors, then the value of net exports is positive.

By subtracting **depreciation** (i.e., the value of capital consumed in production of final outputs) from GNP, we obtain the value of **net national product** (NNP). By subtracting the value of indirect business taxes, such as sales taxes and excise taxes, from NNP, we obtain the value of **national income** (NI). National income is the portion of GNP that can be distributed to the owners of the factors of production as compensation to employees, proprietors' income, rental income, net interest, and corporate profits.

For analytic purposes, the economy can be divided into four sectors—the household sector, the business sector, the government sector, and the foreign sector. The household and business sectors combined represent the **private sector** of the domestic economy; the government sector is sometimes called the public sector. **Private disposable income** is the income received by the private sector; this figure is larger than the figure for **personal disposable income**, because the latter excludes the portion of after-tax gross income of businesses that was not distributed to households during the time period for which data calculations were made.

The government receives its income in the form of tax revenue. **Government outlays** include government purchases, transfers, and interest payments. A **government budget surplus** exists when taxes exceed government outlays. A **government budget deficit** exists when taxes are less than government outlays.

All after-tax income received by the various market participants is either spent or saved. **Saving** is the income received but not spent in some time period. **Private saving** is the private disposable income that is not spent. **Personal saving** is the personal disposable income that is not spent. **Government saving** is tax revenue left over after paying for government outlays. **National saving** is the sum of private saving and government saving; this is the portion of national income that is available to finance investment plus net export expenditures.

Saving is a **flow variable** because it is measured per unit of time. Because saving finances the purchase of assets and the reduction of liabilities, saving creates **wealth**. **Wealth** is a **stock variable** because it is measured at a point in time. The **national wealth** of the United States is the total value of domestic physical assets and net foreign assets owned by U.S. residents. The total value of **net foreign assets** is positive if the value of foreign assets, both physical and financial, exceeds the value of foreign liabilities of domestic residents.

All macroeconomic variables have both nominal values and real values. Current market values are **nominal** values, and values calculated using the prices of some fixed base year are **real** values. Because nominal values do not distinguish between changes in physical quantities and changes in price, **nominal GNP** could increase at the same time that **real GNP** decreased, remained unchanged, or increased, given appropriate changes in the average level of product prices.

Calculation of the average level of product prices in some year relative to the price level in some base year provides a **price index** for these products. A **variable-weight price index** compares the average price of products in the current period with what they would have cost in the base year. One complexity, however, is that some of the goods and services may not have been produced in the base year. A **fixed-weight index** compares the current price level to the base-year price level of some fixed set of goods and services that were produced in the base year. One complexity, however, is that these products may no longer be produced in the current year. The **GNP deflator** is a variable-weight price index that is used to measure changes in the average price of all goods and services. Real GNP is derived by dividing nominal GNP by the GNP deflator. The **consumer price index** (CPI) is a fixed-weight index used to measure changes in the average price of a fixed basket of consumer goods and services. The rate of inflation in consumer products for some year is the percentage rate of increase in the CPI.

Market participants must also be able to calculate the real interest rate from the nominal interest rate. The **nominal interest rate** is the current market rate of return on lending and borrowing money. The **real interest rate** is calculated by subtracting the rate of inflation from the nominal interest rate. Most lending and borrowing decisions, however, are based on the **expected real interest rate**, because the rate of inflation is not known with certainty at the time most lending/borrowing decisions are made. To calculate the expected real interest rate from the nominal interest rate, analysts must use one of several techniques to estimate the expected rate of inflation.

Questions

These questions test your understanding of the **key terms**, **key relationships**, and **key diagrams** highlighted in your text.

Multiple Choice Questions: Circle the letter corresponding to the correct answer to each question.

1.   National income accounts:

    a.   can be understood only by accountants.
    b.   clearly identify who owes how much to whom.
    c.   provide macroeconomists with much of the data needed for macroeconomic analysis, research, and forecasting.
    d.   avoid the technical problems of aggregating data.
    e.   exist for only the most developed countries.

2.   The product approach to calculating GNP:

    a.   adds together the market values of final goods and services produced by domestic factors of production in some time period.
    b.   multiplies the values of inputs by the values of outputs to achieve a product value.
    c.   is superior to the income approach because, unlike the income approach, it gives us the real value.
    d.   adds together the market values of final goods, intermediate goods, and goods added to inventories.
    e.   includes the market value of goods and services produced by households for their own consumption but excludes the value of the underground economy.

3.   Gross national product:

    a.   is identical to gross domestic product in the United States and Canada.
    b.   will exceed gross domestic product if a substantial value of domestic factors of production are employed in foreign countries and only a small value of foreign-owned resources are employed in the domestic economy.
    c.   will always exceed gross domestic product for a closed economy.
    d.   will be higher in a private sector economy than in an economy where there is also a public sector that taxes the private sector.

4.   Unlike final goods and services, intermediate goods and services:

    a.   are purchased by businesses.
    b.   are purchased by government.
    c.   are not exported.
    d.   are completely used up in the current time period.
    e.   become part of inventory investment.

5.   Fixed business investments include purchases of:

    a.   capital equipment and structures.
    b.   land and energy.
    c.   long-term bonds.

d.   inventory investments.
e.   residential housing.

6.   Government purchases:

a.   are recorded as either consumption or investment in the national income accounts, since those are the only two types of goods produced.
b.   are larger than private sector purchases in the post-World War II U.S. economy.
c.   do not include purchases of foreign goods.
d.   are less than government outlays.
e.   are the value of goods and services bought by the federal government.

7.   Which of the following is not a government transfer?

a.   a transfer of money from the defense budget to the space exploration budget.
b.   Social Security payments.
c.   Medicaid.
d.   Medicare.
e.   unemployment insurance.

8.   The largest national income account that is affected by changes in both depreciation rates and sales tax rates is:

a.   private disposable income.
b.   personal income.
c.   NI.
d.   NNP.
e.   GNP.

9.   The principal actors in the private sector national economy are:

a.   domestic households.
b.   domestic households and businesses.
c.   domestic businesses.
d.   domestic businesses and government.
e.   domestic and foreign households.

10.   The principal reason that private disposable income is preferred to personal disposable income is that:

a.   private income includes both personal income and impersonal income.
b.   private income includes disposable and nondisposable income.
c.   private disposable income is an after-tax figure, whereas personal disposable income is a before-tax figure.

d.   the income earned by the private sector is ultimately owned and controlled by households, even if some of it is retained by businesses in the current time period.

e.   private disposable income is real income, whereas personal disposable income is nominal income.

11.   Which of the following equations describes a government budget deficit?

a. $T < (G + TR + INT)$.
b. $(T - G) > (TR + INT)$.
c. $T > G$.
d. $(T + TR + INT) > G$.
e. $(T - TR - INT) > G$.

12.   For a given level of private disposable income, an increase in private saving would:

a.   reduce exports.
b.   reduce the government budget deficit.
c.   reduce investment.
d.   reduce wealth.
e.   increase the private saving rate.

13.   Which of the following equals national saving (S)?

a. $(Y - T + TR + TR) - C$.
b. $Y - (C + G)$.
c. $T - (G + TR + INT)$.
d. $Y - (C + I + G + NX)$.
e. $Y - (I + NX)$.

14.   Wealth:

a.   is a flow variable, measured per unit of time.
b.   is a flow variable, measured at a point in time.
c.   is a stock variable, measured at a point in time.
d.   is a stock variable, measured per unit of time.
e.   and saving are flow variables.

15.   National wealth is the value of:

a.   domestic and foreign physical and financial assets.
b.   domestic physical and financial assets.
c.   domestic physical assets plus net foreign physical and financial assets.
d.   net foreign assets.
e.   domestic financial wealth.

16.   An increase in real GNP:

a.   requires that nominal GNP increase.
b.   could be achieved while nominal GNP declined.

    c.   is inflationary.
    d.   requires that nominal GNP decrease.
    e.   is always smaller than an increase in nominal GNP.

17.   The consumer price index is a:

    a.   fixed-weight index that measures the current price level of a base-year basket of consumer goods and services.
    b.   fixed-weight index that measures the current price level of a current basket of consumer goods and services.
    c.   a variable-weight index that measures the current price level of a current basket of consumer goods and services.
    d.   a variable-weight index that measures the current price level of a base-year basket of consumer goods and services.
    e.   a price index, but neither a fixed-weight nor variable-weight index.

18.   The nominal interest rate equals:

    a.   the real interest rate minus the expected rate of inflation.
    b.   the real interest rate minus the inflation rate.
    c.   the real interest rate plus the expected rate of inflation.
    d.   the expected real interest rate minus the inflation rate.
    e.   the expected real interest rate plus the expected rate of inflation.

Short-Answer Essay Questions

1.   **National output, income, and expenditure**: a) State the fundamental identity of national income accounting. b) How does an "identity" relationship differ from an "equality" relationship? c) Define GNP. d) Identify and briefly describe three approaches to measuring GNP. e) If you were given the value of GNP, how would you calculate the value of NNP, NI, and private disposable income?

2.   **Consumption**: a) Briefly define consumption. b) Give an example of each of the following: consumer durables, nondurable goods, and services. c) Approximately what share of GNP does personal consumption expenditures represent? d) Approximately what share of personal consumption expenditures do services represent? e) How are consumption and the private saving rate related?

3.   **Investment**:   a) What does investment have to do with capital goods? b) Give an example of each of the following types of business fixed investment: equipment and structures. c) Why is spending on new houses and apartments a part of fixed investment? d) Why are household purchases of human capital not a part of investment? e) Briefly describe the role that inventory investment plays in the income-expenditure identity.

4.   **Government output, purchases, and outlays**:   a) In the product approach to calculating GNP, how is the market value of government output determined? b) Do government outlays represent approximately 20% of GNP? Briefly explain. c) Are combined state and local government purchases small compared to federal government purchases? Briefly explain. d) How does the government obtain income to spend? e) How could the government achieve a budget surplus?

5.   **Net exports**:   a) What share of GNP is produced by foreigners? b) In calculating GNP by the income approach, what is the figure used for foreign income? c) Why are net exports added in to the expenditure calculation of GNP? d) When is a good that was produced in a foreign country and purchased by Americans not an import? e) If net exports represent only plus or minus 1% of a nation's GNP, is it fair to say that international trade is unimportant for that nation? Briefly explain.

6.   **Saving and wealth**:   a) Briefly state one way that each of the following could be increased: private saving, government saving, and national saving. b) State the "uses of saving identity." c) Use the "uses of saving identity" to show the effect of an increase in the government budget deficit on investment. d) Does saving create wealth? Briefly explain. e) Is the saving rate in the U.S. high compared to other major OECD countries, and did this saving rate increase in the 1980s?

7.   **Price indexes, inflation, and real variables**:   a) Identify three macroeconomic real variables that are calculated from nominal variables using price indexes. b) Briefly state the difference between a fixed-weight and variable-weight price index. c) If the CPI is 3.50 for the current year, how much inflation has there been since the base year? d) If the CPI increased to 3.75 over the next year, what would be the inflation rate for that year? e) Why do lenders add the expected rate of inflation into the interest rate they charge borrowers?

Answers to Multiple Choice Questions

1.	c	7.	a	13.	b
2.	a	8.	c	14.	c
3.	b	9.	b	15.	c
4.	d	10.	d	16.	b
5.	a	11.	a	17.	a
6.	d	12.	e	18.	e

Answers to Short-Answer Essay Questions

1. **National output, income, and expenditure**

a) The fundamental identity of national income accounting is:

    total product = total income = total expenditure

b) An equation that expresses an identity is always true by definition, regardless of the particular values of the variables. For an identity, any change in the total value of variables on the right-hand side of the equality will be accompanied by an equal change in the total value of the variables on the left-hand side. For an equation that expresses an equality that is not an identity, a change in the total value of variables on one side of the equality will create an inequality.

c) GNP = gross national product = the market value of final goods and services produced by domestic factors of production during a specified time period.

d) The three approaches to measuring GNP are called the product approach, income approach, and expenditure approach. The product approach adds together the market values of the goods and services produced by domestic factors of production during a specified time period (e.g., one-quarter of a year or one year). The income approach adds together the compensation to employees, interest income, rental income, proprietors' income, profits, and tax income earned by the owners of the domestic factors of production employed to produce the output. The expenditure approach adds together the consumption,investment, government, and net export spending on the goods and services produced by domestic factors of production.

e) Calculation of NNP, NI, and private disposable income from GNP:

    1) NNP = net national product = GNP - depreciation.

    2) NI = national income = NNP- indirect business taxes.

3)   Given that GNP = Y,

private disposable income = $Y - T + TR + INT$.

2.   Consumption

a)   Definition: Consumption is the domestic household purchases of domestic and foreign final goods and services during some specified time period.

b)   Examples:

1)   Consumer durables: long-lived consumer goods, such as family automobiles, refrigerators, lawn mowers, home computer, household furniture.

2)   Nondurable goods: short-lived consumer goods, such as household purchases of food, clothing, fuel, cosmetics, prescription drugs.

3)   Services: consumer products that cannot be dropped on your foot, such as education services, medical services, legal services, accounting services, travel agency services, restaurant and hotel services.

c)   Personal consumption expenditures currently represent approximately two-thirds of GNP for the United States.

d)   Services represented approximately 53% (i.e., 35/66 x 100) of personal consumption expenditures for the United States, per Table 2.1.

e)   Private saving = $S_{private}$ = $(Y - T + TR + INT) - C$ = private disposable income - consumption. For a given level of private disposable income, a reduction in consumption will increase the saving rate. Likewise, an increase in the private saving rate will reduce consumption for a given level of private disposable income.

3.   Investment

a)   There are two major types of investment: fixed investment and inventory investment. Fixed investment is the purchase of capital goods for business fixed investment in equipment and structures, and for residential investment. In brief, fixed investment is the purchase of capital goods.

b)   Examples:

1)   Business equipment: includes tools and machines, such as harvesters for farms, printing presses for newspaper businesses, tractors for construction companies, cash

registers for retail stores, office equipment, furniture, company-owned vehicles, and so on.

2)   Business structures: include construction of plant facilities that house the businesses, such as factory buildings, warehouses, retail store buildings, and so on.

c)   Construction of residential houses and apartments are treated as investment in capital because they provide a service over such a long period.   The investment is done by the business that constructs the residential dwellings, rather than the individuals that buy them; business invest. A great deal of economic output is directly or indirectly dependent on the health of the residential construction industry.

d)   In brief, households do not invest; they consume.   Household spending, such as university tuition payments to acquire human skills and training, is consumption spending, even though such spending may increase the productivity of labor and promote technological progress.   Attempts to include part of these expenditures as investment spending would confront severe measurement problems.

e)   The income - expenditure identity states that: $Y = C + I + G + NX$.   This equation suggests that all the goods and services produced are sold.   If all the goods and services produced are not sold in the recorded time period, inventory investment increases by the amount of the unsold goods to satisfy the identity condition.   From an accounting viewpoint, the unsold goods are recorded as being sold to the firms that produced them.

4.   **Government output, purchases, and outlays**

a)   In national income accounting, the cost of producing government output is the recorded market value of that output.

b)   No.   Government purchases currently represent approximately 20% of GNP for the United States, but government outlays exceed purchases by the value of transfers and interest payments on government debt.

c)   No.   Combined state government and local government purchases exceed federal government purchases.   State and local government purchases represented 60% (i.e., 12/60 × 100) of total government purchases for 1989, per Table 2.1.

d)   The income of the government is its tax revenue.   If it spends more than its tax revenue, it must borrow the income needed to finance the budget deficit from the private sector and foreign sector. Taxes and borrowings finance government spending.

e) The government has a budget surplus when its tax revenue (T) exceed its outlays ($G + TR + INT$). Starting from a balanced budget, it could achieve a budget surplus by increasing taxes and reducing outlays.

5. Net exports

a) None. All of GNP is produced by domestic factors of production, including domestic labor.

b) Zero. In calculating GNP by the income approach, the foreign sector earns no income, because it does not contribute any resources to the production of domestic GNP. Foreigners earn only foreign income.

c) Net exports = exports - imports. Exports are added to the expenditure calculation of GNP because they represent foreign spending on the goods and services produced by domestic factors of production. Imports are subtracted because they were included in the figures for consumption, investment, and government purchases.

d) A good produced in a foreign country exclusively by American-owned factors of production is not an import to America when purchased by Americans. Owners of domestic factors of production do not import the goods they produce, even if they exclusively produce them in foreign countries. U.S. imports are produced by foreign-owned factors of production.

e) No. Table 2.1 shows, for example, that net exports for the U.S. in 1989 represented only 1% of GNP, but 12% of U.S. outputs were exported and 13% of foreign outputs were imported. Even if 50% were exported and 51% were imported, the net figure would still be 1%. Even 1% of a $5 trillion dollar economy is $50 billion dollars. Even if only 5% of U.S. goods were traded, a small reduction in that trade could significantly affect the health of the U.S. economy, if critical imports suddenly became unavailable to U.S. businesses (e.g., certain capital goods).

6. Saving and wealth

a) How to increase saving:

    1) Private saving: could be increased by increasing private disposable income for a given saving rate or by reducing consumption for a given level of private disposable income.

2)   Government saving: could be increased by increasing taxes for a given amount of government outlays or by reducing outlays for a given level of taxes.

3)   National saving: could be increased by increasing private saving or government saving.

b)   The following equation is the "uses of saving identity:"

$$S_{private} = I + (G + TR + INT - T) + NX$$

c)   An increase in the government budget deficit is an increase in the value of $(G + TR + INT - T)$, which causes $(I + NX)$ to decline by the amount of the increase in the budget deficit, so that the total value on the right-hand side remains unchanged and equal to the given value of private saving, unless $S_{private}$ also increases.

d)   Yes. National saving finances increases in domestic physical assets (I) and increases in net foreign assets (NX); saving creates wealth in the sense of financing it. For example, saving could finance the purchase of business computers; this increase in capital would be an increase in wealth.

e)   The 1960–1988 data presented in Figure 2.4 in the parent text shows that the United States has a low national saving rate compared to the other major OCED countries, and that the U.S. saving rate declined during the 1980s.   Over the entire period, we observe a trend decline in the national saving rate for OECD countries.

7.   **Price indexes, inflation, and real variables**

a)   All macroeconomic variables have both real and nominal values. GNP, C, and I provide three examples of real variables calculated from data on their nominal values.

b)   Price indexes measure the current average price of goods and services compared to the average price in some base year. A fixed-weight index measures the prices of a fixed set of goods and services produced in the base year; a variable-weight index measures the prices of a current set of goods and services.

c)   If the CPI = 3.50, there has been 250% inflation since the base year. On average, goods that cost $1.00 in the base year now cost $3.50, which is $2.50 more than in the base year.

d)   If the CPI increased from 3.50 to 3.75 in the next year, the inflation rate for that year would be [(3.75 - 3.50)/3.50] = .07 = 7%.

e)   Inflation decreases the purchasing power of each dollar borrowed. Lenders have to charge an inflation premium equal to the inflation rate during the loan period to have the loan value returned by the borrower. However, lenders and borrowers may not know with certainty the inflation rate at the time the loan is made, so the loan is based on the expected rate of inflation. The nominal interest rate equals the expected real interest rate plus the expected rate of inflation.

CHAPTER 3

THE REAL ECONOMY: OUTPUT, EMPLOYMENT, AND INVESTMENT

A Review of Chapter Highlights

Economic models identify the cause-effect relationships
among economic variables. Models are tools used in economic
analysis to explain current macroeconomic events and to predict
future events.   This chapter highlights a labor market model of
employment and production, a goods market model, and a larger
FE line - *IS* curve model that contains both a labor market
and a goods market.

Economic models lend themselves to **supply and demand
analysis** of economic events. For a given supply curve and a
given demand curve, **equilibrium** in some markets is achieved at
the output or input level at which the curves intersect. A
change in supply or demand will shift the respective curves,
which will cause some or all of the equilibrium values of the
variables in the model to change.

Economists define the **long run** as a period of time in which
all markets (in the model) clear; in the long run, all markets
are in equilibrium. **Disequilibrium**, which means lack of
equilibrium, is the opposite of equilibrium. In the **short-run
adjustment period** between long-run equilibrium points in time, at
least one market is in disequilibrium. In this chapter, we
compare the long-run equilibrium values of macroeconomic
variables before some event occurs, with the long-run equilibrium
values after the event; this is sometimes called **comparative
statics analysis**. In this comparative statics analysis of a
market-clearing model of the macroeconomy, we assume that markets
normally operate in equilibrium, except for brief time periods in
which a change in some market condition causes the economy to
establish new equilibrium values. This chapter highlights the
classical model of **perfectly flexible wage-price adjustments**,
which is an example of a market-clearing model. Although the
Keynesian model of the macroeconomy has a short run,
disequilibrium focus, Keynesians do not disagree with the long-
run effects of events, as outlined in this chapter; this suggests

that the short-run Keynesian model is better viewed as a complement to the long-run models than as a substitute for them.

In the classical model of the **labor market**, **labor demand** and **labor supply** jointly determine the equilibrium level of **employment**. The labor demand curve is also the marginal product of labor curve. A productivity shock or a change in the capital stock will shift the labor demand curve. The labor supply curve identifies the number of units of labor supplied at each possible real wage. A change in labor's preference for work, relative to leisure, or a change in the size of the labor force will shift the labor supply curve. At the equilibrium real wage, the amount of labor supplied equals the amount of labor demanded. At the equilibrium real wage, there is no **unemployment**, since all those who are willing to work are also able to work.

Given full employment, the **production function** determines the equilibrium level of **output**, called **full-employment output**. The production function specifies how changes in the **factors of production** create changes in the level of output. Per the **law of diminishing marginal returns**, adding labor to a given amount of capital (or adding capital to a given amount of labor) causes output to increase at a declining rate. This is important because firms always operate in the diminishing returns region of their respective production functions. The production functions let us calculate the **marginal product of labor** and the **marginal product of capital** at various levels of employment. The marginal product of labor is the increase in output produced by adding one unit of labor (e.g., one worker) to production, holding capital constant. The marginal product of capital is the increase in output produced by adding one unit of capital to production, holding labor constant.

An **adverse productivity shock** will shift the production function down to a lower level of output at each possible level of employment and capital stock. A **beneficial productivity shock** will shift the production function up to a higher level of output at each possible level of employment and capital stock.

For a given level of output, **desired saving** and **desired investment** curves jointly determine the equilibrium levels of consumption spending, government spending, and **investment spending** in the **goods market**. In equilibrium, the goods that are not purchased by consumers or by government are purchased by investors; all the goods produced are sold.

A change in desired saving at each possible real interest rate will shift the desired saving curve. Shift variables for the desired saving curve include output, expected future output, and government purchases. A change in the desired level of investment at each possible real interest rate will shift the desired investment curve. Shift variables for the desired investment curve include the expected future marginal product of capital and corporate taxes.

Questions

These questions test your understanding of the **key terms**, **key relationships**, and **key diagrams** highlighted in your text.

Multiple Choice Questions: Circle the letter corresponding to the correct answer to each question.

1. If a market is in equilibrium:

    a. prices will adjust quickly to disequilibrium levels.
    b. quantities will adjust quickly to disequilibrium levels.
    c. prices will rise in the long run.
    d. prices will fall in the long run.
    e. the quantity that buyers demand equals the quantity that sellers supply.

2. The factors of production include:

    a. capital, labor, energy, and materials.
    b. households, firms, and government.
    c. supply factors and demand factors.
    d. wages, interest, rents, and profits.
    e. human capital, real capital, and financial capital.

3. The production function shows the effect on:

    a. labor employment when output is increased.
    b. labor employment when capital is increased.
    c. goods production when production of services declines.
    d. consumer goods when production of intermediate goods is increased.
    e. output when labor is increased.

4. An increase in the productivity of capital will always:

    a. increase the unemployment rate.
    b. increase the full-employment level of output.
    c. lower the rate of return to capital.
    d. shift the production function down to the right.
    e. move us up along a given production function to a lower level of output.

5. The law of diminishing marginal returns explains why:

    a. the labor supply curve is not vertical.
    b. nominal wages are sticky in a downward direction.
    c. the labor demand curve is negatively sloped.
    d. households save only a small share of their income.
    e. the average productivity of labor is always below the marginal productivity of labor.

6.   The marginal product of capital:

    a.   is the output produced by adding one more unit of
          capital to the production process, holding labor
          employment constant.
    b.   equals the output produced per unit of capital
          employed.
    c.   declines, then increases as more units of capital are
          employed.
    d.   increases, then declines as more units of labor are
          employed.
    e.   depends on the product price.

7.   The marginal product of labor:

    a.   exceeds the average product of labor at high levels of
          employment.
    b.   decreases as more capital is added to the production
          process.
    c.   depends on the product price.
    d.   beyond some level of employment, declines as more labor
          is added to the production process.
    e.   equals the output produced per unit of labor employed.

8.   Which of the following would not produce an adverse supply
      shock?

    a.   an increase in the personal income tax rate.
    b.   a decline in the productivity of labor.
    c.   an increase in saving.
    d.   a decline in the supply of capital.
    e.   an increase in wage demands by labor.

9.   The real wage:

    a.   is the nominal wage divided by the price level.
    b.   automatically increases with the cost of living.
    c.   is determined by labor-management negotiations within
          each firm in an industry when labor markets are purely
          competitive.
    d.   is set by explicit contract in the classical model.
    e.   is the nominal wage multiplied by the price level.

10.   Classical economists believe that a market economy will
       normally:

    a.   suffer from extended periods of sustained unemployment.
    b.   achieve full-employment output.
    c.   degenerate into pure monopolies in most industries.
    d.   suffer from money illusion—errors in predicting the
          average price of products.
    e.   eliminate the problems of economic scarcity.

11. As we move down along the Keynesian *IS* curve:

    a. investment spending declines but savings increases.
    b. investment spending and savings both decline.
    c. investment spending and savings both increase.
    d. investment spending increases but savings does not change.
    e. the interest rate and national income both decline.

12. The full-employment line:

    a. determines the level of aggregate demand.
    b. increases with the price level.
    c. determines the equilibrium level of output.
    d. is independent of labor supply.
    e. would increase if the unemployment rate declined.

13. In the production function equation, an increase in the productivity of labor is represented by:

    a. an increase in F.
    b. an increase in N.
    c. an increase in K.
    d. an increase in A.
    e. a reduction in K.

14. The symbol, N, is fixed in the full-employment output equation. N represents:

    a. only labor supply.
    b. labor supplied = labor demanded.
    c. only labor demand.
    d. only output supplied.
    e. output supplied = output demanded.

15. In the goods market equilibrium equation for a closed economy, the total demand for goods equals:

    a. $C^d + I^d$
    b. $C^d + I^d + G$
    c. $C + I + G$
    d. $C + I + G^d$
    e. $C + I + T$

16. One way of writing the goods market equilibrium equation for a closed economy is:

    a. $Y + C + G = S$
    b. $Y + C^d + G^d = S$
    c. $Y - C^d - G = S^d = I^d$
    d. $Y - C^d - G - S^d = I^d$
    e. $Y - C^d + S^d = I^d$

17. In the production function diagram, a beneficial supply shock is shown by:

   a.   an upward shift in the production function, except at the origin.
   b.   a movement up along the production function.
   c.   a downward shift in the production function, except at the origin.
   d.   an increase in the convexity of the curve.
   e.   a movement down along the production function.

18. In the saving-investment diagram, an increase in national income would:

   a.   shift both the saving and investment demand curves to the right.
   b.   shift the saving curve to the left.
   c.   shift the investment demand curve to the right.
   d.   not shift the curves.
   e.   shift the saving curve to the right.

Short-Answer Essay Questions

1.   **Labor market determination of output and employment:**
     a) Draw a labor market diagram and a production function diagram with labor as the variable factor of production. Label the axes and curves. b) On the diagrams, label the equilibrium values of N, W/P, and Y. c) State the "law of diminishing marginal returns" and briefly explain how your diagrams illustrate this law. d) Use your diagrams to show the effects of a beneficial productivity shock on N, W/P, and Y. e) Draw new labor market diagrams and use the diagrams to show the effects of a decline in the size of the labor force.

2.   **Goods market determination of investment:** a) Draw a saving-investment diagram of the product market. Label the axes and curves. b) Identify two shift variables (i.e., nonprice determinants) for the desired saving curve (S) and state whether desired saving is negatively related or positively related to each of these variables. c) Identify two shift variables for the desired investment demand curve and state whether desired investment is negatively related or positively related to each of these variables. d) Briefly explain how the diagram depicts goods market equilibrium, given that it explicitly shows a demand for only one type of good. e) Would an increase in desired saving prevent some capital goods suppliers from being able to sell some of their output? Briefly explain.

3.   *IS* **curve representation of goods market equilibrium:** a) Draw a saving-investment diagram. Label the axes and

curves. b) Show how to use your S-I diagram to construct an IS curve. Label the axes and curve for the IS diagram. c) Identify two variables that are changing in value as we move down the IS curve and state the direction in which they are changing. d) Draw another IS diagram and use the diagram to show the effect on the equilibrium level of desired investment (I^d) of a decline in desired investment demand. e) Is the IS curve supply curve? Briefly explain.

4.   **The full-employment (FE) line:** a) Draw an FE line diagram. Label the axes and curves. b) Briefly describe the relationship between output and the interest rate in this diagram and explain why this relationship exists. c) Identify changes in three variables that would cause the FE line to shift to the right. d) Give an example of an adverse productivity shock. e) Briefly explain the importance, in this model, of the classical assumption that wages are perfectly flexible.

5.   **Equilibrium in the goods and labor markets:** a) Draw an IS curve–FE line diagram. Label the axes, curves, and equilibrium values. b) What markets are in equilibrium in this diagram? c) How important is the position of the IS curve in determining the equilibrium level of output? Briefly explain. d) Use the diagram to show the effects of a temporary increase in energy prices. Label the new equilibrium values. e) Could a change in government spending offset the effect of an increase in energy prices on the interest rate? Briefly explain.

6.   **Productivity (supply) shocks:** Use the following diagrams to show the effects—if any exist—of human capital investments in education in some previous time period that now create a beneficial productivity shock: a) a production function diagram, for which labor is the variable factor of production; b) a labor market diagram; c) a saving-investment diagram; d) an IS curve–FE line diagram. e) Why would an increase in energy prices in this time period reduce our ability to measure the economic benefits of the human capital investments in education?

7.   **Causes of real economic growth:** a) Identify three causes of economic growth that are highlighted by the production function equation and state one reason for each of these changes to occur. b) Identify two causes of economic growth highlighted in the goods market equation and briefly state one reason for each of these changes to occur.

Answers to Multiple Choice Questions

1.	e	7.	d	13.	d
2.	a	8.	c	14.	b

3.	e	9.	a	15.	b
4.	b	10.	b	16.	c
5.	c	11.	c	17.	a
6.	a	12	c	18.	e

Answers to Short-Answer Questions

1.   **Labor market determination of output and employment**

a)

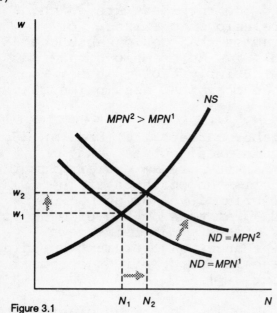 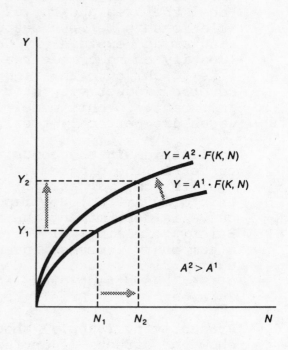

Figure 3.1

b)   The equilibrium values are: N_1, w_1, and Y_1.

c)   The law of diminishing marginal returns states that, if more units of labor are added to production beyond some level of employment, when the amount of capital employed is fixed, then output will increase at a declining rate. The slope of the production function is the marginal product of labor (*MPN*); the curve is concave because diminishing marginal returns causes the slope to decline as more labor is added to production in the short run. The labor demand curve (*ND*) is the set of *MPN* values at various levels of employment; the labor demand curve is negatively sloped, because firms experience diminishing marginal returns to labor in the short run.

d)   A beneficial productivity shock is shown by the increase in A to A_2. This increases the marginal product of labor schedule to MPN^2, which causes employment to increase to N_2, the real wage to increase to w_2, and output to increase to Y_2.

e)

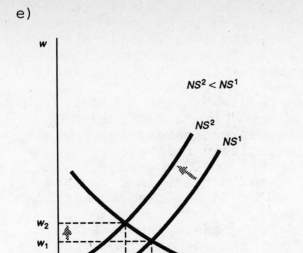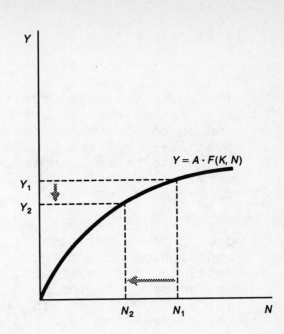

Figure 3.2

A decline in the labor force to NS^2, causes labor employment to decline to N_2, real wage to increase to w_2, and output to decline to Y_2.

2.   **Goods market determination of investment**

a)

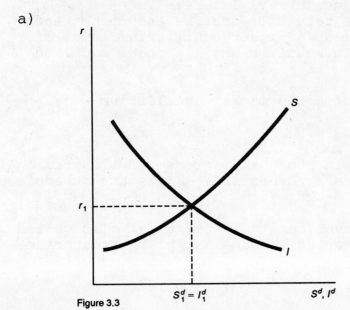

Figure 3.3

b)   Two shift variables for the desired saving schedule (S) are current income and expected future income. Saving is positively related to current income but negatively related to expected future income. An increase in current income will cause the saving to increase; the S curve will shift to the right. An increase in expected future income will cause the saving to decline; the S curve will shift to the left.

c)   Two shift variables for the desired investment schedule (I) are the expected future marginal product of capital (MPK) and corporate taxes. Desired investment demand is positively related to MPK but negatively related to corporate taxes. An increase in MPK would increase I; the curve would shift to the right. An increase in corporate taxes could decrease I; the curve would shift to the left.

d)   There are three types of demand for goods: investment demand, consumer demand, and government demand. Desired consumption demand and government demand for goods partly determine the position of the desired saving curve; a change in desired consumption demand or government demand would shift the S curve. The level of goods supplied, which is called real income, also determines the position of the desired saving curve. In equilibrium, the goods supplied that are not demanded by consumers or government are demanded by investors. Goods market equilibrium exists when $S^d = I^d$, because all the goods supplied are demanded (i.e., purchased and sold).

e)   No. An increase in desired saving would shift the saving curve to the right. At the initial interest rate, $S^d > I^d$, but the flexible interest rate will decline enough to return the market to equilibrium at a higher equilibrium level of saving and investment. In equilibrium, all goods supplied are sold.

3.   *IS* **curve representation of goods market equilibrium**

a)   See Figure 3.4 on page 37.

b) IS is constructed by showing that an increase in Y shifts S to the right, which causes r to decline. IS is the schedule of (Y, r) points where $I^d = S^d$.

c)   As we move down an IS curve, national output (Y, also called national income) is increasing and the market interest rate (r) is declining.

d)   See Figure 3.5 on page 37.

e)   The IS curve is not a supply curve; it is a goods market equilibrium curve. At every point along the IS curve, the supply of goods equals the demand for goods. As we move down an IS curve, the supply of savings and the supply of investment goods are increasing.

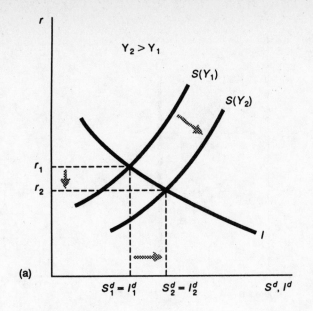

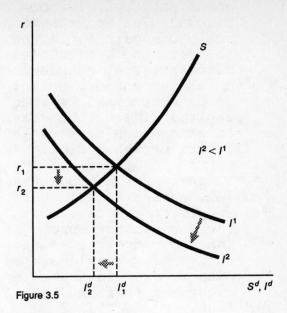

Figure 3.5

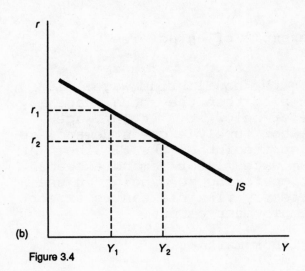

Figure 3.4

4.   The full-employment output (*FE*) line:

a)   See Figure 3.6 on page 38.

b)   Output is independent of the current interest rate, as shown
by the vertical *FE* line. In the short run, by definition,
the amount of capital employed in production is fixed ($K = \bar{K}$) and the productivity of resources is fixed (A is some
fixed number). Given these assumptions, output depends only
on the amount of labor employed, and equilibrium employment,
determined in the labor market, is independent of the
interest rate. The interest rate does partly determine the

amount of capital goods
purchased—as we've seen in
the goods market diagram.
However, the current level
of output does not depend
on the amount of capital
goods bought, since that
capital will not be added
to production until some
future market period.

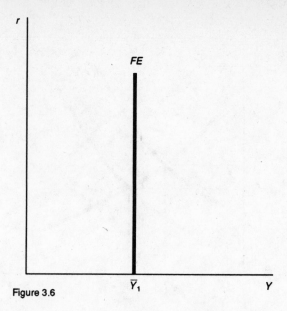

Figure 3.6

c)   An increase in productivity
(A), an increase in the
supply of capital, or an
increase in the supply of
labor would increase the
full-employment level of
output, as illustrated by a
rightward shift in the FE
line.

d)   A decline in the
productivity of labor is an example of an adverse
productivity shock.

e)   Full employment exists only at the equilibrium wage. If
wages were not perfectly flexible, then the actual wage may
be above the equilibrium wage or below it. At any wage
above the equilibrium wage, labor supply exceeds demand; so
the economy is not operating at a point on the FE line. At
any wage below the equilibrium wage, labor demand exceeds
supply, so the economy is not operating at a point on the FE
line. Only when wages are perfectly flexible can we expect
the economy to achieve full-employment output.

5.   **Equilibrium in the goods and labor markets**

a)   See Figure 3.7 on page 39.

b)   Both the labor market and the goods market are in
equilibrium in this diagram at (Y_1, r_1). Any point on the
FE line represents labor market equilibrium. Any point on
the IS curve represents goods market equilibrium. The
equilibrium point in the IS curve-FE line diagram, is on
both curves.

c)   In this long-run, market-clearing model, the position of the
IS curve is not even a partial determinant of the
equilibrium level of output. Output is completely
determined by the production function, for a given
equilibrium level of employment, as determined by the labor
market. Output is independent of the IS curve. Even if the
IS curve were to shift, output would remain unchanged.

d)   A temporary increase in
      energy prices causes the *FE*
      line to decline to FE^2,
      which causes output to fall
      to Y_2 and the market
      interest rate to rise to
      r_2.

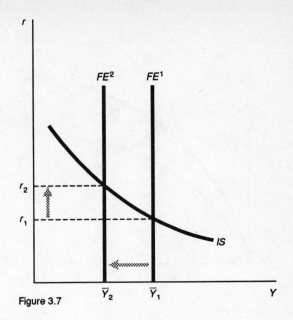

Figure 3.7

e)   Yes. An increase in energy
      prices would shift the *FE*
      line to the left, along a
      given *IS* curve.
      Consequently, the
      equilibrium interest rate
      would rise and output would
      fall. A decline in
      government spending would
      increase saving, which
      would cause the *IS* curve to
      shift to the left, along
      the new *FE* line (FE^2).
      Consequently, the interest
      rate could fall back to its initial value.

6.   **Productivity (supply) shocks**

a-d) See Figure 3.8 on page 40.

e)   An increase in energy prices in this time period would cause
      an adverse productivity (i.e., supply) shock, which would
      tend to offset the beneficial productivity shock of
      increases in labor's education level. We would observe only
      the net effects of both events. We would not be able to
      measure the effects of each event separately if they
      occurred at the same time and affected the values of the
      same market variables.

7.   **Causes of real economic growth**

a)   The production function shows that economic growth could be
      caused by: an increase in the equilibrium quantity of labor
      supplied, an increase in the equilibrium quantity of capital
      supplied, and an increase in productivity (i.e., an
      increase in the productivity of labor or capital). An
      increase in the number of working-age, able-bodied people in
      the economy would cause more labor to be supplied.   A
      decline in wealth taxes would cause more capital to be
      supplied. An increase in the opportunities or incentives to
      acquire education would cause more people to become more
      educated, which would increase the productivity of labor,
      which would increase productivity.

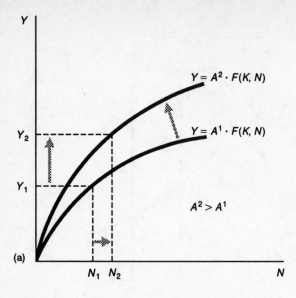

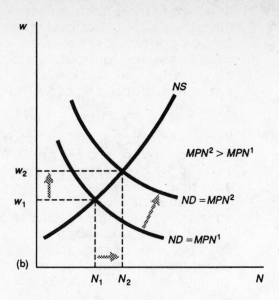

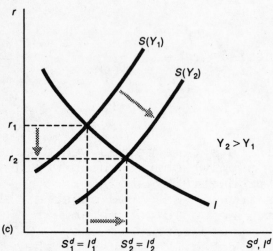

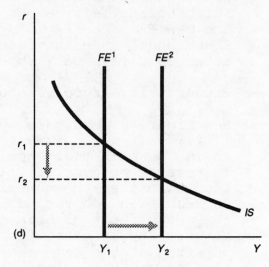

Figure 3.8

b)   An increase in the equilibrium level of investment spending
      will increase the quantity of capital that can be used to
      produce goods in future time periods; such an increase,
      therefore, increases economic growth. The goods market
      equation shows that an increase in the "expected future
      productivity of capital" would increase desired investment,
      which would increase the equilibrium level of investment and
      saving. It also shows that a reduction in government
      spending would increase desired saving, which would increase
      the equilibrium level of investment and saving. Certain

types of consumption spending will also promote economic
growth. For example, household spending on education,
nutrition, and exercise represent consumption spending that
increases economic growth.

CHAPTER 4

THE ASSET MARKET, MONEY, AND PRICES

A Review of Chapter Highlights

Money is the set of assets that are widely used to make payments. Since many different assets have been used as money in different countries and at different time periods, a conceptual definition of money has to be quite general. One conceptual approach is to provide a functional definition of money. Whatever functions as money is money.

Money has three principal functions: it serves as a medium of exchange, a unit of account, and a store of value. As a **medium of exchange**, money is used to pay for items in exchange. Using money as a payment mechanism lowers the costs of trading resources, products, and assets; thereby, the use of money promotes exchange and production for exchange in a market economy. As a **unit of account**, the value of resources, goods, and assets are denominated in money units; each unit costs so many dollars. Using money as a unit of account lowers trading costs by greatly reducing the number of exchange value calculations we need to make in a market economy. As a **store of value**, money is one possible asset that can be used to hold wealth. For example, if a farmer wanted to save the market value of some of her apple crop for five years, it would be cheaper to sell the apples now and save the money, than it would be to store the apples now and sell them in five years for money. In brief, money is a form of wealth that can be used for making payments.

A way to define money empirically is to measure the number of units of the money assets. The total number of dollar units of some specific set of money assets is called a **monetary aggregate**. **M1** is a monetary aggregate of the assets that are principally used to make payments; M1 consists of currency plus checkable deposits in banks and thrifts. **M2** is a monetary aggregate that includes M1 but also has a number of assets that are largely used for saving (i.e., storing value). M2 consists of M1 plus saving accounts, small time deposits, money market accounts, overnight repurchase agreements and overnight

Eurodollars. The **supply of money**, or stock of money, is the number of dollars in a particular monetary aggregate; for example, there is an M1 money supply and an M2 money supply.

The supply of money is controlled by the central bank of the United States, which is called the Federal Reserve. The Federal Reserve controls the supply of money primarily through **open market operations**. The Federal Reserve can increase the money supply by an open market purchase of government bonds and can reduce the money supply by an open market sale of government bonds.

Money is one asset among the set of assets that people hold in their portfolios. Each wealth-holder must make **portfolio allocation decisions** to determine how much of their wealth to allocate to each of the alternative assets. The three principal determinants of portfolio allocation decisions are expected return, risk, and liquidity. **Expected return** is the rate of return or interest rate that an asset is expected to earn per unit of time. **Risk** is a measure of the degree of uncertainty that the actual return will be significantly different from the expected return. **Liquidity** is a measure of the trading costs that will be incurred, if you quickly trade the asset for money; for a quick sale, less liquid assets will have to be sold further below their market values. Wealth-holders prefer assets with higher rates of return, lower risk, and more liquidity; for assets with a given liquidity, they will demand more of those assets that pay higher risk-adjusted, expected rates of return.

In addition to being the most liquid asset, money earns a nominal rate of return equal to i^m. The **demand for money** in the macroeconomy is the total amount of money that people want to hold in their portfolios in some time period. Real money demand is nominal money demand divided by the price level. The principal determinants of real money demand are specified by the **money demand function**. The money demand function tells us that the demand for real money balances is positively related to real income and the nominal interest rate on money but negatively related to the nominal interest rate on nonmonetary assets.

The demand for money is related to the income **velocity** of money; the inverse of velocity is the portion of nominal income demanded as money $[1/V = k = M^d/(PY)]$. Velocity can also be defined as the dollar value of output purchased per dollar of the money supply; so it tells us, on average, how many times each dollar is spent on final goods and services produced (i.e., the turnover rate of money). According to the classical **quantity theory of money**, velocity is a constant number, so nominal money demand is proportional to nominal GNP. Data presented in Figure 4.1 show empirically that velocity was not constant over the 1960–1990 period; although velocity did increase at a fairly stable trend rate in this period until 1980.

To simplify our analysis of the asset market, we can aggregate all wealth into monetary assets and nonmonetary assets. Given this aggregation, asset market equilibrium is achieved if and only if money market equilibrium is achieved. The **LM** curve depicts the various real output, real interest rate (*Y, r*) points at which money market equilibrium and, consequently, asset market equilibrium, is achieved.

The macroeconomy is in **general equilibrium** when the labor market, goods market, and asset market are simultaneously in equilibrium. In a general equilibrium model of the economy, **money neutrality** exists if a change in the nominal money supply causes the price level to change proportionally but has no real economic effects. Given the classical assumption of flexible prices, money is neutral in the complete *IS-LM* model, but money is not neutral under the Keynesian assumption of slow price adjustments.

Questions

These questions test your understanding of the **key terms**, **key relationships**, and **key diagrams** highlighted in your text.

Multiple Choice Questions: Circle the letter corresponding to the correct answer to each question.

1.   Which of the following statements best defines money?

    a.   Income is money.
    b.   Wealth is money.
    c.   Time is money.
    d.   The root of all evil is money.
    e.   The set of assets that can be used to make payments is money.

2.   Which of the following best illustrates the medium of exchange function of money?

    a.   The price of a new car is $25,000.
    b.   A penny saved is a penny earned.
    c.   A person owes $10,000 on his credit card.
    d.   You pay $3.00 to purchase a bag of apples.
    e.   Time is money.

3.   The number of units of one good that trade for one unit of alternative goods can be determined most easily when:

    a.   there is one unit of account.
    b.   the goods all weigh about the same.
    c.   the goods are all new.
    d.   the goods are actively traded through barter.
    e.   money is used as a medium of exchange.

4.   The most widely used money assets:

    a.   include government bonds.
    b.   do not include bank deposits.

c.   include credit cards.
d.   and nonmonetary assets are used as a store of value.
e.   have zero risk.

5.   One of the criticisms of standard monetary aggregates is
     that:

a.   they cannot be measured.
b.   the sum of the assets they contain is not weighted by
     the frequency at which they are used to make payments.
c.   they cannot be controlled by the central bank.
d.   fluctuations in their size are purely inflationary.
e.   they are never updated to include the assets actually
     used in modern transactions.

6.   Which of the following is not included in M1?

a.   demand deposits.
b.   NOW accounts.
c.   money market accounts.
d.   other checkable deposits.
e.   currency.

7.   Compared to M1, the assets in M2:

a.   are more liquid.
b.   are held more as a store of value.
c.   are more homogeneous.
d.   are more stable in value.
e.   have a higher velocity.

8.   The shortest reporting period for publication of data on the
     size of the money supply and on money supply growth is:

a.   weekly.
b.   semimonthly.
c.   daily.
d.   monthly.
e.   annually.

9.   An open market purchase by the Federal Reserve will:

a.   increase the nominal interest rate.
b.   reduce the price level.
c.   increase the supply of corporate bonds on the open
     market.
d.   reduce real GNP.
e.   increase the nominal money supply.

10. Which of the following portfolio allocation decisions
     represents the best individual response to an increase in
     the interest rate on nonmonetary assets?

a.   Sell some stocks and use the money to buy bonds.
b.   Sell some bonds and use the money to buy stocks.
c.   Trade some money for nonmonetary assets.
d.   Sell some land and use the money to buy nonmonetary
      assets.
e.   Reduce your assets and increase your liabilities.

11.   Instability in money demand for M1 during the mid-1970s and
       early 1980s is most closely related to changes in:

a.   Federal Reserve chairmen.
b.   the risks of nonmonetary assets.
c.   real GNP.
d.   the assets included in M1, due to financial innovation
      and changes in the financial system.
e.   the liquidity of M1 assets.

12.   In part, money is demanded because:

a.   it usually has a higher expected return than
      nonmonetary assets.
b.   it is relatively low risk.
c.   it is relatively high risk.
d.   it usually has a lower expected return than nonmonetary
      assets.
e.   money is relatively illiquid.

13.   The liquidity of an asset indicates:

a.   how many years before the asset matures.
b.   how quickly the asset can be sold at market value.
c.   how easily the asset is physically damaged by frequent
      exchange.
d.   the costs of transporting the asset to market.
e.   how much the purchasing power of the asset can be
      lowered by inflation.

14.   The nominal demand for money is proportional to:

a.   nominal income.
b.   real income.
c.   the nominal interest rate.
d.   the nominal interest rate on money.
e.   the price level.

15.   The money demand function specifies:

a.   the variables that determine how much money is held in
      a specific time period.
b.   the uses of money.
c.   the value of money.

d.   how much real income will increase if money demand
     increases by 5%.
e.   which market actors demand money.

16. According to the classical quantity theory of money:

a.   velocity increases with nominal income.
b.   velocity is positively related to the real interest
     rate.
c.   velocity is a constant number.
d.   velocity is proportional to price.
e.   velocity is unstable.

17. The *LM* curve is positively sloped because, if real income
     increases:

a.   the price level must increase to clear the money
     market.
b.   the nominal interest rate on money must increase to
     clear the asset market.
c.   the price level must increase to clear the goods
     market.
d.   the real interest must increase to clear the goods
     market.
e.   the real interest rate on nonmonetary assets must
     increase to clear the asset market.

18. In the complete *IS-LM* model, if a change in the money supply
     quickly moves the economy from one general equilibrium point
     to another, then:

a.   money has a real interest rate effect.
b.   money is neutral.
c.   money has an unemployment effect.
d.   money supply increases are not inflationary.
e.   money has a real income effect.

Short-Answer Essay Questions

1.   **Money supply**: a) Identify and briefly describe the three
     principal uses of money. b) What overall economic benefit
     does money provide to a market economy? c) What are the
     major components of M1? d) What are the major components of
     M2? e) What determines the supply of money?

2.   **Portfolio allocation**: a) Define portfolio allocation
     decision. b) Identify and briefly define the three
     principal determinants of portfolio allocation decisions. c)
     What is the principal economic goal of market actors in
     making portfolio allocation decisions? d) How often are
     portfolio allocation decisions made? e) Compare and

contrast money and nonmonetary assets in terms of expected return, risk, and liquidity.

3. **Money demand:** a) What is the difference between nominal money demand and real money demand? b) State the money demand function. c) Identify three possible causes of an increase in money demand. d) Briefly explain how money demand and velocity are related. e) Do modern classicals and Keynesians accept the traditional quantity theory of money assumption that velocity is approximately constant? Briefly explain.

4. **The *LM* curve:** a) Draw a money supply–money demand diagram. Label the axes and curves. b) Show how to use the money supply–money demand diagram to construct an *LM* curve diagram. c) Define the *LM* curve. d) Draw another *LM* curve diagram and use the diagram to show the effects of an increase in money demand.

5. **Supply shocks, demand shocks, monetary policy, and inflation in a complete *IS-LM* model of the economy:** In answering the following questions, assume that prices are flexible: a) Draw a complete *IS-LM* model diagram and use it to show the effects of an adverse supply shock. b) Draw a complete *IS-LM* model diagram and use it to show the effects of an increase in money demand. c) Draw a complete *IS-LM* model diagram and use it to show the real effects of a decline in desired investment. d) Given flexible prices, could monetary policy be used to offset the real interest rate effects of an adverse supply shock or a decline in desired investment? Briefly explain. e) Identify two causes of inflation.

6. **Velocity:** a) Why did the velocity of M1 increase above its trend rate of increase in the 1974–1976 period? b) Assuming slow price adjustments, what are the expected short run effects on Y, r, and P of an increase in velocity? c) Why did the velocity of M1 decline in the early 1980s? d) Assuming slow price adjustments, what are the expected short run effects on Y, r, and P of a decline in velocity? e) Does the empirical evidence for the 1974–1983 period support the classical quantity theory of money belief that velocity is constant? Briefly explain.

Answers to Multiple Choice Questions

1.	e	8.	a	15.	a
2.	d	9.	e	16.	c
3.	a	10.	c	17.	e
4.	d	11.	d	18.	b
5.	b	12.	b		

6. c   13. b
7. b   14. e

Answers to Short-Answer Essay Questions

1. **Money supply**

a) The three principal uses of money are as a:

   1) medium of exchange: Money is used to pay for the factors of production, goods and services, and nonmonetary assets. For example, you may be able to buy a bag of apples for $3.00.

   2) unit of account: Money is the standard of value used to compare the market values of dissimilar resources, goods, and assets. For example, the dollar is the monetary standard for the United States; the value of other things are measured in dollar units.

   3) store of value: Money is used as a way of holding wealth. For example, money in NOW account deposits and savings account deposits represent using money as a store of value.

b) The principal economic benefit of using money in a market economy is that it lowers trading costs. By lowering trading costs, the use of money encourages people to allocate their factors of production to their highest valued uses to produce for exchange in a market economy, which increases real GNP.

c) The principal components of M1 are currency, demand deposits, other checkable deposits, and travelers checks. Currency includes coins and Federal Reserve notes (i.e., paper money). Other checkable deposits are checking accounts at banks and thrifts that earn interest (e.g., NOW accounts).

d) The principal components of M2 are M1, savings account deposits, small time deposits, money market accounts, overnight repurchase agreements, and overnight Eurodollars. Small time deposits are certificates of deposits (CDs) of less than $100,000 denomination. Money market accounts include money market mutual funds (MMMFs) and money market deposit accounts (MMDAs).

e) The Federal Reserve determines the supply of money. The Federal Reserve is the central bank of the United States.

2.   **Portfolio allocation**

a)   Definition: By making a portfolio allocation decision, a market actor determines how much of various assets to use to hold one's wealth.

b)   The three principal determinants of portfolio allocation decisions are:

   1)   expected return: the predicted percentage increase in value that an asset will pay on average, when the actual rate of return is not known with certainty.

   2)   risk: a measure of the degree to which the actual return could significantly differ from the expected return. The higher the risk, the greater the range of probable rates of return above and below the expected rate of return.

   3)   liquidity: a measure of the trading costs incurred when an asset has to be sold quickly. The more illiquid an asset is, the lower we have to drop the price below market value to achieve a quick sale.

c)   The principal goal of market actors in making portfolio allocation decisions is to maximize their income. Given their liquidity preferences, individuals and firms attempt to maximize their earnings by choosing the combination of assets that will provide the maximum risk-adjusted, expected return on the portfolio.

d)   Portfolio allocation decisions may be made whenever a market actor's preferences for risk or liquidity change, and whenever the expected return, risk, and liquidity of one or more assets changes.

e)   Nonmonetary assets earn higher expected rates of return, are higher risk, and are less liquid than money.

3.   **Money demand**

a)   Real vs. nominal money demand:

   1)   Real money demand (MD) = L = amount of money held, measured in terms of the goods it will buy.

   2)   Nominal money demand = $P \times L$ = market value of the money held = value of goods and services that the money held could purchase.

b)   The money demand function is:

$$M/P = L(Y, i, i^m)$$

The demand for real money balances is a function of real income (Y), the nominal interest rate (i), and the nominal interest rate on money (i^m). A change in the value of Y, i, or i^m will change the real quantity of money demanded.

c)   Given that ($i = r$ + expected rate of inflation), the real quantity of money demanded would increase if real income increased, the expected rate of inflation decreased, or the nominal interest rate on money increased.

d)   The inverse of velocity is the portion of nominal income demanded as money $[1/V = M/(PY)]$ or $[M/P = Y/V]$, where V is velocity, M is nominal money demand, and M/P is real money demand.

e)   No. Both classicals and Keynesians believe that real money demand depends on Y, i, and i^m; therefore velocity is not constant.

4.   The *LM* curve

a)   A money supply (*MS*) - money demand (*MD*) diagram. The second money demand curve is added to help answer part (b).

$$MS = M/P$$

$$MD = L(Y,\ i,\ i^m)$$

$$Y_2 > Y_1$$

b)   Constructing an *LM* curve: The linear *LM* curve is drawn in (Y, r) space, by connecting the (Y, r) equilibrium points in the above money supply–money demand diagram, with a money demand curve for each level of real GNP. See Figure 4.2 on page 52.

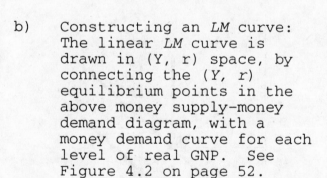

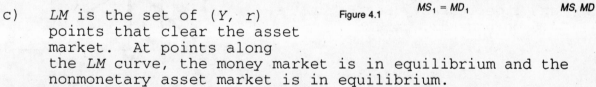

Figure 4.1

c)   *LM* is the set of (Y, r) points that clear the asset market. At points along the *LM* curve, the money market is in equilibrium and the nonmonetary asset market is in equilibrium.

(d)   Effect of an increase in *MD* on the asset market: r increases at a given level of real GNP. See Figure 4.3 on page 52.

$$MD_2 > MD_1$$

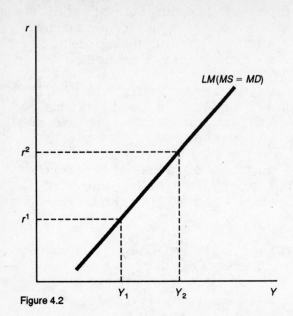

Figure 4.2

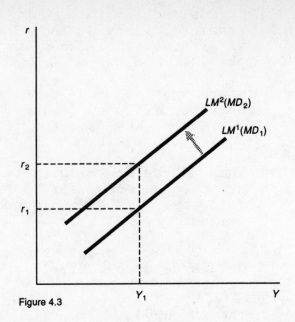

Figure 4.3

5.   **Supply shocks, demand shocks, monetary policy, and inflation in a complete *IS-LM* model of the economy:** Answers assume that prices are flexible.

a)   Effects of an adverse supply shock: Y decreases, r increases, P increases.

$$P_2 > P_1$$

b)   Effects of an increase in money demand: P decreases. See Figure 4.5 on page 53.

$$L_2 > L_1$$

$$P_2 < P_1$$

c)   Effects of a decline in investment: P decreases and r decreases. See Figure 4.6 on page 53.

$$I_2 < I_1$$

$$P_2 < P_1$$

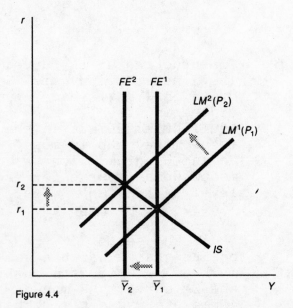

Figure 4.4

d)   No. Given flexible prices, monetary policy cannot shift the *LM* curve; therefore, it cannot offset either of these

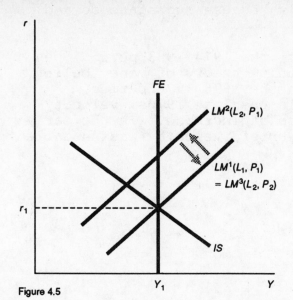

Figure 4.5

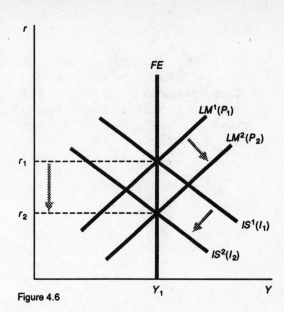

Figure 4.6

changes. Although the Federal Reserve can change the
nominal money supply, any change in M creates a proportional
change in P, so that the real money supply, M/P, does not
change.

e)   Two causes of inflation are adverse supply shocks and
     increases in the nominal money supply.

6.   **Velocity**

a)   In the 1974–1976 period, velocity increased because real
     money demand declined for a given level of real income. Real
     money demand for M1 declined principally because an increase
     in inflation and the addition of money market accounts and
     repurchase agreements to M2 lowered the relative rate of
     return on M1 deposits.

b)   Assuming slow price adjustments, the short-run effects of an
     increase in velocity are: money demand declines, which
     shifts the LM curve down so that Y increases; r declines;
     and P increases. Given slow price adjustments, the increase
     in P is less than proportional in the short run, but P
     slowly increases because aggregate demand exceeds output.

c)   In the early 1980s, velocity declined because real money
     demand increased for a given level of real GNP. Real money
     demand for M1 increased principally because a decline in
     inflation and the addition of NOW accounts to M1 increased
     the relative rate of return to M1 deposits.

d)   Assuming slow price adjustments, the short-run effects of a
     decline in velocity are: money demand increases, which

shifts the *LM* curve up so that *Y* decreases; *r* increases; and *P* decreases. *P* declines slowly because aggregate demand is less than output.

e)   No. The empirical evidence for the 1974–1983 period does not support the classical quantity theory of money belief that velocity is constant. In the 1976–1976 period, velocity increased rapidly. In the late 1970s, velocity resumed its previous trend rate of increase. In the early 1980s, velocity declined. In brief, velocity was unstable during the 1974–1983 period.

CHAPTER 5

CONSUMPTION AND SAVING: THE PRESENT VERSUS THE FUTURE

A Review of Chapter Highlights

Forward-looking consumers consider their current and future
resources, as well as their preferences for current and future
consumption, in making their consumption and saving decisions.
For each possible level of current consumption, the **budget
constraint** determines future consumption, for given values of
initial wealth, current income, expected future income, and the
real interest rate. The **budget line** is a graph of the budget
constraint, depicting the set of current consumption, future
consumption (C, C^f) combinations available to a consumer.

The current resource value of income payments received n
periods in the future, $Y^f/(1 + r)$, is called the **present value** of
these resources. The current resource value of initial wealth
and current income is the same as their present value, since
these economic resources are available in the present (i.e.,
current) time period. The **present value of lifetime resources
(PVLR)** is the current dollar value of a consumer's initial
wealth, current income, and expected future income. *PVLR*
determines the budget constraint by determining the present value
of lifetime consumption [i.e., $PVLR = C + C^f/(1+r)$]. An increase
in *PVLR* causes the budget line to shift to the right by the
amount of the increase.

Because of their **consumption-smoothing motive**, households
(i.e., individuals and families) tend to spend a fairly stable
share of their economic resources in each time period to maximize
their **utility** (i.e., happiness, satisfaction, or well being)
intertemporally. Consistent with the consumption-smoothing
motive, the **permanent-income theory** predicts that consumption
spending will change more in response to permanent changes in
one's income than for temporary changes in one's income.

The **life-cycle model** is also consistent with the
consumption-smoothing motive; it predicts that consumption
changes much less than income, as individuals' advance through
life from the early working years, to the high-income years, to
retirement years.

The **bequest motive** causes people to save more and consume less in each time period, so that they can leave an estate of accumulated wealth for their heirs.

By restricting the amount of future income that can be borrowed, a **borrowing constraint** potentially affects the consumption and saving decision. A **nonbinding borrowing constraint** has no effect on an individual's consumption and saving decision, because the person does not desire to borrow more than they are able to borrow. A **binding borrowing constraint** reduces current consumption, because it reduces the amount of future income that can be borrowed. A binding borrowing constraint does not force people to save, but it does reduce dissaving. When there is a binding borrowing constraint, people spend any available current income or wealth on current consumption.

Questions

These questions test your understanding of the **key terms**, **key relationships**, and **key diagrams** highlighted in your text.

Multiple Choice Questions: Circle the letter corresponding to the correct answer to each question.

1. Which of the following behaviors is not characteristic of a forward-looking consumer?

    a. The individual reduces his saving when his expected future income increases.
    b. The individual dissaves during retirement years.
    c. The individual reduces saving during a temporary recession.
    d. The individual reduces saving during his middle-age, high-income years.
    e. The individual's saving decision is not affected by a nonbinding borrowing constraint.

2. Which of the following variables does not directly determine the budget constraint?

    a. initial wealth.
    b. future consumption.
    c. the real interest rate.
    d. current income.
    e. expected future income.

3. The slope of the budget line is:

    a. $-1/(1 + i)$
    b. $1/(1 - i)^n$
    c. $(1 + r)$

(d). $-(1 + r)$
e. $1/(1 + r)$

4. Which of the following changes would reduce the present
    value of a given future real income payment?

    (a).   The real interest rate increases.
    b.   The real interest rate declines.
    c.   The future payments will be received one year earlier
          than initially expected.
    d.   The individual learns that she will not be allowed to
          borrow against the future income.
    e.   Inflation will be lower than expected between the
          current period and the receipt of the future payment.

5. An increase in the present value of lifetime resources
    (*PVLR*) will always:

    a.   increase saving.
    b.   reduce consumption.
    (c).   create a parallel shift to the right of the budget line
          by the amount of the increase in *PVLR*.
    d.   increase the slope of the budget line, because it will
          allow for more future consumption at any given level of
          current consumption.
    e.   cause the individual's preference for current
          consumption to increase.

6. The fact that consumption is more stable than income over
    time, is best explained by:

    a.   the income effect.
    b.   utility maximization.
    (c).   the consumption-smoothing motive.
    d.   binding borrowing constraints.
    e.   impatience.

7. The principal reason that consumers buy goods is that
    buying goods increases their:

    a.   real income.
    b.   wealth.
    c.   *PVLR*.
    d.   consumption opportunities.
    (e).   utility.

8. According to Friedman's permanent-income theory, a temporary
    increase in income will:

    (a).   increase saving more than for a permanent increase in
          income.
    b.   increase consumption more than for a permanent increase
          in income.

    c.   increase an individual's *PVLR,* more than for a permanent increase in income.

    d.   not affect current consumption and saving, because these depend only on permanent income.

    e.   will not increase the value of their future assets.

9.   According to Modigliani's **life-cycle model**, individuals usually:

    a.   dissave during their middle-age, high-income years.

    b.   dissave during their early working years and retirement years.

    c.   save for the future.

    d.   save throughout their working years but dissave during their retirement years.

    e.   have high saving rates through their lifetimes, so that they can provide large bequests.

10.   An increase in the bequest motive for a high percentage of households would:

    a.   increase the real interest rate.

    b.   increase inflation.

    c.   shift the budget line to the right.

    d.   reduce present values.

    e.   reduce aggregate consumer spending.

11.   Which of the following best illustrates a borrowing constraint?

    a.   Your parents refuse to give you a no-interest loan.

    b.   A bank wants you to pay interest on a loan while you are going to school.

    c.   A bank wants to charge you a relatively high interest rate on a loan.

    d.   You face a strict limit on your credit card balance.

    e.   A bank will give you a loan only if you appear able to pay it back.

12.   A nonbinding borrowing constraint:

    a.   reduces saving.

    b.   creates a positive income effect.

    c.   does not affect the consumption and saving decision.

    d.   causes individuals to consume all of their initial wealth and current income.

    e.   causes individuals to dissave.

13.   One reason why the Japanese had higher saving rates in the 1980s than Americans is that:

    a.   unlike the Japanese, Americans are not forward-looking consumers.

b.   unlike the Japanese culture, the American culture does not encourage saving.

c.   binding borrowing constraints were reduced in the 1980s for many American households.

d.   a higher percentage of American households provide large bequests.

e.   during the 1980s, temporary income declined in America while permanent income declined in Japan.

14.   According to the budget constraint equation, which of the following changes would reduce future consumption for a net saver?

a. Y^f increases.
b. C increases.
c. r increases.
d. a increases.
e. Y increases.

15.   The present value equation shows that:

a.   at low interest rates, there is no point in saving.
b.   an increase in saving will lower the interest rate.
c.   the longer you have to wait for a payment, the lower its present value.
d.   people should not borrow money at high interest rates.
e.   present values increase with the interest rate.

16.   An alternative view of the budget constraint is that the present value of lifetime consumption equals:

a. $Y + Y^f/(1 + r) + a$
b. $Y + a + Y^f$
c. $Y + Y^f(1 + r) + a$
d. $C + C^f$
e. $C(1 + r) + C^f$

Short-Answer Essay Questions

1.   **Consumption and saving motives:** a) Why do individuals save? b) What is an intertemporal consumption decision? c) Can the consumption decision and saving decision be made separately? Briefly explain. d) Briefly describe the behavior predicted by the consumption-smoothing motive. e) How would a decline in an individual's bequest motive affect his consumption and saving?

2.   **Present values:** a) Define present value. b) Write out the present value equation. c) Assuming an interest rate of 5 percent, calculate the present values of a $1000 payment received in one year, in two years, and in three years. d) Identify four variables that determine the present value of

lifetime resources. e) How would a decline in an individual's *PVLR* affect her budget line?

3. **Budget constraints and preferences**: a) Draw a budget line diagram. Label the axes. b) What would cause the slope of the budget line to increase (i.e., become steeper)? c) Identify two variable changes that would cause the budget line to shift to the right. d) What economic cost of current consumption is illustrated by the budget line? e) Use the diagram to show the effect of an increase in one's preference for future consumption.

4. **Permanent-income theory:** a) Define the terms temporary income and permanent income. b) Compare and contrast the effects on consumption and saving of an increase in temporary income with the effects of an increase in permanent income. c) Is the permanent-income theory consistent with the consumption-smoothing motive? Briefly explain. d) How does the permanent-income theory help us to understand why consumption fell more in the 1973–1975 recession than in the 1981–1982 recession? e) State one advantage of the life-cycle model over the permanent-income theory in explaining consumption.

5. **Life-cycle model:** a) Identify the three principal stages of consumption and saving in Modigliani's life-cycle model. b) Briefly explain the hump-shaped pattern of saving in the life-cycle model. c) Is the life-cycle model consistent with the consumption smoothing motive? Briefly explain. d) Does the life-cycle model explain the behavior of people who are forward-looking, or those who are relatively impatient, or both? Briefly explain. e) Does the life-cycle model explain the behavior of people with low bequest motives, high bequest motives, both? Briefly explain.

6. **Borrowing constraints:** a) Why does a nonbinding borrowing constraint not affect consumption and saving? b) State the effects on consumption and saving of a binding borrowing constraint. c) Draw a budget line diagram for a consumer who faces a binding borrowing constraint. Label the preferred consumption combination. d) Use your diagram to show the effect of a relaxation of the binding borrowing budget constraint. e) Does the life-cycle model explain the behavior of people with nonbinding borrowing constraints, binding borrowing constraints, or both? Briefly explain.

7. **Explaining the Japanese saving rate:** a) State and briefly explain four reasons why the Japanese saving rate exceeded the American saving rate in the 1980s. b) Which, if any, of these reasons is a determinant of individuals opportunities to save? c) Which, if any, of these reasons is a determinant of individuals' preferences for saving?

d) Identify one change that would increase the aggregate saving rate in the United States. e) Evaluate the following statement: The American saving rate is far too low, thus government policymakers must do whatever is needed to raise the saving rate in America to equal the Japanese saving rate.

Answers to Multiple Choice Questions

1.	d	8.	a	15.	c
2.	b	9.	b	16.	a
3.	d	10.	e		
4.	a	11.	d		
5.	c	12.	c		
6.	c	13.	c		
7.	e	14.	b		

Answers to Short-Answer Essay Questions

1.   Consumption and saving motives

a)   Individuals save to increase their future consumption and provide for bequests. Unless individuals save, their future consumption cannot exceed their future income. Individuals save to pay for expensive goods and services, such as cars, houses, and education. They save to pay for items that they could not easily finance out of their monthly budgets, such as property taxes and large medical emergencies. They save to accumulate wealth that will finance their consumption during retirement years. They save to earn interest income that can supplement or replace their labor income.

b)   Intertemporal means between time periods. An intertemporal consumption decision is an individual's determination of how much of the present value of her lifetime resources to spend on consumer goods and services in the current time period, and how much to save for consumption in the future. Forward-looking consumers make intertemporal consumption decisions to maximize their happiness intertemporally (i.e., over some planning horizon that extends beyond the current time period).

c)   No. The consumption decision cannot be made separately from the saving decision, since saving is defined as the income that is not spent on consumer goods and services (i.e., $Y - C = S$). We could call it the consumption and saving decision, since the shares of our income allocated to consumption and saving, at any point in time, is made by one decision. By choosing how much to consume, we have chosen how much to save. Alternatively by choosing how much to save, we have chosen how much to consume. In general, the economic benefits (i.e., utility) of consuming and saving are simultaneously considered in making each consumption/ saving decision.

d) The consumption-smoothing motive suggests that individuals prefer to have a fairly stable level of consumption across different time periods, so consumption varies less than income over the business cycle and over the life-cycle. In terms of a budget line diagram, the consumption-smoothing motive predicts that people will generally choose a (C, C^f) combination that is near the middle of the budget line, rather than being near either end.

e) A decline in an individual's bequest motive would increase his consumption and reduce his saving.

2.   **Present values**

a) Present value is the current dollar value of future payments. Present value calculations tell us how much future income payments are worth in today's dollars.

b) For a nominal income payment (Y^f) received n periods in the future, the present value is: $Y^f/(1 + i)^n$, where i is the nominal interest rate. For a real income payment received n periods in the future, the present value is: $Y^f/(1 + r)^n$, where r is the real interest rate.

c) Given a 5% interest rate, the present values of $1000 received one year, two years, and three years in the future are, respectively:

1) $1000/(1 +.05) = \$1000/1.05 = \$952.38$
2) $\$1000/(1 + .05)^2 = \$1000/1.1025 = \$907.03$
3) $\$1000/(1 + .05)^3 = \$1000/1.1576 = \$863.86$

d) The four variables that determine the present value of lifetime resources (*PVLR*) are current income, future income, the real interest rate, and initial wealth:

$$PVLR = Y + Y^f/(1 + r) + a$$

e) A decline in an individual's *PVLR* would cause her budget line to shift to the left by the amount that *PVLR* declined.

3.   **Budget constraints and preferences**

a) Budget line diagram. See Figure 5.1 on page 63.

b) The slope of the budget line is $[-(1 + r)]$, where r is the real interest rate. An increase in r would increase the slope, by making it a larger negative number. The slope is defined as the change in the value of the variable on the vertical axis (C^f) per unit change in the value of the variable on the horizontal axis (C).

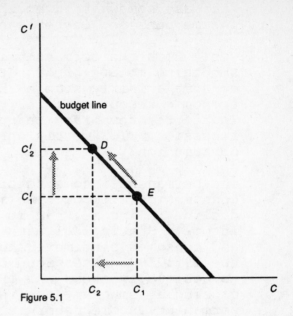

Figure 5.1

c)   Two variable changes that would make the budget line shift to the right are: 1) an increase in current income (Y); 2) an increase in expected future income (Y^f). This can be seen from the budget constraint equation, which defines the budget line: $C^f = (Y + a - C)(1 + r) + Y^f$

d)   The slope of the budget line, $-(1 + r)$, is the per unit economic cost of current consumption in terms of units of future consumption foregone. For every dollar of goods bought today, $(1 + r)$ dollars of future consumption of goods is given up. Likewise, the economic benefit (i.e., reward) for every dollar saved is $(1 + r)$ dollars of additional consumption spending in the future.

e)   In part (a), an increase in preference for future consumption is shown by a movement along a given budget line to a point where C is smaller, but C^f is larger. In the diagram, we move from point E to point D.

4.   **Permanent-income theory**

a)   Definitions:

   1)   Temporary income: income that is transitory or short-lived. A temporary change in income changes current income but not future income.

   2)   Permanent income: income that is not transitory. A permanent change in income changes both current income and future income.

b)   Current consumption and future consumption would increase more, while saving would increase less, for a given increase in permanent income compared to the same current period increase in temporary income. The temporary increase in income will be mostly saved, so future consumption will increase somewhat, even though the temporary increase in income does not increase expected future income.

c) Yes. Both the permanent-income theory and the consumption-smoothing motive predict that individuals will choose to consume a fairly stable share of their current and future economic resources (i.e., *PVLR*) in each time period. Therefore, temporary changes in income, as might occur in a recession, will mostly change saving, rather than current consumption.

d) The permanent-income theory predicts that current consumption will decline more in response to a permanent decline in income than it will for a temporary decline in income. Statistical data on measures of consumer confidence and consumer sentiment show that most people believed that the 1973-1975 recession would cause their permanent income to decline; whereas the 1981-1982 recession was perceived as causing a temporary decline in their income. As the permanent-income theory predicts, consumption declined more in the 1973-1975 recession than in the 1981-1982 recession.

e) One advantage that the life-cycle model has over the permanent-income theory of consumption and saving is that unlike the permanent-income theory, the life-cycle theory can show how changes in the age distribution of a country's population can cause the saving rate to change.

5. Life-cycle model

a) The three stages of Modigliani's life-cycle model are: the early working years (adults under 40), middle-age working years (ages 40-65), and retirement years (over 65).

b) Changes in saving over these three periods provide a "hump-shaped" saving pattern. A brief description and explanation follows.

1) In the early working years: individuals dissave at declining rates until about age 35, when they achieve low, but increasing saving rates as they age. During these relatively low-income years, adults are acquiring education, buying and furnishing their first homes, and raising their young children.

2) During the middle-age working years: saving rates continue to increase with age until about age 55, when they begin to decline to a zero saving rate at age 65. During these relatively high-income years, adults are able to reduce their liabilities and increase their saving to finance their children's education and their retirement.

3)   During the retirement years: people again dissave at an increasing rate for several years, after which they dissave at a fairly constant rate during retirement. After a few years with no labor income, people usually learn to maintain a fairly stable standard of living during retirement.

c)   Yes. Both the life-cycle model and the consumption-smoothing motive predict that individual's attempt to maintain a fairly stable standard of living over the different time periods of their lifetime. As a result, consumption changes less than income in different time periods.

d)   Both. Like many economic theories, the life-cycle model is quite general; therefore, it predicts the behavior of most people. Relatively impatient people are still forward-looking consumers, even though they save less of their income in any time period, compared to more forward-looking consumers. Most people will exhibit the same hump-shaped pattern of saving over their life cycle.

e)   Both. Compared to people with high bequest motives, individuals or families with low bequest motives will save more in any time period, so that they can leave an estate of accumulated wealth for their heirs. The life-cycle model is general enough to be used to predict the basic pattern of saving behavior of people with different bequest motives.

6.   Borrowing constraints

a)   A nonbinding borrowing constraint does limit one's potential opportunities to borrow, but the constraint doesn't affect consumption and saving because the individual does not choose to borrow above the borrowing limit. An individual facing a nonbinding borrowing constraint does not want to borrow more than she is allowed to borrow.

b)   A binding borrowing constraint reduces current consumption, because it prevents the individual from borrowing against his future income to increase current consumption above current income and initial wealth. The individual chooses to save nothing with or without the constraint, but the binding borrowing constraint reduces dissaving—it reduces the negative saving.

c)   A budget line diagram with a binding borrowing constraint shows the individual consuming at the point where the budget line and borrowing constraint line intersect. See Figure 5.2 on page 66.

d)   A decline in a binding borrowing constraint is shown by the borrowing constraint line shifting to the right. This lets the individual move to a consumption combination (C, C^f) where C has increased and C^f has decreased, such as from D to E.

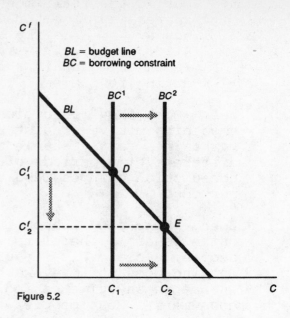

Figure 5.2

e)   Both. The life-cycle model does require that people borrow some of their future income during their early working years, but this could be achieved by acquiring a home mortgage loan, a car loan, a school loan, or even a loan from other family members. Some young adults may wish to borrow more than they can borrow, but few are unable to borrow at all. During the retirement years, most people borrow from themselves by selling their wealth to finance consumption in excess of income.

7.   Explaining the Japanese saving rate

a)   The following factors help to explain why the Japanese saving rate exceeded the American saving rate during the 1980s:

1)   population age structure: A higher percentage of Japanese were in their peak saving years, per the life-cycle model, and they generally expected to live longer than Americans.

2)   income growth: The growth rate of national income has been higher in Japan than in America over the past forty years, so the working adults saved relatively more in Japan than America, while the retired Japanese dissaved relatively less than Americans. Therefore, the aggregate saving rate was higher in Japan than America.

3)   housing and land prices and mortgage markets: The Japanese must save more than Americans because Japanese land prices and housing prices are much higher and downpayment requirements for their mortgages are higher than in America.

4)   bequest motive: Hayashi's research suggests that the Japanese have higher bequest motives than most

Americans, so they must save more of their income in each time period.

b)   Population age structure and income growth are two principal determinants of individuals' opportunities to save.

c)   Housing and land prices and downpayment requirements in mortgage markets, as well as bequest motives, are principal determinants of individuals' preferences for saving.

d)   The U.S. saving rate would increase if banks increased their downpayment requirements for housing loans.

e)   Economists can say that the U.S. saving rate is low today compared to some other time periods or compared to some other countries. Economists can identify and measure the various economic costs and benefits of a low saving rate compared to a high saving rate. Furthermore, economists can identify the causes of a low saving rate. However, economic theory cannot tell us that the saving rate is "too low" or that it "should or must" be increased; these statements rely on social value judgments, which are beyond the scope of economic theory. Economists believe that American individuals and families are saving what they want to save, given their preferences and market opportunities or incentives to save. Government policies can change the U.S. saving rate by changing market opportunities or incentives to save. However, economic theory alone cannot tell us whether government policies "should" attempt to do this. It would be hard to prove that the current Japanese saving rate is the ideal one for America. We can say that economists do not generally endorse "whatever it takes" kind of policies; economists weigh the expected benefits of any change against the costs and generally endorse those policies that they believe will increase a nation's standard of living.

CHAPTER 6

SAVING, INVESTMENT, AND THE REAL INTEREST RATE

A Review of Chapter Highlights

Two of the determinants of desired saving are the expected real interest rate and the tax rate on interest earnings.

A change in the expected real interest rate has two opposing effects on desired saving for both net savers and borrowers; these are the substitution effect and the income effect. The **substitution effect** of an increase in the expected real interest rate is an increase in desired saving. Households and firms save more, because the rate of return to saving increases, relative to the rate of return on current consumption. The **income effect** of an increase in the expected real interest rate is a decline in desired saving. Households and firms reduce their desired saving, to achieve some target level of wealth, because an increase in the rate of return increases their wealth. Desired saving is positively related to the expected real interest rate if the substitution effect is stronger than the income effect. Empirical evidence suggests that the substitution effect does exceed the income effect, but not by much.

Assuming that the substitution effect is stronger than the income effect, desired saving is negatively related to the tax rate on interest earnings, because savers are interested in their **after-tax rate of return.** An increase in the tax rate on savings reduces desired saving, if people are more responsive to a decline in the relative reward to saving than to a decline in the present value of their lifetime income.

The **expected real after-tax rate of return** on saving is the nominal after-tax interest rate minus the expected rate of inflation. Desired saving would be independent of the expected rate of inflation, if changes in the expected rate of inflation created proportional changes in the nominal after-tax rate interest rate, leaving the expected real after-tax rate of return unchanged.

Investment is the purchase of capital goods to add to firms' existing capital stocks. For each firm, the **desired capital stock** is the amount of real capital that maximizes the firm's profits. Three principal determinants of desired capital stock are the user cost of capital, the tax rate on capital goods, and the expected future marginal product of capital.

The **user cost of capital** is the sum of the interest cost and the depreciation cost of the real capital investment. Desired capital stock is negatively related to the user cost of capital. An increase in the user cost will reduce the equilibrium level of desired capital stock.

To maximize profits, when firms' revenues are taxed, each firm will purchase just enough capital to equate the expected future marginal product of capital to the **tax-adjusted user cost of capital** on the last unit of capital purchased. Although several taxes exist that affect after-tax profits (e.g., corporate profits tax, depreciation schedules, and investment tax credits), the **effective tax rate** is the revenue-tax equivalent of all these taxes.

Gross investment is the increase in capital stock plus depreciation of existing capital. **Net investment** is gross investment minus depreciation, which equals the increase in capital stock. Net investment by a firm in some year is the increase in capital stock needed to achieve the desired capital stock—the level needed to maximize profits.

In analyzing the effects of a tax change on desired saving, desired investment, and the expected real interest rate, the analysis can be simplified by assuming a lump-sum tax change. A **lump-sum tax change** is a fixed dollar amount (e.g., $100) by which each household's taxes are increased or reduced. Lump-sum tax changes do not change market incentives to save and invest.

The **Ricardian Equivalence Proposition** contends that a temporary government budget deficit created by a lump-sum tax cut will have no real effect on the economy. The proposition assumes, however, that households do not face borrowing constraints. If a sufficient number of households in the economy face binding borrowing constraints, a tax cut will cause the saving curve to shift to the left, thereby lowering the equilibrium level of desired saving and desired investment, while increasing the equilibrium real interest rate. A government budget deficit caused by a temporary increase in government spending would also shift the saving curve to the left.

A leftward shift in the saving curve will cause the *IS* curve to shift up. By changing taxes and government spending, fiscal policies would cause the *IS* curve to shift, if they caused the saving curve to shift. A fiscal policy that causes the IS curve to shift up is an **expansionary fiscal policy**. A fiscal policy, such as a temporary decline in government spending, that causes the *IS* curve to shift down is a **contractionary fiscal policy**.

Questions

These questions test your understanding of the **key terms**, **key relationships**, and **key diagrams** highlighted in your text.

Multiple Choice Questions: Circle the letter corresponding to the correct answer to each question.

1.   The substitution effect of a decline in the real interest rate would:

   a.   at least partially offset the income effect.
   b.   cause desired saving to increase.
   c.   sometimes increase and sometimes decrease desired saving; the theoretical effect is ambiguous.
   d.   never be greater than the income effect.
   e.   have the same effect as the income effect.

2.   An increase in the personal income tax rate on interest income received by households will:

   a.   unambiguously increase desired saving.
   b.   unambiguously decrease desired saving.
   c.   decrease saving if the income effect is larger than the substitution effect.
   d.   decrease saving if the income effect is smaller than the substitution effect.
   e.   will not affect the nominal rate of return on saving.

3.   The expected real after-tax rate of return on saving is the after-tax nominal rate of return minus expected:

   a.   future income.
   b.   future wealth.
   c.   future capital gains.
   d.   rate of interest.
   e.   rate of inflation.

4.   The desired level of capital stock will increase if the:

   a.   user cost of capital increases.
   b.   expected future marginal product of capital increases.
   c.   effective tax rate increases.
   d.   price of capital increases.
   e.   investment tax credit decreases.

5.   An increase in the price of capital goods will:

   a.   increase the expected future marginal product of capital.
   b.   reduce the expected future marginal product of capital.
   c.   increase the interest cost and the depreciation cost of capital.
   d.   increase the interest cost but not affect the depreciation cost of capital.
   e.   not affect the interest cost of capital.

6.   In calculating the tax-adjusted user cost of capital, the user cost of capital is:

    a.   multiplied by the tax rate.
    b.   multiplied by (1 - tax rate).
    c.   divided by (1 - tax rate).
    d.   divided by the tax rate.
    e.   added to the tax rate.

7.   The effective tax rate is:

    a.   another name for the corporate profits tax rate.
    b.   the inflation-adjusted corporate profits tax rate.
    c.   the risk-adjusted corporate profits tax rate.
    d.   increases with investment tax credits.
    e.   is the revenue-tax rate equivalent of the actual tax rates.

8.   The level of capital stock increases:

    a.   always for the macroeconomy.
    b.   if gross investment exceeds depreciation.
    c.   if net investment plus depreciation exceeds zero.
    d.   if many firms make investments.
    e.   if the price of capital goods declines.

9.   The principal effect of net investment on the economy is to:

    a.   increase the unemployment rate.
    b.   increase real national output and income.
    c.   increase inflation.
    d.   decrease the real interest rate.
    e.   increase the expected marginal product of capital.

10.   Which of the following illustrates a lump-sum tax change?

    a.   Each household's tax liability increases by $1000.
    b.   The marginal income tax rate increases by 5% for people who earn over $100,000.
    c.   The marginal income tax rate increases by 2% for all income brackets.
    d.   The sales tax rate increases by 2%.
    e.   The FICA tax rate increases by 1%.

11.   According to the Ricardian Equivalence Proposition, a temporary government budget deficit, created by cutting taxes:

    a.   will cause desired consumption to increase.
    b.   will cause future taxes to increase but will have no real economic effects.
    c.   will have the same real economic effects as a budget deficit, created by raising government spending.

d.   would have the same real effects whether or not
      consumers face binding borrowing constraints.
e.   will cause desired saving to increase.

12.   Which of the following is an expansionary fiscal policy?

a.   tax reform legislation.
b.   an increase in taxes.
c.   a decline in government spending, when households
      face binding borrowing constraints.
d.   a decline in taxes, when households do not face binding
      borrowing constraints.
e.   an increase in government spending.

13.   Contractionary fiscal policies cause:

a.   the saving curve to shift to the left.
b.   the *IS* curve to shift to the right.
c.   the *FE* line to shift to the left.
d.   the *IS* curve to shift to the left.
e.   the *LM* curve to shift to the left.

14.   The government budget constraint shows that, for a given
      level of government spending, a decline in current tax
      revenue will:

a.   cause future government spending to increase.
b.   create permanent government budget deficits.
c.   cause future tax revenue to increase by more than
      the decline in current tax revenue, when future
      government spending remains unchanged.
d.   cause the interest rate to decrease.
e.   cause the present value of government spending
      to increase.

15.   An increase in current income would cause a consumer's
      budget line to:

a.   shift to the right, and an increase in the real
      interest rate would cause the budget line to pivot in a
      clockwise direction through the no-borrowing, no-
      lending point.
b.   shift to the left, and an increase in the real interest
      rate would cause the budget line to pivot in a
      clockwise direction through the no-borrowing, no-
      lending point.
c.   remain at its initial position, and an increase in the
      real interest rate would shift the budget line to the
      right.
d.   remain at its initial position, and an increase in the
      real interest rate would shift the budget line to the
      left.

e.   shift to the right, and an increase in the real
      interest rate would cause the budget line to pivot
      counterclockwise through the initial consumption point.

Short-Answer Essay Questions

1.   **The real interest rate and the saving decision**: a) Draw a
      consumer's budget line diagram for a two-period model.
      Label the axes and the initial consumption point at the no-
      lending, no-borrowing point. b) Identify the slope of the
      budget line and explain why the slope is negative. c) Use
      the diagram to show the effect of an increase in the real
      interest rate on desired consumption. d) Briefly state the
      income effect and the substitution effect of an increase in
      the real interest rate for a saver. e) Draw a budget line
      diagram for a borrower and use the diagram to show the
      income effect and the substitution effect of an increase in
      the interest rate.

2.   **Tax incentives for saving**: a) Identify two types of taxes
      on interest earnings. b) Does an increase in the tax rate
      on interest earnings reduce desired saving? Briefly
      explain. c) According to most empirical research studies,
      how strong is the overall effect of a change in the expected
      real interest rate on desired saving? d) State the expected
      real after-tax rate of return equation. e) How would the
      expected real after-tax rate of return be affected by each
      of the following events: 1) taxes increase; and 2)
      expected inflation declines.

3.   **The real interest rate, the user cost of capital, and the
      investment decision**: a) Draw a MPK^f curve and user cost of
      capital curve. Label the axes, curves and equilibrium
      values. b) Briefly explain why MPK^f curve has a negative
      slope. c) How would desired investment be affected by a
      decline in the user cost of capital? d) State one reason
      why investment is a volatile component of total spending and
      explain how this volatility could be shown in your diagram.
      e) Use your diagram to show the effects of a technological
      advance.

4.   **Taxes and the desired capital stock**: a) State the user cost
      of capital equation. b) How would each of the following
      changes affect the user cost of capital: 1) an increase in
      the price of capital goods; and 2) an increase in the real
      interest rate. c) State the desired capital stock equation.
      d) How would each of the following changes affect the level
      of desired capital stock: 1) an increase in the capital
      gains tax; and 2) an increase in the depreciation rate of
      capital goods. e) Briefly define the "effective tax rate."

5.   **The saving-investment diagram**: a) Draw a saving-investment diagram. Label the axes, curves, and equilibrium values. b) Define the investment curve and explain its slope. c) Define the saving curve and explain its slope. d) Use the diagram to show the effect of a government budget deficit, created by a temporary increase in government purchases. e) What does the Ricardian Equivalence Proposition tell us about the expected real economic effects of a temporary government budget deficit? Briefly explain.

6.   **Fiscal policies and the *IS* curve**: a) Identify two fiscal policy instruments. b) Give an example of an expansionary fiscal policy. c) Give an example of a contractionary policy. d) Draw an *IS* curve diagram. Label the axes and curve. e) Use the diagram to show the effect of a contractionary fiscal policy.

Answers to Multiple Choice Questions

1.	a	8.	b	15.	a
2.	d	9.	b		
3.	e	10.	a		
4.	b	11.	b		
5.	c	12.	e		
6.	c	13.	d		
7.	e	14.	c		

Answers to Short-Answer Essay Questions

1.   The real interest rate and the saving decision

a)   A consumer's budget line diagram for a two-period model, with consumption at the no-lending, no-borrowing point.

b)   The slope of the budget line is $-(1 + r)$, where r is the real interest rate. The negative slope of the budget line shows that $(1 + r)$ units of future consumption are given up for each unit of current consumption. The negative slope illustrates that for a given *PVLR*, there exists a trade-off between current consumption and future consumption; each unit of

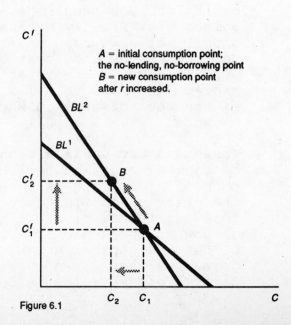

A = initial consumption point; the no-lending, no-borrowing point
B = new consumption point after r increased.

Figure 6.1

current consumption incurs the opportunity of cost of $(1 + r)$ units of future consumption. Likewise, each dollar of saving increases future consumption by $(1 + r)$ dollars.

c) As shown in part (a), an increase in the interest rate causes the budget line to pivot in a clockwise direction around the no-lending, no-borrowing point. The substitution effect of the interest rate increase causes current consumption to decline; C_1 declines to C_2. There is no income effect, when an individual initially consumes at the no-lending, no-borrowing point; unless the consumer saves or dissaves, the interest rate does not affect his income.

d) Income and substitution effects an increase in the real interest rate, for a saver:

   1) Substitution effect: An increase in the real interest rate will cause an individual to increase his saving and decrease his current consumption, because the relative rate of return to saving has increased. An increase in the real interest rate reduces consumption because it increases the opportunity cost of consumption.

   2) Income effect: An increase in the real interest rate will cause an individual to reduce his saving and increase current consumption, because the higher rate of return on saving means that he needs to save less to achieve any given level of future consumption.

e) Budget line diagram for a borrower. Since both the income effect and the substitution effect cause a borrower to save more and consume less, current consumption declines from C_1 to C_2.

2. Tax incentives for saving

a) The personal income tax and the estate tax both tax interest earnings.

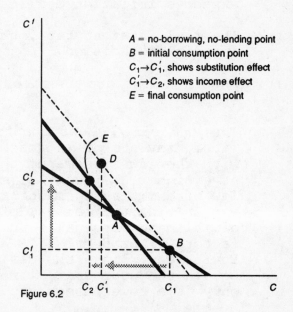

Figure 6.2

Interest earned on saving is taxed at the personal income tax rate of each household. The estate tax is a tax on the value of accumulated saving (i.e., wealth), when it is left to the next generation.

b)   An increase in the tax rate on interest earnings has the same effect on desired saving as a decline in the interest rate, since it reduces the after-tax real interest rate. Given the usual assumptions that most people are savers and that the substitution effect is stronger than the income effect, saving would decline in the macroeconomy. Individual savers, however, could choose to increase or decrease saving, since the income effect may be stronger or weaker than the substitution effect for them. Borrowers would decrease saving. Individuals who neither borrow nor lend would decrease saving.

c)   Empirical researchers have not been able to agree on the strength of the effect of a change in the real interest rate on desired saving. Most researchers believe that desired saving is positively related to the interest rate but that the relationship between the variables is weak, because of the opposing income and substitution effects for savers.

d)   The expected real after-tax rate of return equation is:

$$r_{\text{after-tax}} = i(1 - t) - \pi^e$$

e)   The expected real after-tax rate of return would decline, if taxes increased. However, $r_{\text{after-tax}}$ would increase, if expected inflation declined.

3.   **The real interest rate, the user cost of capital and the investment decision**

a)   An MPK^f curve and user cost curve diagram. See Figure 6.3 on page 77.

b)   The MPK^F curve shows quantity of capital goods demanded (i.e., investment) at each possible user cost. Consistent with the law of demand, the MPK^f curve has a negative slope; at a higher user cost (i.e., price), less is demanded. The law of diminishing marginal returns provides a theoretical explanation for the law of demand. Per the law of diminishing marginal returns, for given amounts of other factors of production, MPK^f declines as capital stock increases. Since the desired capital stock is where MPK^f equals the user cost, more capital stock will be purchased only at a lower user cost.

c)   Desired investment is the equilibrium level of capital stock purchases, where MPK^f = user cost. A decline in the user cost requires that MPK^f increase, to achieve a new equality. MPK^f measures the marginal benefit of employing capital, and user cost measures the marginal cost of employing capital. The desired capital stock equation illustrates the general economic efficiency rule of buying something up to the level where its marginal benefit equals its marginal cost.

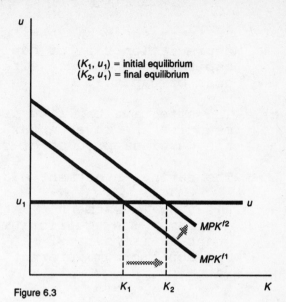

(K_1, u_1) = initial equilibrium
(K_2, u_1) = final equilibrium

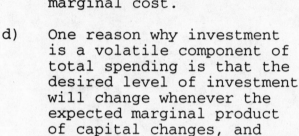

Figure 6.3

d)   One reason why investment is a volatile component of total spending is that the desired level of investment will change whenever the expected marginal product of capital changes, and such expectations are volatile. For example, good news about the macroeconomy tends to increase the expected marginal product of capital, because investors become more optimistic; whereas bad news tends to decrease the expected marginal product of capital, because investors become more pessimistic.

e)   As shown in part (a), a technological advance causes the MPK^f schedule to shift to the right. This increases the equilibrium level of capital stock purchases, from K_1 to K_2. The equilibrium user cost (u_1) does not change, because the user cost curve is horizontal. The horizontal user cost curve illustrates that the individual firm can buy all it wants at one user cost.

4.   **Taxes and the desired capital stock**

a)   The user cost of capital equation is:

$$u = rp_k + dp_k = (r + d)p_k$$

where: r = the expected real interest rate

d = the depreciation rate for capital

p_k = the real price of capital goods

b)   The user cost of capital would increase, if the price of capital goods increased or the real interest rate increased.

c)   The desired capital stock equation is:

$$MPK^f = u/(1 - \tau) = (r + d) \, p_k/(1 - \tau)$$

d)   An increase in the capital gains tax or an increase in the depreciation rate of capital goods would reduce desired capital stock, since either would increase tax-adjusted user cost of capital.

e)   The effective tax rate is a theoretical construct that measures the revenue-tax equivalent of the actual taxes on the marginal product of capital.

5.   **The saving-investment diagram**

a)   A saving-investment diagram. The equilibrium quantity is where $S_1 = I_1$. The equilibrium interest rate is r_1.

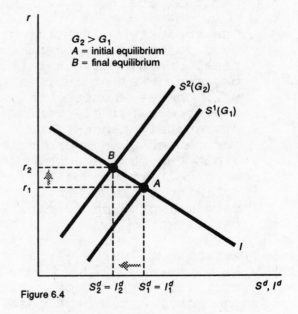

Figure 6.4

b)   By definition, the investment curve is the set of (I^d, r) points, which depict the various aggregate levels of desired capital stock purchases that all firms in the macroeconomy are willing and able to buy at various real interest rates. The slope of the investment demand curve is negative, because a decline in the real interest is needed to induce firms to purchase more capital goods at lower MPK^f values. MPK^f declines as capital stock purchases increase, per the law of diminishing marginal returns.

c)   By definition, the saving curve is the set of (S^d, r) points, which depict the various aggregate levels of saving that all households, firms, and levels of government are willing and able to supply (i.e., make available for investment) at various real interest rates. Consistent with the law of supply, the saving curve is positively sloped. The interest rate is the rate of return on funds saved. An increase in the interest rate raises the rate of return to saving, which causes desired saving to increase.

d)   As shown in part (a), a government budget deficit, created by a temporary increase in government purchases, causes the saving curve to shift to the left. The equilibrium level of desired saving and desired investment declines, from $S_1 = I_1$ to $S_2 = I_2$. The equilibrium interest rate increases, from r_1 to r_2.

e) According to the Ricardian Equivalence Proposition, a temporary government budget deficit created by a tax cut will not have any real economic effect, because it will not shift the saving curve. A necessary condition for the theory to hold is that no significant share of households face binding borrowing constraints. The Ricardian Equivalence Proposition does not imply that a temporary government budget deficit created by an increase in government purchases will have any real economic effects.

6. Fiscal policies and the *IS* curve

a) Taxes and government spending are fiscal policy instruments (i.e., tools). A change in tax rates and a change in government purchases represent changes in fiscal policy. b) An increase in government purchases is an example of an expansionary fiscal policy; it would cause the *IS* curve to shift up. A cut in taxes is expansionary, if there are binding borrowing constraints.

b) An increase in government purchases is an example of an expansionary fiscal policy; it would cause the *IS* curve to shift up. A cut in taxes is expansionary, if there are binding borrowing constraints.

c) A decrease in government purchases is an example of a contractionary fiscal policy; it would cause the *IS* curve to shift down. A rise in taxes is contractionary, if there are binding borrowing constraints.

d) An *IS* curve diagram.

e) As shown in part (d), a contractionary fiscal policy causes the *IS* curve to shift down. At a given level of real output (Y_1), the equilibrium real interest rate declines, from r_1 to r_2.

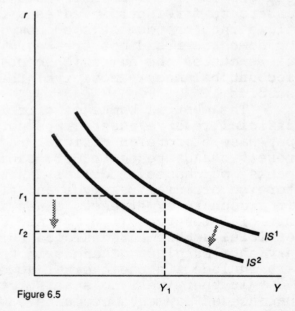

Figure 6.5

CHAPTER 7

SAVING AND INVESTMENT IN THE OPEN ECONOMY

A Review Of Chapter Highlights

The two principal **balance of payments accounts** are the current account and the capital account. The **current account** measures the values of currently produced net exports of goods, services, and income from foreign assets, plus the value of net unilateral transfers into the domestic national economy. The value of net exports of goods is called the **merchandise trade balance.** **Unilateral transfers** are the international flow of funds, such as foreign aid transfers, that do not represent payments for goods, services, or assets. If the **current account balance** has a negative value, the country has a current account deficit.

The **capital account** measures the net value of international trade in existing real and financial assets, including net changes in official reserves assets. The sale of domestic assets to foreigners creates a **capital inflow**; foreign income flows into the domestic economy. The purchase of foreign assets by domestic residents creates a **capital outflow**; domestic income flows out of the domestic economy. If the value of the **capital account balance** is positive, the country has a capital account surplus.

The central banks of different countries also buy and sell **official reserve assets** internationally. The Federal Reserve's purchase of foreign official reserve assets increases U.S. reserves and creates a U.S. capital outflow. Foreign central banks' purchases of dollar-denominated reserve assets increases foreign official reserves and creates a U.S. capital inflow. If a country experiences a net increase in the value of its official reserves (i.e., a net capital outflow) it has an **official settlements balance** surplus, also called a **balance of payments** surplus. Changes in the official settlements balance are included in the capital account balance.

If there were no statistical measurement errors in the balance of payments accounts data, the sum of the current account balance and the capital account balance would always equal zero. The **statistical discrepancy** is the net value of measurement errors in the balance of payments account. The statistical discrepancy has a positive value if the current account deficit is larger than the capital account surplus.

Total domestic spending on current domestic output ($C + I + G$) is called **absorption**. In goods market equilibrium, output equals absorption plus net exports. If output exceeds absorption, the country has a current account surplus; since foreigners purchase the excess output that domestic residents did not purchase, all of the output is sold in the current period in which it is produced.

A country that engages in international transactions has an open economy. It lends the value of its current account surplus to other countries, which enables foreigners to buy more output than they produced in the current period; the outflow of funds gives the country a capital account deficit. Alternatively, a country borrows the value of its current account deficit; the inflow of funds gives it a capital account surplus. An economy that is too small to affect the world real interest rate by its lending and borrowing is called a **small open economy**. The **world real interest rate** is the lending rate and borrowing rate in a perfect international capital market equilibrium. A **large open economy** lends or borrows enough to affect the equilibrium world real interest rate by its behavior. For example, an increase in international lending by a large open economy, by increasing the supply of savings in the world capital market, will lower the world real interest rate.

Questions

These questions test your understanding of the **key terms, key relationships**, and **key diagrams** highlighted in your text.

Multiple Choice Questions: Circle the letter corresponding to the correct answer to each question.

1.   The two principal accounts in the balance of payments accounts are the:

    a.   merchandise trade account and the current account.
    b.   merchandise trade account and the services trade account.
    c.   net exports account and income payments account.
    d.   current account and capital account.
    e.   capital account and the official settlements account.

2.   Which of the following transactions would not be included in the current account of the home country?

    a.   A consumer good is imported into the home country.
    b.   A capital good is imported into the home country.

c.   A foreign student pays tuition to a university in the home country.

d.   A home country resident receives income on his foreign assets.

e.   A home country resident makes a deposit in a foreign bank.

3.   Probably the principal reason why the merchandise trade balance gets so much attention in the news media is that:

a.   the news media love bad news.

b.   news reporters prefer to report international data much more than domestic data.

c.   the balance is reported quarterly, whereas most of the other data is reported only semiannually.

d.   the balance is reported monthly, whereas most of the other data is reported only quarterly.

e.   it tells us how well domestic suppliers of goods and services can compete in international markets.

4.   If a foreigner working in the United States sends 50% of his income to his family in his home country, the transaction will show up in the U.S. balance of payment accounts as:

a.   an income payment outflow.

b.   a capital account outflow.

c.   a unilateral transfer outflow.

d.   a current account deficit.

e.   a capital account surplus.

5.   A country has a current account surplus if:

a.   the value of its exports exceeds the value of its imports.

b.   the value of its net exports of services exceeds the value of its net exports of goods.

c.   it receives more income from foreign assets than it pays to foreigners for foreign-owned domestic assets.

d.   its financial inflows exceed its financial outflows.

e.   it sells more currently produced goods than existing assets to foreigners.

6.   The two principal accounts in the capital account are the:

a.   net capital inflows and net capital outflows.

b.   net capital inflows and the net change in official reserves.

c.   short-term capital and long-term capital accounts.

d.   debt capital and equity capital accounts.

e.   new capital and existing capital accounts.

7.   To achieve a net reduction in its foreign indebtedness, an LDC country must:

    a.   reduce its GNP growth rate.
    b.   stop importing.
    c.   export a higher value of goods and services than it imports.
    d.   not accept any capital inflows.
    e.   form a debtor cartel with other LDC debtors.

8. An economic benefit of capital outflows is that they:

    a.   reduce domestic unemployment.
    b.   reduce domestic saving.
    c.   increases domestic investment.
    d.   create future income payment inflows.
    e.   increase domestic output.

9. A country's capital account surplus will decrease if:

    a.   its current account deficit decreases.
    b.   its income payment inflows on foreign assets decrease.
    c.   its domestic residents working abroad reduce the income they send home to their families.
    d.   foreigners increase their purchases of its existing assets.
    e.   its residents reduce their purchases of existing foreign assets.

10. A negative value for the U.S. official reserve assets line in the balance of payments accounts means that:

    a.   U.S. residents have sold more gold to foreigners than they bought.
    b.   U.S. residents bought more gold from foreigners than they bought.
    c.   the U.S. central bank has increased its holdings of foreign reserve assets.
    d.   the U.S. central bank has decreased its holdings of foreign reserve assets.
    e.   the U.S. has a balance of payments deficit.

11. The official settlements balance:

    a.   is always negative when there is a current account deficit.
    b.   always equals zero.
    c.   declines when U.S. official reserves increase.
    d.   is always positive when the capital account is positive.
    e.   is also called the balance of payments.

12. If a country has a balance of payments deficit, then:

    a.   its capital outflows exceeded its capital inflows.
    b.   it cannot compete in international markets.

c.   it reduced its holdings of official reserve assets.
d.   it has a current account deficit.
e.   it must increase its exports.

13.   In the balance of payments accounts for the United States, the statistical discrepancy figure:

a.   would never exceed $10 billion.
b.   is the measurement error in the current account.
c.   is the measurement error in the capital account.
d.   used to exceed $10 billion, but recent improvements in the quality of data reduced the error to under $5 billion by 1990.
e.   exceeded $70 billion in 1990.

14.   Which of the following represents absorption?

a. $C^d + I^d$
b. $C^d + I^d + G$
c. $C^d + I^d + G + NX$
d. $Y + NX$
e. $I^d + NX$

15.   In a saving-investment diagram for a small open economy:

a.   the saving curve is vertical at some fixed level of output.
b.   the saving curve is horizontal at some fixed interest rate.
c.   the $I + NX$ curve is negatively sloped.
d.   the interest rate is fixed at the world real interest rate.
e.   equilibrium requires that $S^d = I^d$.

16.   In a model of two open economies, the real interest rate will increase in one economy:

a.   if saving declines in the other small economy.
b.   if saving declines in the other large economy.
c.   if investment declines in the other small economy.
d.   if investment declines in the other large economy.
e.   if investment increases in its small economy.

17.   A large open economy:

a.   dominates world trade in one or more products.
b.   is physically larger than all small open economies.
c.   has a larger population than all small open economies.
d.   is a lender in international markets.
e.   lends or borrows enough in the international capital market to influence the world real interest rate.

18. The goods market equilibrium equation in an open economy shows that:

a. $NX = S^d - I^d$
b. $S^d + NX = I^d$
c. $S^d + I^d = NX$
d. $S^d = I^d$
e. $NX = Y - S^d$

Short-Answer Essay Questions

1. **Balance of payments accounting**: a) Identify and briefly define the two principal accounts in the balance of payments accounts. b) Briefly explain why the sum of the two principal accounts is zero. c) Identify two types of transactions that would create capital inflows. d) Why do central banks buy and sell official reserve assets? e) Briefly evaluate the economic significance of a merchandise trade deficit compared to a current account deficit.

2. **Goods market equilibrium in an open economy**: a) State the goods market equilibrium equation for an open economy. b) How would a current account surplus be affected by a decline in investment. Briefly explain. c) How would a current account surplus be affected by a decline in saving? Briefly explain. d) State the absorption equation for goods market equilibrium in an open economy. e) Use the absorption equation to identify two possible causes of a decline in the current account balance.

3. **Saving and investment in a small open economy**: a) Define the term "small open economy." b) What determines the interest rate in a small open economy? c) Draw a saving-investment diagram for a small open economy that lends internationally. Label the axes, curves, and equilibrium values. d) Can it be determined whether or not the country has a current account surplus? Briefly explain. e) Could this country become a net debtor internationally without changing its willingness to save or invest at various interest rates? Briefly explain.

4. **LDC debt crisis**: a) Briefly explain why LDC countries are typically net borrowers in international capital markets. b) Why is the LDC debt problem now called a "crisis?" c) Identify and briefly explain two causes of the LDC debt crisis. d) Why do debtor countries have to be net exporters to service their debt; why don't they pay off the debt with domestic income? e) If the debt burden on LDCs has become severe, should they default on their foreign loans? Briefly discuss.

5.   **Saving and investment in a large open economy:** a) Is the
      U.S. a large open economy? Briefly explain. b) When there
      are so many countries involved in international
      transactions, is a two-economy model too simplistic? c)
      Draw a goods market equilibrium diagram for the home country
      and foreign country in a two-economy model, making the home
      country a net borrower. Label the axes, curves, and
      equilibrium values. d) Identify the line segments on your
      graphs that show the current account deficit or surplus of
      each country, and state how these line segments are related.
      e) Identify one event in the home country that would cause
      the world real interest rate to increase, and identify one
      event in the foreign country that could offset this effect.

6.   **Twin deficits of the 1980s:** a) What was the principal cause
      of the U.S. government budget deficits of the 1980s? b) Use
      the goods market equilibrium equation to explain the
      expected effect, if any exists, of the government budget
      deficit on U.S. net exports. c) Use the absorption version
      of the goods market equilibrium equation to explain the
      expected effect, if any exists, on U.S. net exports. d)
      According to the Ricardian Equivalence Proposition, what is
      the expected effect on U.S. net exports of the government
      budget deficit, and why might the proposition fail to
      predict the actual effect? e) What is the expected effect
      of the government budget deficit on the U.S. capital account
      balance? Briefly explain.

Answers to Multiple Choice Questions

1.	d	8.	d	15.	d
2.	e	9.	a	16	b
3.	d	10.	c	17	e
4.	c	11.	e	18.	a
5.	a	12.	c		
6.	b	13.	e		
7.	c	14.	b		

Answers to Short-Answer Essay Questions

1.   **Balance of payments accounting**

a)   The two principal accounts in the balance of payments
      accounts are the current account and the capital account.

      1)   The current account measures the value of net exports
            of currently produced goods, services and assets, plus
            the value of net unilateral transfers into a country.

2)   The capital account measures the value of net capital inflows into a country from trade in existing real and financial assets.

b) $(CA + KA = 0)$, because every international transaction is a swap of goods, services or assets and the two sides to any transaction always have offsetting effects on the current account and the capital account. Capital account surpluses (i.e., net borrowing from foreigners) finance (i.e., pay for) current account deficits. Current account surpluses finance capital account deficits (i.e., net lending to foreigners).

c)   Two types of transactions that create capital inflows are: 1) foreigners' purchases of existing domestic assets; and 2) foreign central banks' purchases of domestic reserve assets.

d)   Central banks buy and sell official reserves to officially settle their international balance of payments account surpluses and deficits. Changes in the official settlements balances cause the capital account balance to be equal but opposite in value to the current account balance.

e)   A current account deficit is more important, because it represents a net export deficit, whereas a merchandise trade deficit maybe offset by a surplus in services trade, net investment income, and net transfers. A net export deficit equals net foreign borrowing in the current time period.

2.   Goods market equilibrium in an open economy

a)   The goods market equilibrium equation for an open economy is: $S^d = I^d + NX$.

b)   The goods market equilibrium equation shows that, for a given level of saving, a decline in investment would increase a current account surplus, where NX equals the current account surplus. A decline in the domestic investment use of available saving would increase the amount of saving available for foreign investment. NX also represents net foreign investment—the net purchase of foreign assets by domestic residents and net lending to foreigners.

c)   The goods market equilibrium equation shows that, for a given level of investment, a decline in saving would create a decline in a current account surplus, where NX equals the current account surplus. Less saving would be available to finance foreign investments, so fewer foreign investments would be made.

d)   The absorption equation for goods market equilibrium in an open economy is: $NX = Y - (C^d + I^d + G)$.

e)   The absorption equation shows that a decline in the right-hand-side value of the equation would cause the current account balance (NX) to decline, to restore equilibrium. A decline in national income (Y) or an increase in any form of desired domestic spending—desired consumption, desired investment, or government purchases—would cause NX to decline.

3.   **Saving and investment in a small open economy**

a)   A *small open economy* is the national economy of a country that engages in (i.e., is open to) international transactions, but whose lending and borrowing in the international capital market is too small to affect the world real interest rate. Many developing countries are small open economies.

b)   Changes in domestic saving or investment in a small open economy do not affect the interest rate at which funds are borrowed and lent in that country; they can borrow or lend all they want at the world real interest rate. The world real interest rate is determined by the aggregate supply of saving and demand for investment in the international capital market.

c)   A saving-investment diagram for a small country that lends internationally:

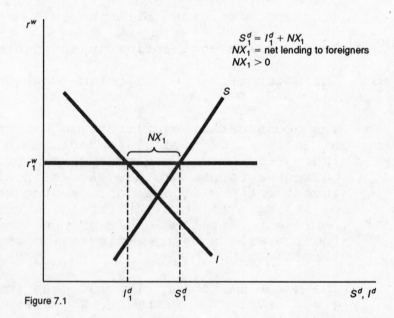

Figure 7.1

d)   In equilibrium, a country that lends internationally must have a current account surplus, because it can only lend the surplus foreign exchange that it earns from selling more exports than it imports. The country's capital account deficit is the value that it lends internationally, which is equal to its current account surplus (NX): $S^d - I^d$ = net capital outflows = $NX > 0$.

e)   Yes. For given domestic saving and investment curves, a
     sufficient decline in the world real interest rate would
     cause $S^d < I^d$, at which point the country would have become
     a net borrower internationally.

4.   LDC debt crisis

a)   Less developed countries (LDCs) are typically net borrowers
     in international capital markets because their supply of
     saving is low relative to their investment demand.
     Consequently, $S^d < I^d$ in these countries, at the world real
     interest rate. In LDCs, the supply of saving is low because
     their national income is relatively low compared to the
     income of developed countries; saving is positively related
     to income. In LDCs, investment demand is high because the
     expected future marginal product of capital (MPK^f) is high
     compared to MPK^f schedules in developed countries.

b)   The LDC debt problem is now called a crisis because
     developed country lenders have incurred extraordinarily
     large losses on these loans for several years and
     substantial future losses are still expected. Some debtor
     countries have threatened to default on the remainder of
     their huge foreign debts, but large defaults could threaten
     the health of some large bank lenders. Furthermore,
     attempts of LDCs to repay their debt impose a major burden
     on their economies.

c)   Two causes of the LDC debt crisis were:

     1)   unexpected global macroeconomic events: including the
          OPEC oil crisis in the 1970s followed by worldwide
          recessions in the 1979-1982 period, both of which
          reduced nonoil-exporting LDC's net exports.

     2)   careless lending and poor investment decisions. Banks
          loaned these countries too much, partly because they
          were lending "recycled petro-dollars," and the LDC
          borrowers did not efficiently invest all the funds in
          projects that would produce enough investment income to
          repay the loans.

d)   Debtor countries have to service their foreign debts with
     the foreign exchange they receive as net exporters of goods
     and services. If a country's capital account deficit equals
     its debt service, it must have an equivalent current account
     surplus to achieve balance of payments equilibrium.

e)   No. The long-term, high economic costs and political costs
     of defaulting on the debt make that option unattractive.
     The IMF, the World Bank, the governments and industry
     leaders of concerned countries are all working to resolve

the LDC crisis on terms that are acceptable to all parties involved.

5.   **Saving and investment in a large open economy**

a)   Yes. The U.S. is an "open economy" because it engages in international transactions; it is a "large economy" because it lends and borrows enough in international capital markets to affect the world real interest rate. Consequently, the United States is a large open economy.

b)   No. A two-economy model could include all the open economies in the world. For example, the U.S. economy could be one economy in the model; all the other national economies in the world together could represent the other economy. Although the two-economy model is a simplification, it is suitable for most economic analysis of international transactions.

c)   A two-economy diagram of goods market equilibrium, with the home country a net borrower:

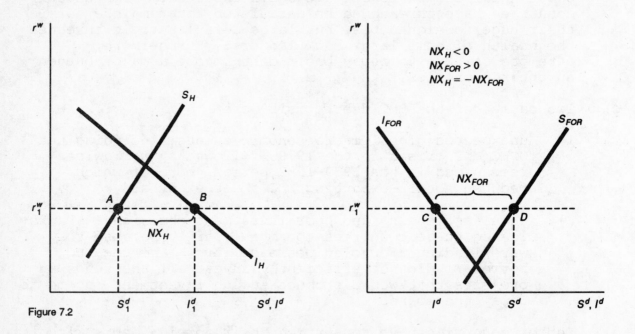

Figure 7.2

d)   The line segment *AB* represents the current account deficit of the home country; this equals the length of the line segment *CD*, which represents the equivalent current account surplus in the foreign country.

e)   A decline in home country saving would cause the world real interest rate to increase, as the home country saving curve shifted to the left. An increase in saving in the foreign large open economy country could offset this effect; the rightward shift in the foreign country saving curve would cause the world real interest rate to decrease.

6. **Twin deficits of the 1980s**

a) The principal cause of the U.S. federal government budget deficits of the 1980s was the Economic Recovery Act of 1981, which cut tax revenue without cutting government spending.

b) The goods market equilibrium equation for an open economy is: $S^d = I^d + NX$. If the government budget deficit reduces saving, for a given investment demand, then net exports (NX) must decline. If $S^d = I^d$, so that $NX = 0$ initially, then the decline in saving creates a current account deficit. This is the "twin deficits" view; a budget deficit creates a trade deficit. However, we cannot say with certainty that the tax cut reduced saving.

c) The absorption version of the goods market equilibrium equation for an open economy is: $NX = Y - (C^d + I^d + G)$. This equation shows that an increase in any type of domestic absorption (i.e., spending on domestic goods), for a given level of national income (Y), causes net exports to decline. For a given level of G, the tax cut is expected to increase C^d and I^d, which would cause NX to decline. However, we cannot say with certainty that the tax cut did increase absorption.

d) According to the Ricardian Equivalence Proposition, a government budget deficit, created by a tax cut, will have no real economic effects, because it will not affect saving. According to this theory, the government budget deficit and the trade deficit are independent events; they are unrelated occurrences. The Ricardian Equivalence Proposition may fail to predict the actual effects of the tax cut, when a significant share of U.S. households face binding borrowing constraints.

e) If the government budget deficit had no effect on the current account balance (NX), then it had no effect on the capital account balance, since these balances are equal but opposite in value in equilibrium. If the budget deficit caused the current account deficit, then it caused the capital account surplus. For balance of payments equilibrium, the capital account surplus is needed to finance the current account deficit (i.e.,the excess domestic spending in foreign markets).

CHAPTER 8

LONG-RUN ECONOMIC GROWTH

A Review of Chapter Highlights

Growth accounting identifies the relative importance of productivity growth, labor growth, and capital growth in determining the average yearly rate of real output (i.e., economic or national income) growth in the long run.

We use real per capita (i.e., per person) income as a measure of a country's standard of living. An increase in real per capita income is the same as an increase in output per worker, if a fixed share of the population work in each year. The Solow model of economic growth studies the behavior of real output per worker in the long run. In the Solow model, output is a positive function of the **capital-labor ratio**, which is the amount of real capital (e.g., equipment and structures) employed on average by each worker in the national economy.

The Solow model shows that an economy would reach a steady state in the long run, if there were no productivity growth. The long run is a period of time in which all markets continuously clear; it is a sustained period of general equilibrium growth. In a **steady state**, output, investment, and consumption increase each year at the same rate of growth as population growth, but output per worker, capital per worker (i.e., the capital-labor ratio), and consumption per worker do not change. Thus, there is no increase in a country's standard of living in a steady state. However, if there is productivity growth, output per worker can continue to grow indefinitely.

Two of the principal causes of productivity growth are technological advances in real capital and increases in human capital. Increases in **human capital** are improvements in the education, skills, health, and mobility of labor and entrepreneurs.

Although there exists a wide gap in the living standards of people in rich and poor countries, the Solow model predicts that their living standards will eventually converge (i.e., become similar). Differences in human capital help to explain the weak empirical support for the Solow model prediction of **convergence**.

Industrial policies and central planning are two types of government policies that might be used by countries to achieve higher average rates of economic growth and higher standards of living in the long run. **Industrial policy** attempts to promote economic growth by subsidizing firms in certain targeted industries, with the expectation that growth in these selected industries will create growth in other industries linked to them. **Central planning** attempts to increase economic growth by giving the central (e.g., federal) government the power to make most economic decisions, with the expectation that a large central government could allocate the factors of production, income, and wealth more efficiently than private market decision makers. Although these government policies offer some possible theoretical benefits, most economic research shows that industrial policies and central planning do not usually promote economic growth and do not usually improve countries' standards of living in the long run.

Questions

These questions test your understanding of the **key terms**, **key relationships**, and **key diagrams** highlighted in your text.

Multiple Choice Questions: Circle the letter corresponding to the correct answer to each question.

1. Which of the following is not an important variable in growth accounting calculations?

    a. productivity growth.
    b. money supply growth.
    c. labor growth.
    d. capital growth.
    e. output growth.

2. The steady state capital-labor ratio will decline if:

    a. the saving rate per worker increases.
    b. the consumption rate per worker declines.
    c. population growth increases.
    d. investment per worker increases.
    e. productivity increases.

3. Which of the following best describes a steady state?

    a. political stability is maintained by the state.
    b. peoples' standard of living is increasing at a stable rate.
    c. each firm in the economy receives a steady stream of income.
    d. an economy that has no output growth.

e.   an economy that is experiencing no change in saving per worker or investment per worker over time.

4.   The rapid recovery of the Japanese and West German economies after World War II is best explained by their:

a.   expansionary monetary policies.
b.   expansionary fiscal policies.
c.   protectionist trade policies.
d.   high level of human capital.
e.   high level of real capital.

5.   According to Solow's model of output growth, the standards of living of people in rich and poor countries:

a.   will eventually converge.
b.   will converge in the short run but will diverge in the long run.
c.   are the same today and will continue to be the same in the future.
d.   will converge for open economies but not for closed economies.
e.   will become increasingly unequal in the near future.

6.   Which of the following is not proposed by advocates of an industrial policy for U.S. high-technology industries?

a.   increased trade protection from high-technology imports.
b.   reduced regulation of high-technology firms.
c.   research and development funding assistance by government to high-technology firms.
d.   reduced business taxes.
e.   elimination of all subsidies to high-technology firms.

7.   One of the principal reasons that many countries are now moving:

a.   toward more central planning is that centrally planned economies have historically outperformed market economies in the long run.
b.   toward more central planning is that living standards have risen more rapidly in the Soviet Union than in Western market economies since World War II.
c.   away from central planning is that market economies have historically outperformed centrally planned economies in the long run.
d.   away from central planning is that central planning is not compatible with socialistic government.
e.   away from central planning is that democratic governments cannot plan for the future without damaging their market economies.

8. In the growth accounting equation, productivity growth is:

    a. the difference between output growth and labor growth.
    b. the difference between output per worker growth and
        labor per worker growth.
    c. the difference between labor growth and capital growth.
    d. the sum of labor growth and capital growth.
    e. output growth minus the sum of labor growth and capital
        growth, weighted by the elasticities of output with
        respect to labor and capital.

9. The per-worker production function relates:

    a. output per worker to capital per worker.
    b. output per worker to production per worker.
    c. output per worker to factors of production per worker.
    d. production per worker to the size of the work force.
    e. production per worker to the size of the capital stock.

10. Steady-state consumption per worker is:

    a. larger in the short run than in the long run.
    b. less than steady-state investment per worker.
    c. less than steady-state saving per worker.
    d. steady-state production per worker minus steady-state
        investment per worker.
    e. larger in large economies than in small economies.

11. According to the steady state equation:

    a. there are constant returns to capital in the long run.
    b. there are increasing returns to labor in the long run.
    c. an increase in saving per worker will produce
        continuing increases in a country's standard of living
        in the long run.
    d. the steady state capital-labor ratio will equate steady
        state saving per worker and investment per worker per
        year in the long run.
    e. for any given rate of saving per worker, there are many
        possible rates of investment per worker that are
        consistent with the steady state condition.

12. In analyzing the sources of economic growth in the U.S.,
    Denison and Jorgenson found:

    a. that economic growth in the 1980s was much higher than
        for other decades since World War II.
    b. that productivity growth declined significantly after
        1973.
    c. that capital growth is usually a more important source
        of economic growth than labor growth.
    d. that labor growth is more variable than capital growth.

    e.   that the U.S. economy achieved steady state growth for the 1948-1982 period.

13.   A decline in the rate of population growth in the U.S. will:

    a.   increase steady-state output per worker.
    b.   not affect steady-state consumption per worker.
    c.   reduce steady-state consumption per worker.
    d.   reduce the capital-labor ratio.
    e.   reduce steady-state saving per worker in the long run.

14.   In a steady-state diagram, if saving per worker initially exceeds investment per worker:

    a.   the economy will enter a recession.
    b.   the economy will experience inflation.
    c.   the capital-labor ratio will increase.
    d.   investment per worker will decline.
    e.   saving per worker will decline.

15.   Economic theory shows that increases in the capital-labor ratio will:

    a.   always reduce steady-state consumption.
    b.   always increase steady-state consumption.
    c.   reduce steady-state consumption, if starting from low capital-labor ratios.
    d.   increase steady-state consumption, starting from low capital-labor ratios.
    e.   reduce steady-state consumption, starting from high capital-labor ratios, and empirical studies show that most countries already invest too much.

16.   In a steady-state diagram, an increase in saving per worker is shown by:

    a.   shifting the saving per worker curve down to the right.
    b.   shifting the saving per worker curve up along a given investment per worker curve to a higher steady state capital-labor ratio.
    c.   moving to the right along a given saving per worker curve to a higher steady-state investment per worker.
    d.   shifting the production function down along an investment per worker curve.
    e.   a pivot of the investment per worker curve to the left, at the origin.

17.   In a steady-state diagram, a decline in productivity:

    a.   is shown by shifting the saving per worker curve down to the right to a lower steady-state capital-labor ratio.

b. is shown by a pivot of the investment per worker curve
    to the left, at the origin.

c. is shown by shifting the saving per worker curve up
    along a given investment per worker curve to a higher
    steady state capital-labor ratio.

d. is shown by a movement to the left along a given saving
    per worker curve.

e. reduces saving and investment but does not change the
    steady-state capital-labor ratio.

Short-Answer Essay Questions

1. **Sources of economic growth**: a) Identify and briefly
    describe the three principal sources of economic growth. b)
    Identify and briefly describe one cause of a change in each
    of these three variables, that would increase economic
    growth. c) State the growth accounting equation. d)
    Define the variable a_N. e) How do we know that the growth
    accounting equation is an identity?

2. **Causes of post-1973 growth slowdown**: Identify and briefly
    explain five causes of the post-1973 growth slowdown in the
    United States.

3. **The Solow model of growth**: a) Draw an investment per
    worker - production per worker diagram. Label the axes and
    curves, and identify the capital-labor ratio where long-run
    consumption is maximized. b) Briefly explain the shape of
    the per-worker production curve. c) Draw a steady-state
    diagram. Label the axes and curves. d) Identify and
    briefly explain the slopes of the two curves. e) If
    investment per worker initially exceeds saving per worker,
    how is the steady state capital-labor ratio achieved?

4. **Fundamental determinants of long-run living standards**: Draw
    steady-state diagrams showing the effect of the following
    changes on the capital-labor ratio: a) a decline in saving
    per worker; b) a decline in population; and c) a decline
    in productivity. d) In the Solow growth model, is
    investment per worker a fundamental determinant of long-run
    living standards? Briefly explain. e) Why does the Solow
    growth model predict convergence in the standards of living
    of people in rich and poor countries, and why does the
    empirical evidence appear to reject the theory?

5. **Government policies to raise long-run living standards**:
    Briefly discuss whether or not the government should adopt
    the following policies to raise long-run living standards:
    a) introduce a 5% national sales tax; b) provide a tax
    credit to firms proportional to their research and
    development expenses; c) require high school students to
    pass some standardized achievement tests at some minimum

performance level before they can graduate; d) adopt a less democratic form of government; e) have the government adopt comprehensive central planning of the national economy.

6.   **From central planning to market economies in Eastern Europe:** a) Identify and briefly describe two theoretical arguments in favor of central planning. b) Does the empirical evidence provided by Eastern European countries support the theoretical arguments in favor of central planning? Briefly explain. c) Identify and briefly describe two theoretical arguments against central planning.   d) Does the empirical evidence provided by Western developed countries support the theoretical arguments against central planning? Briefly explain. e) Use Solow's growth model to explain why many Eastern European countries are moving away from central planning toward market economies.

Answers to Multiple Choice Questions

1.	b	8.	e	15.	d
2.	c	9.	a	16.	b
3.	e	10.	d	17.	a
4.	d	11.	d		
5.	a	12.	b		
6.	e	13.	a		
7.	c	14.	c		

Answers to Short-Answer Essay Questions

1.   **Sources of economic growth**

a)   The three principal sources of economic growth are:

   1)   labor growth: increases in the work force.
   2)   capital growth: increases in the amount of capital employed in the economy.
   3)   productivity growth: increases in output for given amounts of labor and capital.

b)   Causes of positive changes in the sources of economic growth:

   1)   labor growth: an increase in the size of the population through immigration or birth and an increase in the share of the population that works (e.g., more women) will increase labor growth.
   2)   capital growth: an increase in the rate of saving will increase capital growth.
   3)   productivity: an increase in human capital and a technological advance will increase productivity.

c)   The growth accounting equation is:

$$\Delta Y/Y = \quad \Delta A/A \; + a_k \quad \Delta K/K + a_N \quad \Delta N/N$$

d) a_N = the output-elasticity of labor = percentage increase in output when labor increases by 1%.

e)   An identity is an equation that is always true. The growth accounting equation is an identity, because the value of productivity growth is always whatever it needs to be to achieve the equality. Because the equality always holds, the equation is an identity.

2.   **Causes of post-1973 growth slowdown**

Five of the significant causes of the post-1973 growth slowdown in the U.S. are:

1)   measurement problems: Actual growth may have exceeded measured economic growth during this period; the slowdown may be, at least in part, an illusion. Production of services now dominates production of goods, but increases in the quality and quantity of services (e.g., haircuts and financial consultant services) are harder to measure than increases in the quality and quantity of goods.

2)   legal and human environment: New legislated regulations to reduce pollution and improve worker safety and health caused some workers and capital to be allocated to meeting these new regulatory requirements, which reduced the amount of labor and capital available to produce goods and services. Increased use of labor and capital to fight crimes and a decline in educational quality (e.g., human capital) also reduced overall factor productivity.

3)   technological depletion: Per the technological depletion hypothesis, there were relatively few valuable technological innovations in this period and the earlier innovations are no longer producing significant productivity gains. Although significant breakthroughs in electronics (e.g., computers) and in biogenetic engineering (e.g., gene-splicing) have been achieved, they have not, as yet, produced significant productivity increases.

4)   commercial adaptation: American firms have been slow during this period to make commercially profitable use of recent scientific and technological breakthroughs; wheras some foreign firms, including Japanese firms, have benefited greatly from these breakthroughs.

5)   oil price increases: The substantial oil price increases in the post-1973 period lowered the amount of output that could be produced from a given amount of capital and labor, thus lowering productivity. Oil price increases caused the prices of all sources of energy to increase, and caused the prices of all intermediate products to increase, thereby significantly increasing final production costs.

3.   The Solow model of growth

a)   An investment per worker-production per worker diagram. Consumption per worker is maximized at k_1.

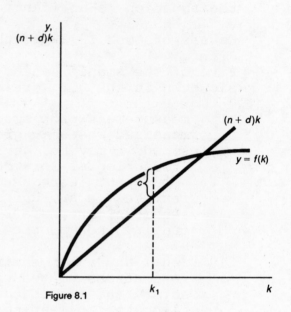

Figure 8.1

b)   The per-worker production curve is positively sloped because adding capital to each unit of labor increases output per worker. The curve is concave (i.e., increasing at a decreasing rate) because of diminishing marginal productivity of capital; output increases at a slower rate than capital when capital is added to production.

c)   A steady-state diagram. At k^*, steady-state saving per worker = steady-state investment per worker.

d)   The slopes of the two curves:

1)   the saving per worker curve is positively sloped, since saving is proportional to output per worker, which increases with the capital-labor ratio.

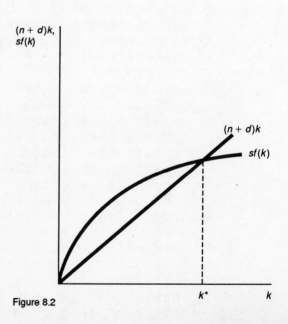

Figure 8.2

2)   the investment per worker curve is positively sloped, since investment per worker equals net

investment per worker (nk) plus depreciation of capital per worker (dk), which both increase with the capital-labor ratio. The positive slope of the investment per worker curve is $(n + d)$, with n and d both having positive values.

e)   If investment per worker initially exceeds saving per worker, then the initial capital-labor ratio exceeds the steady-state capital-labor ratio. However, the capital-labor ratio will decline, because saving is insufficient to provide enough capital to maintain the initial capital-labor ratio. The capital-labor ratio will continue to decline until it reaches the steady-state capital-labor ratio.

4.   Fundamental determinants of long-run living standards

a)   A steady-state diagram. A decline in saving per worker causes the steady-state capital-labor ratio to decline from k_1 to k_2.

b)   A steady-state diagram. A decline in population causes the steady-state capital-labor ratio to increase from k_1 to k_2. See Figure 8.4 on page 102.

c)   A steady-state diagram. A decline in productivity causes the steady-state capital-labor ratio to decline from k_1 to k_2. See Figure 8.5 on page 102.

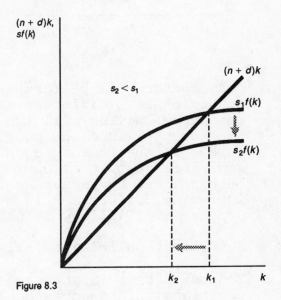

Figure 8.3

d)   No. In the Solow growth model, steady-state investment per worker does not change over time in the long run, so investment growth is proportional to labor growth plus depreciation $(n + d)$. The rate of investment is not an independent variable but a dependent variable, determined by population growth and the depreciation rate of capital.

e)   The Solow model predicts that the standards of living of two closed-economy countries with different capital-labor ratios will eventually converge, if they have the same production function, saving rate, and population growth rate. This is because they will have the same steady-state capital-labor ratio, toward which both economies move, and the steady-state capital-labor ratio determines their long-run standard of living. If the two countries have open economies,

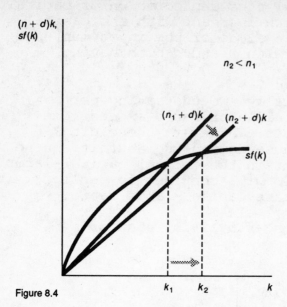

Figure 8.4

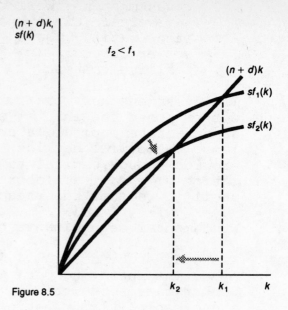

Figure 8.5

convergence will be faster and will occur even if the two countries have different saving per worker functions; in this case, saving will flow out of the rich, high saving rate country into the poor country, until the saving per worker is the same in each country. The lack of strong empirical support for Solow's prediction of convergence may be explained by variables that are missing from the model, including differences in human capital, political stability, and the availability of natural resources.

5.   **Government policies to raise long-run living standards**

Economic theory alone cannot fully answer "should" questions, since those questions require us to say what we "want" or "prefer." Although science cannot tell us what we want, it can help us to make policy decisions by identifying the economic costs and benefits of alternative choices. Among economists, there are those who favor and those who oppose each of the following policies: I offer one argument for and one argument against each policy proposal.

a)   A national sales tax

PRO: An increase in tax revenue, that lowered private consumption and was not spent by the government, would represent an increase in national saving. The Solow model shows that this increase in saving would produce a one-time jump in the country's standard of living.

CON: Although the tax increase may increase saving per
     worker, the government should not be using its taxation
     power to manage the aggregate saving rate. Households
     and firms can better decide how much they want to save
     without this kind of government intervention.

b)   A tax credit for research and development

PRO: A tax credit would raise the after-tax rate of return
     to firms investing in research and development, which
     would increase the rate of technological advances in
     the economy, thus increasing productivity. The Solow
     model shows that continuing productivity increases will
     produce continuing improvements in a country's standard
     of living.

CON: A tax credit for research and development will reduce
     government tax revenue and may not increase research
     and development (R&D) expenditures very much, since
     firms would get the credit for all of the R&D dollars
     they would have spent without the tax credit.

c)   Standardized achievement tests

PRO: Making students pass standardized achievement tests
     would encourage them, their parents, and their teachers
     to make sure they received a better education than they
     now receive, which would raise productivity. The Solow
     model shows that a one-time increase in productivity
     will provide a one-time jump in the country's standard
     of living.

CON: Although it is probably true that we don't achieve
     higher academic standards than we demand, standardized
     achievement tests would not necessarily represent
     higher aggregate standards; they could cause standards
     to fall to minimum required levels in many schools.
     Much of the enriching, motivating diversity of American
     education would be lost in a homogenized education
     system, even if Americans policymakers could agree on
     the desired standards and acceptable tests.

d)   A less democratic form of government

PRO: One of the problems with a broadly democratic,
     representative, popularly-elected government is that
     government leaders are subject to a lot of short-run
     political pressures to fund the pet projects of special
     interest group lobbies. Avoiding these inefficient,
     politically-inspired projects would increase
     productivity. The Solow model shows that a one-time
     productivity improvement would create a one-time jump
     in a country's living standard.

CON: Government by the people, of the people, and for the people must be sensitive to the will of the people if it is going to act in the interests of the people. A government that is sheltered or isolated from the will of the people is unlikely to be more efficient in satisfying the demands of the people.

e)   Comprehensive central planning

PRO: Comprehensive planning for the long-run development of the economy by government leaders would be more effective than the ad hoc uncoordinated, often conflicting decisions made by government leaders today. The Solow model shows that a one-time productivity improvement would produce a one-time increase in a country's standard of living.

CON: Although government planning for the limited economic role that governments should have in market economies may be beneficial, empirical research has convincingly shown that comprehensive planning by government in the economy is highly inefficient compared to decentralized planning by millions of individual market participants, coordinated by a market system of prices.

6.   **From central planning to market economies in Eastern Europe**

a)   Two arguments in favor of central planning are:

1)   lower unemployment rate: The planning commission of the central government can allocate all of the available labor to produce planned outputs. Thus, central planning will avoid the lost income costs of unemployment found in market economies.

2)   everyone's basic needs will be met: Enough resources will be allocated to necessities production to satisfy everyone's basic economic needs. The extreme problems of absolute poverty found in market economies will be avoided.

b)   No. Central planning by Eastern European Countries has not eliminated the income losses from inefficient employment and it has not eliminated poverty.

1)   unemployment: Although apparent (i.e., official) unemployment may be less with central planning, disguised unemployment (i.e., employed but unproductive workers) is more problematic and generally inefficient use of labor is widespread under central planning, all of which create income losses.

2)   poverty: Absolute poverty, by Western standards, is widespread in Eastern European countries. Since the amount of income each person receives is independent of how much each produces in centrally planned economies, people have little incentive to be productive, so productivity is very low and technological advances are relatively infrequent. The size of the overall pie that can be distributed to households is so small that basic needs still cannot be met.

c)   Two theoretical arguments against central planning are:

1)   an inefficient output mix: In centrally planned economies, firms do not produce what consumers want to buy, so consumers' wants are not met; central planners decide what will be produced (i.e., the output mix) and decide who will receive it (i.e., distribution of outputs to households).

2)   inflexible, legally set prices: With flexible price adjustments in a market economy, markets generally clear at equilibrium prices, but with the inflexible legal prices of central planners, prices and output levels cannot quickly adjust to market-clearing levels. Generally, there is an excess supply of some goods and an excess demand for others, since prices are not determined by demand and supply in centrally-planned economies.

d)   Yes. In market economies, unlike centrally planned economies, consumers are able to choose what they will buy (i.e., consumer sovereignty exists), and market prices and output levels quickly adjust to changes in supply and demand by moving toward their equilibrium levels.

e)   Solow's growth model shows that higher standards of living are promoted by higher productivity. Higher productivity is more easily achieved under market economies than under centrally-planned economies, because market economies are more efficient and provide greater incentives to achieve technological advances.

CHAPTER 9

BUSINESS CYCLES

A Review of Chapter Highlights

The NBER's **business cycle chronology** gives the dates for the peaks and troughs and identifies the number of months of contraction and expansion for the thirty complete business cycles experienced by the U.S. since 1854.

A **contraction**, also called a **recession**, is a downturn in aggregate economic activity that follows a peak in the business cycle. A severe recession of long duration is called a **depression**. A business cycle contraction bottoms out at a **trough**, followed by an **expansion** in aggregate economic activity. An expansion that includes rapid real GNP growth is called a **boom**. An expansion rises to a **peak**, which completes one cycle.

In addition to being measured from peak to peak, a **business cycle** can also be measured from trough to trough. A peak is an upper **turning point** and a trough is a lower turning point in a business cycle.

Business cycle fluctuations are deviations from the normal growth path of many aggregate economic variables, including changes in the economic growth rate, unemployment rate, inflation rate, and in other macroeconomic variables. The tendency for many economic variables to move together in a predictable way over business cycles is called **comovement**. The tendency for both contractions and expansions to last a while, once begun, is called **persistence**.

Comovements of aggregate economic variables over the business cycles are called business cycle facts. We study the business cycle facts, in part, by analyzing the direction and timing of changes in the values of these economic variables over the business cycles.

An economic variable that moves in the same direction as aggregate economic activity over the cycle is **procyclical**. An economic variable that moves in the opposite direction as aggregate economic activity over the cycle is **countercyclical**. An **acyclical** variable has no predictable pattern of change in value over the business cycle. The more sensitive a variable is

to business cycles, the more it changes in value over a cycle;
acyclical variables are insensitive to business cycles.

A variable that reaches its peaks and troughs before
aggregate economic activity is a **leading variable**. A variable
that reaches its peaks and troughs at about the same time as
aggregate economic activity is a **coincident variable**. A variable
that reaches its peaks and troughs after aggregate economic
activity is a **lagging variable**. Movements in leading variables
lead the cycle, movements in coincident variables coincide with
movements in the cycle, and movements in lagging variables lag
behind the cycle. The **index of leading indicators** is a weighted
average of thirteen leading variables, which is used to forecast
business cycles.

Government policy attempts to reduce business cycle
fluctuations in aggregate economic activity are called
stabilization policies. Classical economists opposed the use of
stabilization policies; they viewed these policies as
unnecessary, ineffective, and undesirable. Keynesian economists
endorsed the use of stabilization policies; they viewed these
policies as necessary, effective, and desirable. Today, new
classicals and new Keynesians still disagree on whether to use
stabilization policies, but their ongoing empirical research has
improved our understanding of business cycle activity and has
brought these schools of economists closer together.

Questions

These questions test your understanding of the **key terms**,
key relationships, and **key diagrams** highlighted in your text.

Multiple Choice Questions: Circle the letter corresponding to
the correct answer to each question.

1.   The NBER's business cycle chronology for the U.S. shows
     that:

     a.   there were no business cycles after 1961.
     b.   there were no business cycles prior to 1929.
     c.   there was no business cycle expansion in the 1930s.
     d.   the onset of major wars usually has caused the economy
          to contract.
     e.   compared to the 1954-1929 period, the post-1945 period
          was characterized by fewer months in contraction and
          more months in expansion.

2.   A business cycle contraction is best described as:

     a.   a decline in aggregate economic variables below their
          normal growth path.
     b.   a decline in real GNP growth.
     c.   an increase in the unemployment rate.

    d.   a decline in the inflation rate.
    e.   a decline in nominal interest rates.

3.   The 1973-1975 period showed that:

    a.   business cycles are easy to accurately forecast.
    b.   business cycles are dead.
    c.   stabilization policies have tamed business cycles.
    d.   Keynesian stabilization policies can quickly offset business cycle contractions without creating inflation.
    e.   business cycle recessions are not entirely temporary events, they sometimes create long-run losses of output.

4.   During the Great Depression:

    a.   Roosevelt's "New Deal" was completely ineffective in pulling the economy out of a contraction.
    b.   Roosevelt proposed a government program of annually balanced budgets and minimal government intervention in economic activity.
    c.   planned investment spending declined substantially.
    d.   output fell but the economy continued to provide full employment.
    e.   the financial market remained healthy despite the collapse of the goods market.

5.   After reaching a trough in November 1982, the U.S. economy expanded until:

    a.   the recession of 1985.
    b.   the recession of 1990.
    c.   the recession of 1988.
    d.   reaching a peak in 1985.
    e.   reaching a peak in 1988.

6.   Which of the following will not likely occur during an expansion?

    a.   real GNP growth.
    b.   declining money supply growth.
    c.   declining unemployment rate.
    d.   increasing average labor productivity.
    e.   increasing consumption expenditures.

7.   One negative aspect of a business cycle boom is:

    a.   a declining rate of unemployment.
    b.   a declining rate of inventory investment.
    c.   a reduction in government budget deficits.
    d.   increasing real wages.
    e.   increasing rate of inflation.

8.   A peak in a business cycle:

     a.   exhibits persistence.
     b.   is where real GNP has stopped growing.
     c.   is an upper turning point.
     d.   is where unemployment peaks.
     e.   occurs periodically.

9.   Listed in order, the phases of a complete business cycle
     are:

     a.   contraction, trough, expansion, peak.
     b.   contraction, recession, depression, expansion.
     c.   trough, expansion, boom, bust.
     d.   expansion, contraction, trough, peak.
     e.   peak, expansion, contraction, trough.

10. The lower turning point in a business cycle is reached by:

     a.   lagging variables before being reached by coincident
          variables.
     b.   lagging variables before being reached by leading
          variables.
     c.   coincident variables before being reached by leading
          variables.
     d.   leading variables before being reached by coincident
          variables.
     e.   all cyclical variables simultaneously.

11. The comovements of cyclical economic variables:

     a.   identify the cause-effect relationships between the
          variables.
     b.   enable economists to accurately forecast the duration
          of most business cycle contractions.
     c.   enable economists to accurately forecast the severity
          of most business cycle contractions.
     d.   are all procyclical.
     e.   are called business cycle facts.

12. Persistence of a business cycle expansion is best measured
     by:

     a.   the number of months from trough to peak.
     b.   the degree of periodicity in the expansion.
     c.   the rate at which real GNP increases during the
          expansion.
     d.   the degree of comovement of economic variables during
          the expansion.
     e.   continuing high rates of unemployment during the
          expansion.

13.   Which of the following is not a procyclical variable?

    a.   unemployment.
    b.   business fixed investment.
    c.   average labor productivity.
    d.   real wage.
    e.   stock prices.

14.   In theory, stabilization policies:

    a.   are procyclical.
    b.   are acyclical.
    c.   are countercyclical.
    d.   are both countercyclical and procyclical.
    e.   exhibit no comovement.

15.   Real interest rates are:

    a.   procyclical, just like nominal interest rates.
    b.   acyclical, while nominal interest rates are procyclical.
    c.   acyclical, just like nominal interest rates.
    d.   countercyclical, while nominal interest rates are procyclical.
    e.   not part of the business cycle facts.

16.   Which of the following is not a leading variable?

    a.   money (M1).
    b.   stock prices.
    c.   average labor productivity.
    d.   residential investment.
    e.   inflation.

17.   When the value of coincident variables are declining, aggregate economic activity:

    a.   will begin to decline within six months.
    b.   might start to decline in the near future, but aggregate economic activity is an unreliable indicator of contractions.
    c.   has been declining for at least six months.
    d.   is declining.
    e.   has just reached a trough.

18.   Lagging variables are aggregate economic variables that reach a peak:

    a.   after leading variables but before coincident variables reach a peak.
    b.   after coincident variables reach a peak.
    c.   two or more years after aggregate economic activity reaches a peak.

d   are insensitive to business cycles.
e.   are countercyclical variables.

19. Consecutive increases in the index of leading indicators
    during the most recent few months of a recession suggest
    that:

    a.   the severity of the recession will increase.
    b.   the recession will be of long duration.
    c.   the recession will become a depression.
    d.   within six months, the economy will be in an expansion.
    e.   the economy will soon recover if the index is rising by
         at least 5%; otherwise the recession will continue.

20. The use of stabilization policies during a recession is
    intended to:

    a.   lower real wages.
    b.   increase inflation.
    c.   reduce unemployment.
    d.   reduce the money supply.
    e.   reduce investment.

Short-Answer Essay Questions

1. **Characteristics of business cycles:** a) Define a business
    cycle. b) Define the following characteristics of business
    cycles: recurrence and persistence. c) Are business cycles
    periodic? Briefly explain. d) Identify and briefly
    describe the three types of possible comovement of economic
    variables in terms of direction and timing.

2. **Comovements:** Identify the comovements (i.e., direction and
    timing) of the following variables over a business cycle:
    a) production; b) unemployment; c) nominal interest rates;
    d) money supply (M1); and e) investment.

3. **Effects of business cycles:** a) Compare and contrast the
    effects of the following business cycle contractions on
    national output and unemployment: 1) 1929–1933; (2)
    1973–1975; 3) 1981–1982. b) Are business cycle
    contractions purely temporary events with only short-run
    real effects? Briefly explain. c) Identify two industries
    that are particularly sensitive to business cycles. d)
    Identify one negative effect of a booming expansion.

4. **Index of Leading Indicators:** a) Define the Index of Leading
    Indicators. b) Briefly describe how the index would
    forecast a contraction. c) What is the measurement problem
    of the index? d) Can the index accurately predict the
    severity and length of a recession? Briefly explain.

e) How reliable is the index in predicting upper and lower turning points in business cycles? Briefly explain.

5.   **Classical and Keynesian approaches to business cycle analysis:** Compare and contrast the classical and Keynesian approaches to business cycle analysis by answering the following questions: a) What causes business cycles? b) How persistent are business cycle contractions? c) How severe is the unemployment effect of contractions? d) How severe are the price effects of contractions? e) Are stabilization policies desirable?

Answers to Multiple Choice Questions

1.	e	8.	c	15.	b
2.	a	9.	a	16.	e
3.	e	10.	d	17.	d
4.	c	11.	e	18.	b
5.	b	12.	a	19.	d
6.	b	13.	a	20.	c
7.	e	14.	c		

Answers to Short-Answer Essay Questions

1.   Characteristics of business cycles

a)   Business cycles are recurrent fluctuations in aggregate economic variables away from their potential growth path. A complete business cycle may start at a peak or at a trough. A peak is followed by a contraction that ends in a trough, which is followed by an expansion, which rises to another peak to begin the next cycle.

b)   Business cycles exhibit recurrence and persistence.

   1)   Recurrence means that each complete cycle is followed by another complete cycle.

   2)   Persistence means that, once begun, each contraction tends to continue. Likewise, once begun, each expansion tends to continue. For example, the 1981-1982 contraction lasted for 16 months, and the 1982-1990 expansion lasted for 93 months. These are persistent events.

c)   No. Business cycles are not periodic. Contractions vary in length and severity; expansions are also irregular in their duration and intensity.

d)   Comovements: Over the business cycle, the values of some variables move together in terms of direction and timing.

1)   Direction: Variables may be procyclical, countercyclical, or acyclical. Procyclical variables change in the same direction as changes in business cycles. Countercyclical variables change in the opposite direction as changes in business cycles. Acyclical variables do not show any consistent directional movement over business cycles.

2)   Timing: Variables may be leading, coincident, or lagging. Leading variables reach the irrespective peaks and troughs before business cycle peaks and troughs. Coincident variables reach their respective peaks and troughs at the same time as business cycle peaks and troughs. Lagging variables reach their respective peaks and troughs after business cycle peaks and troughs.

2.   Comovements

a)   Production: is a procyclical and coincident variable.

b)   Unemployment: is a countercyclical variable whose timing is unclassified by the NBER.

c)   Nominal interest rates: are procyclical and lagging.

d)   Money supply (M1): is a procyclical and leading variable.

e)   Residential investment: is a procyclical and leading variable.

3.   Effects of business cycles

a)   Among these particular contractions, the effects on output and employment were largest for the 1929-1933 contraction. The 1973-1975 contraction had the second largest output effect, but the 1981-1982 contraction had the second-largest unemployment effect. At their troughs, the effect were:

	Percent Decline in Output	Unemployment Rate
1929-1933	30%	25%
1973-1975	4.3%	9%
1981-1982	3.2%	11%

b)   No. At least some contractions have long-run permanent effects, in that the economy does not return to its prerecession growth path. An example is the 1973-1975 recession. One researcher concluded that, on average, 70% of contractions are temporary and 30% are permanent.

c) Consumer durables and investment goods industries are
    particularly sensitive to business cycle fluctuations. The
    auto industry is an example of an industry producing a
    consumer durable. The steel industry is an example of an
    industry producing an investment good.

d) A booming expansion tends to overheat the economy, creating
    an increase in inflation. Booms are also likely to be
    followed by busts.

4. **Index of Leading Indicators**

a) The Index of Leading Indicators is a weighted average of
    eleven economic variables that tend to reach their peaks and
    troughs before respective business cycle peaks and troughs.

b) A decline in the index for three consecutive months during
    an expansion forecasts that a contraction will begin in the
    next three to six months.

c) The measurement problem is that the measures of the
    variables in the index are revised two months after being
    initially reported, and revised again two months later.
    These revisions, however, may be large enough to change the
    directional movement of the index from that initially
    reported. These errors in measurement may give off false
    alarms and, therefore, are troublesome.

d) No. The Index of Leading Indicators does not forecast the
    severity and length (i.e., duration) of recessions. During
    a contraction, it tells us only that the contraction will
    continue beyond or end in the next several months, but it
    does not tell us how long it may continue beyond the next
    quarterly period.

e) Partly because of measurement problems and partly because of
    the ever-changing structure of the U.S. economy, the Index
    of Leading Indicators is not perfectly reliable in
    forecasting peaks and troughs, but it is a valuable tool for
    predicting these business cycle turning points.

5. **Classical and Keynesian approaches to business cycle
    analysis**

a) Classical economists emphasize the supply-side causes of
    business cycle fluctuations; Keynesians emphasize the
    demand-side causes of most contractions and expansions.

b) The classical and Keynesian models are both consistent with
    the fact that business cycles tend to be persistent.
    Contractions often last more than a year and a complete
    business cycle may take a decade.

c)   Classicals believe that rapid wage and price adjustments
     will prevent a contraction from creating as much
     unemployment as the Keynesians predict. Output and
     unemployment adjust first in the Keynesian model, followed
     by wage and price adjustments.

d)   According to classical economists, wage and price
     adjustments will be large enough to quickly return the
     economy to full employment. In contrast, Keynesians believe
     that wages and prices are slow to adjust downward; so output
     declines and unemployment increases before complete wage-
     price adjustments are achieved.

e)   Classicals believe that business cycles represent the
     economy's best response to supply shocks; therefore,
     stabilization policies are unnecessary and socially
     undesirable. Keynesians believe that the market economy
     will not adjust quickly to demand shocks; therefore,
     stabilization policies are necessary and socially desirable.

CHAPTER 10

THE LABOR MARKET

A Review of Chapter Highlights

Aggregate labor demand (*ND*) is the number of workers (*N*) that all
firms and governments in the national economy are willing to
employ at various real wage rates ($w = W/P$) in some time period.
In real terms, each purely competitive firm will demand the
number of workers needed to equate the real wage and the marginal
product of labor. In nominal terms, each firm will demand the
number of workers needed to equate the nominal wage and the
marginal revenue product of labor, which is the revenue produced
by the last worker hired. The aggregate labor demand curve is
negatively sloped so that more labor is demanded at a lower real
wage.
       Aggregate labor supply (*NS*) is the number of workers who are
willing to work at various real wage rates in some time period.
At each possible real wage, individuals will supply the amount of
labor that maximizes their utility from income and leisure.
Leisure is the time not allocated to working in the market
economy. The aggregate supply of labor curve is positively
sloped so that more labor is supplied at a higher real wage.
       A change in the real wage has both a substitution effect and
an income effect on the amount of labor supplied. An increase in
the real wage is an increase in the relative rate of return to
work compared to leisure; the **substitution effect** tells us that
people respond by substituting some work for leisure. However,
an increase in the real wage also increases labor's real income
for a given amount of work; the **income effect** tells us that
people respond by substituting some leisure for work. Assuming
that the positive substitution effect of a temporary increase in
the real wage is more powerful than the negative income effect,
the aggregate labor supply curve is positively sloped.
       The personal income tax is a tax on labor income.
Economists contrast the effects of a change in the average tax
rate with the effects of a change in the marginal tax rate on the
supply of labor. The **average tax rate** on labor income is the
percentage of all labor income that is paid in taxes.   The
marginal tax rate on labor income is the percentage of the last

dollar earned that is paid in taxes. An increase in the average tax rate, holding the marginal tax rate constant, would create a pure income effect, which would cause labor supply to increase. An increase in the marginal tax rate, holding the average tax rate constant, would create a pure substitution effect, which would cause labor supply to decrease. **Supply-side economics** contends that a decline in the marginal tax rate on labor that also decreases the average tax rate significantly increases aggregate labor supply, because the substitution effect exceeds the income effect. Economists have several measures of employment and unemployment. The **labor force** is the number of adults in the national economy who are working or actively looking for work in the market economy. The **unemployment rate** is the percentage of people in the labor force who are unable to secure employment. The **participation rate** is the percentage of the adult population that is in the labor force. The **employment ratio** is the percentage of the adult population that is working. **Discouraged workers** are adults who have stopped participating in the labor force because they have lost hope of finding a job; if job opportunities increased for them, they would enter the labor force. Discouraged workers are not counted as unemployed, because they are not part of the labor force. However, the existence of discouraged workers causes the unemployment rate to understate the percentage of adults who would be willing to work, if market opportunities for employment were better.

Continuous unemployment for an individual over some time period is called an **unemployment spell**. The **duration** of an unemployment spell is its length in weeks or months. **Frictional unemployment** has a short duration for most people, because it is the unemployment of readily employable people, who are temporarily unemployed upon entering the labor force or after quitting one job to search for another. Some people, however, are **chronically unemployed**, which means that they tend to suffer long or frequent spells of unemployment. **Structural unemployment** has a long duration for most people. Structurally unemployed people tend to be chronically unemployed because they lack the job skills, education, or personal attributes demanded by employers. Structural changes in the economy, such as those created by technological progress and by changes in competition, create structural unemployment.

Frequently, structurally unemployed workers must upgrade their technical training or university education, or relocate to gain employment. According to the **dual labor market theory**, some workers may acquire enough job skills training by working in the secondary labor market to enable them to gain employment in the primary labor market. However, most jobs in the secondary labor market offer few opportunities for job skills training.

The unemployment rate is never zero, because some frictional unemployment and some structural unemployment always exist.

Questions

These questions test your understanding of the **key terms**, **key relationships**, and **key diagrams** highlighted in your text.

Multiple Choice questions: Circle the letter corresponding to the correct answer to each question.

1.   At the profit-maximizing level of employment for an individual firm:

   a. $w = MRPN$.
   b. $W = MRPN$.
   c.   adding one more worker would cause $MRPN$ to exceed w.
   d.   adding one more worker would cause $MRPN$ to increase.
   e.   the firm will maximize $(w - MRPN)$.

2.   Which of the following does not illustrate leisure?

   a.   repairing your home.
   b.   a night out for dinner and dancing.
   c.   studying for an upcoming economics exam.
   d.   enjoying a productive day at the office.
   e.   figuring out how to pay your household bills on your limited income.

3.   If your real wage temporarily increases, the substitution effect suggests that you will:

   a.   retire early.
   b.   continue working, but reduce the number of hours worked.
   c.   continue working 40 hours per week, even if you could work more.
   d.   offer to increase the number of hours you work.
   e.   substitute towards leisure, whose relative rate of return has increased.

4.   The income effect of an increase in labor's expected future real wage will:

   a.   reduce aggregate labor supply.
   b.   increase aggregate labor supply.
   c.   reduce aggregate labor demand.
   d.   increase aggregate labor demand.
   e.   not change current labor market conditions.

5.   For the highest income earners in the United States, the 1981 and 1986 Federal personal income tax changes:

   a.   lowered their marginal tax rate, without changing their average tax rate.
   b.   lowered their marginal and average tax rates.

    c.   lowered their marginal tax rate, but raised their
          average tax rate.
    d.   raised their marginal and average tax rates.
    e.   lowered their average tax rate, without changing their
          marginal tax rate.

6.   A temporary increase in the marginal tax rate on labor
income, with the average tax rate held constant creates:

    a.   a pure income effect, causing aggregate labor supply to
          increase.
    b.   a pure income effect, causing aggregate labor supply to
          decrease.
    c.   a pure substitution effect, causing aggregate labor
          supply to decrease.
    d.   a pure substitution effect, causing aggregate labor
          supply to increase.
    e.   an increase in aggregate labor demand, because the
          income effect exceeds the substitution effect.

7.   The empirical evidence for the Federal tax changes on labor
income in the 1980s suggests that supply-side economists:

    a.   overestimated the reduction in labor supply that the
          tax reductions would create.
    b.   overestimated the income effect on labor supply.
    c.   underestimated the reduction in labor supply that the
          tax increases would create.
    d.   underestimated the substitution effect on labor supply.
    e.   overestimated the increase in labor supply that the tax
          reductions would create.

8.   For married couples, several empirical studies have found
that a permanent increase in the real wage of the:

    a.   husband or wife will reduce the labor supply of the
          spouse.
    b.   husband will increase the labor supply of his wife.
    c.   wife will increase the labor supply of her husband.
    d.   wife will reduce the labor supply of her husband,
          although a permanent real wage increase for the
          husband, will not reduce her labor supply.
    e.   husband will reduce the labor supply of his wife,
          although a permanent real wage increase for the wife
          will not reduce his labor supply.

9.   The Bureau of Labor Statistics principally determines the
unemployment rate:

    a.   by totaling the reported layoffs by big business
          in the last month.
    b.   as the number of people collecting welfare payments.

c. as the number of people collecting unemployment
    benefits.
d. by a random interview of people on the street.
e. by a survey of about 60,000 households.

10. The labor force participation rate is the percentage of the:

a. population that is employed.
b. population that is willing to work but unable to find
    jobs.
c. adult population that is unemployed.
d. adult population that is working or actively looking
    for work.
e. adult population that is employed.

11. The employment ratio will increase if:

a. the labor force increases.
b. the adult population increases.
c. the population increases.
d. the labor force decreases.
e. employment grows faster than the adult population.

12. Discouraged workers are discouraged because:

a. their employers continue to underpay them.
b. they are working part-time, but they want full-time
    work.
c. they don't have jobs and are unable to find jobs in
    their specialties.
d. their employers are too demanding.
e. their bosses won't listen to their ideas about
    how to cut costs and improve product quality.

13. An increase in the legal minimum wage is most likely to
     create an unemployment spell for:

a. teenaged, unskilled workers.
b. middle-aged, skilled workers.
c. female workers.
d. professional workers.
e. plumbers and electricians.

14. In the United States, the duration of most unemployment
     spells is:

a. less than two weeks.
b. about two months or less.
c. approximately one year.
d. two or three years.
e. four or more years.

15. The type of unemployment for which the net economic costs
    are most likely to be small is:

    a.   structural unemployment.
    b.   frictional unemployment.
    c.   seasonal unemployment.
    d.   cyclical unemployment.
    e.   chronic unemployment.

16. Most of the chronically unemployed workers in the U.S.
    economy are unemployed because:

    a.   they are too old or too young to work.
    b.   they are too sick or too disabled to work.
    c.   they do not want to work; they would rather live on
          welfare.
    d.   of frictional unemployment.
    e.   they do not have the job skills and personal attributes
          their employers demand of labor.

17. The kind of unemployment created by technological progress
    and by changes in competition is called:

    a.   progressive unemployment.
    b.   competitive unemployment.
    c.   frictional unemployment.
    d.   structural unemployment.
    e.   capitalist unemployment.

18. According to the dual labor market theory, jobs in the
    secondary labor market can be characterized as:

    a.   progressive jobs.
    b.   full-time, permanent jobs.
    c.   dead-end, low-wage jobs.
    d.   jobs for highly educated workers.
    e.   jobs for skilled workers.

19. In a labor market diagram:

    a.   labor demand is a positively sloped curve.
    b.   labor supply is a negatively sloped curve.
    c.   the quantity of labor demanded equals the quantity of
          labor supplied at the equilibrium real wage.
    d.   a change in labor supply creates a change in labor
          demand.
    e.   a temporary adverse productivity shock causes the
          labor supply curve to shift to the left.

Short-Answer Essay Questions

1. **Labor demand**: a) Draw an aggregate labor demand curve. Label the axes and curve. b) Identify and briefly explain the slope of the curve. c) Identify two shift variables for the labor demand curve and state whether labor demand is positively related or negatively related to each of these variables. d) Can the quantity of labor demanded change without a change in labor demand? Briefly explain. e) State the employment rule that an individual firm uses to determine how much labor to employ, and use the rule to show when a firm is employing too much labor.

2. **Labor supply**: a) Draw an aggregate labor supply curve. Label the axes and curve. b) Identify and briefly explain the slope of the curve. c) Identify four shift variables and state whether labor supply is positively related or negatively related to each of these variables. d) Explain the income and substitution effects of an increase in the real wage. e) State the decision rule that an individual worker uses to determine how much labor to supply, and use the rule to show when an individual is supplying too much labor.

3. **Aggregate labor demand and supply**: a) Briefly explain how to use labor demand curves for individual firms and labor supply curves for individual workers to develop aggregate labor demand and supply curves. b) Draw a labor market diagram. Label the axes, curves, and equilibrium values. c) Draw a corresponding aggregate production function diagram. Label the axes, curve, and equilibrium values. d) Use the diagrams to show the real effects of a temporary beneficial supply shock. e) Would an increase in the capital stock create an increase in the level of employment? Briefly explain.

4. **Unemployment**: a) Briefly describe the method by which the Bureau of Labor Statistics determines the unemployment rate. b) Identify two types of unemployment and briefly explain the cause of each type. c) Are race, age, gender, and education determinants of unemployment? d) Does the duration of a typical unemployment spell depend on the type of unemployment? Briefly explain. e) Identify two government policies or programs that attempt to reduce unemployment.

5. **The Laffer Curve, tax reform, and labor supply**: a) Draw a Laffer Curve diagram and state the relationship between tax revenue and (marginal and average) tax rate. b) Use the Laffer Curve analysis to explain the expected effect on the quantity of labor supplied of a tax reduction, according to supply-side economists. c) What critique of the supply-side conclusions did Fullerton's empirical research provide? d)

Does the income and substitution effects analysis of the expected effects of an increase in the after-tax real wage support the supply-side conclusion? Briefly explain. e) What was the actual effect of the 1980s tax changes on the quantity of labor supplied, and does this empirical evidence support the supply-side conclusion?

6. **The minimum wage law:** a) Briefly describe the minimum wage law. b) What kinds of labor are most likely to be affected by the minimum wage law? c) Draw a labor supply-labor demand diagram, and use the diagram to show the effects of a minimum wage law on the labor market. d) Draw an *IS-LM* and *FE* line diagram, and use the diagram to show the effects of a minimum wage law on the product market and money market. e) Is the minimum wage law an effective way to reduce poverty? Briefly explain.

Answers to Multiple Choice Questions

1.	b	8.	a	15.	b
2.	d	9.	e	16.	e
3.	d	10.	d	17.	d
4.	a	11.	e	18.	c
5.	b	12.	c	19.	c
6.	c	13.	a		
7.	e	14.	b		

Answers to Short-Answer Essay Questions

1. Labor demand

a) An aggregate labor demand curve diagram.

$w = W/P$ = real wage per unit of labor time (e.g., per hour per worker)

N = units of labor time (e.g., number of workers)

b) The labor demand curve has a negative slope, which means that at a lower real wage, more labor will be demanded. The labor demand curve is the same as the marginal product of labor (*MPN*) schedule. *MPN* declines as N increases, because of diminishing

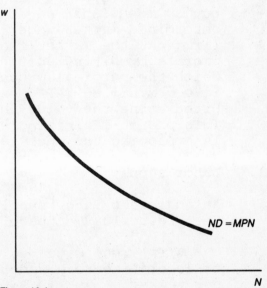

Figure 10.1

marginal returns to labor. At each possible real wage, firms are willing to employ the amount of labor needed to equate the real wage and the marginal product of labor ($w = MPN$). Because adding labor reduces *MPN,* firms will add labor only at a lower real wage for each worker employed.

c)   Two shift variables for labor demand are:

1)   productivity (*A*): labor demand is positively related to productivity. A beneficial productivity shock will increase labor demand, shifting the curve to the right. An adverse productivity shock will decrease labor demand, shifting the curve to the left.

2)   capital stock (*K*): labor demand is positively related to capital stock. Adding capital to production will increase the demand for labor, shifting the labor demand curve to the right. A decline in the level of capital stock employed will decrease labor demand, shifting the labor demand curve to the left. Capital principally complements labor in production, but an increase in capital may reduce the labor/capital ratio (*N/K*), since capital is, to some extent, a substitute for labor in production.

d)   Yes, moving along a given labor demand curve to another real wage changes the quantity of labor demanded, without changing labor demand. Labor demand is the entire set of (*N,w*) points, depicting various quantities of labor demanded at each possible real wage.

e)   Industry supply and demand for each type of labor will determine the real wage that each competitive firm will pay for a given type of labor. Each firm in the industry can buy as much labor as it wants to buy at the industry-determined market wage; the market real wage is given to the firm. At the market real wage, the firm will maximize profits by hiring enough labor to minimize the amount by which the marginal product of labor exceeds the real wage (i.e., minimize ($MPN \geq w$). When $MPN = w$, the last worker hired earns the value that he contributes to production. This profit-maximizing employment rule shows that the firm is employing too much labor, if $MPN < w$.

2.   Labor supply

a)   An aggregate labor supply curve diagram.
See Figure 10.2 on page 125.

$w = W/P$ = real wage per unit
of labor time (e.g., per hour
per worker)

N = quantity of labor supplied (e.g., number of workers)

b)   The labor supply curve is positively sloped, indicating that more labor time will be supplied at a higher real wage. The change in the real wage along a given labor supply curve is a change in the current real wage, holding the expected future real wage constant (i.e., a temporary change in the real wage). A permanent change in the real wage is a change in the current real wage and a change in the expected future real wage. Along a given labor supply curve, a temporary increase in the real wage increases the reward to working, which causes workers to increase the amount of labor time they are willing to work; as the real wage increases, workers substitute away from leisure and towards work.

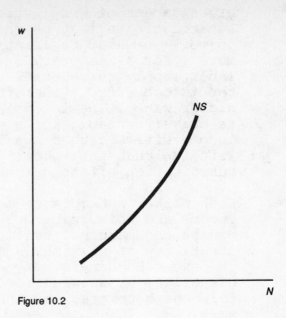

Figure 10.2

c)   Shift variables for labor supply include:

1)   wealth: labor supply is negatively related to wealth. An increase in workers' wealth will reduce labor supply, shifting the labor supply curve to the left.

2)   expected future real wage: labor supply is negatively related to workers' expected future real wage. An increase in the expected future real wage will reduce labor supply, shifting the labor supply curve to the left.

3)   government purchases: labor supply is positively related to government purchases. An increase in government purchases will increase labor supply, shifting the labor supply to the right.

4)   average tax rate: labor supply is positively related to the average tax rate. An increase in the average tax rate will increase labor supply, shifting the labor supply curve to the right.

d)   An increase in the real wage has an income effect and a substitution effect on the quantity of labor supplied. The income effect is that it increases labor's income for a given amount of work, which induces labor to work less. The substitution effect is that it increases the rate of return to work compared to leisure, which induces labor to work more. For a temporary real wage increase, along a given labor supply curve, the substitution effect is stronger than the income effect; therefore, more labor is supplied at a higher wage. The income effect makes the labor supply curve relatively steep. For a permanent real wage increase, the income effect causes the labor supply curve to shift to the left, so that the income effect could exceed the substitution effect on the amount of labor supplied.

e)   Each worker attempts to maximize her utility from labor income and leisure by working the number of hours needed to equate the marginal utility of income to the marginal disutility of working. The marginal utility of income is the expected benefit of the last hour worked. The marginal disutility of working is the expected cost, in terms of foregone happiness, of the last hour of leisure traded for work.

3.   **Aggregate labor demand and supply**

a)   If the labor demand curves by all individual firms and government are summed horizontally, the resulting curve is the aggregate labor demand curve. Horizontal summation requires that the amounts of labor demanded at each possible real wage are added together. If the labor supply curves of all individual workers are summed horizontally, the resulting curve is the aggregate labor supply curve.

b)   An aggregate labor demand-labor supply diagram.

Equilibrium = (N_1, w_1)

$ND^2 > ND^1$

c)   An aggregate production function diagram. See Figure 10.4 on page 127.

N = labor employed (e.g., number of workers per hour durings some time period, such as a month or year)

Y = aggregate output (i.e., real GNP produced during this time period)

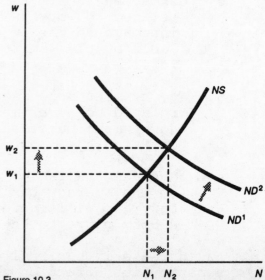

Figure 10.3

Equilibrium = (N_1, Y_1)
$A^2 > A^1$

d) A temporary beneficial
    supply (i.e., productivity)
    shock causes the slope of
    the production function
    (*MPN*) to increase at every
    level of employment. Since
    the labor demand curve is
    the schedule of *MPN* values,
    the labor demand curve also
    shifts upward. In the
    diagrams, A^1 increases to A^2
    and ND^1 increases to ND^2.

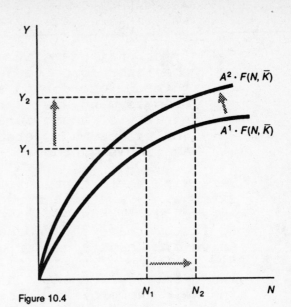

Figure 10.4

e) Yes. Assuming that the
    additional capital stock
    does not simply substitute
    for labor, the expected
    effects are similar to a
    beneficial supply shock.
    An increase in K increases the slope of the production
    function at every level of N, and causes ND to shift to the
    right along a given labor supply curve. The equilibrium
    level of employment (N) increases.

4. **Unemployment**

a) The Bureau of Labor Statistics (BLS) undertakes a survey of
    about 60,000 households each month to estimate the
    unemployment rate. The BLS categorizes people into three
    categories: employed, unemployed, and not in the labor
    force. The employed have jobs. The unemployed are actively
    looking for work and would accept a position at the market
    wage, if they could find one. About half the population of
    the United States are "not in the labor force;" these people
    are neither working nor unemployed. Among the people who
    are "not in the labor force" are those who are too young to
    work, too old to work, or too sick to work; some are
    students, some are homemakers, some are rich and prefer not
    to work.

b) Two types of unemployment are:

    1) structural unemployment: caused by changes in market
        structures creating a mismatch in the job skills of
        unemployed workers and those skills required by firms
        looking for workers to fill vacancies. Examples of
        structural changes that create structural unemployment
        include technological advances and changes in foreign
        competition. Structurally unemployed labor must often

relocate or acquire further education or technical training to gain employment.

   2)   frictional unemployment: created by people entering the labor force to search for a job and by people quitting one job to search for a better one. Unemployment spells for the frictionally unemployed are usually of short duration, since these people have the job skills and personal attributes needed to fill available vacancies.

c)   Yes, with the exception of gender. Black Amercians, for example, have a higher unemployment rate than white Americans. Teenagers have a higher unemployment rate than adults over age 20. Workers who did not finish college or university have a higher unemployment rate than those who did. Although women have a higher unemployment rate than men historically, there has been no significant difference in their unemployment rates in recent years in the United States. The demographics of race, age, and education are important determinants of unemployment.

d)   Yes. The duration of a typical unemployment spell for frictional unemployment is relatively short; the duration of a typical unemployment spell for structural unemployment is relatively long.

e)   Education policies and industrial policies attempt to reduce structural unemployment. Fiscal stabilization policies and monetary stabilization policies attempt to reduce cyclical unemployment.

5.   The Laffer curve, tax reform, and labor supply

a)   A Laffer curve diagram shows the relationship between tax rate and tax revenue. A maximum-revenue tax rate (t^*) exists; increasing the tax rate above this rate lowers tax revenue. The Laffer curve shows that to increase tax revenue, government may need to lower the tax rate. See Figure 10.5 on page 129.

T = tax revenue = tY

t = tax rate

b)   Assuming that the current tax rate exceeds the maximum revenue tax rate, supply-side economists reasoned that a reduction in the marginal and average tax rate would increase the quantity of labor supplied sufficiently to increase tax revenue. The tax rate reduction raises the after-tax return to labor compared to leisure, causing more labor to be supplied.

c)   Fullerton's empirical
      research concluded that the
      maximum-revenue tax rate
      (t^*) for the U.S. in 1981
      was about 79%, which was
      twice as high as the
      existing tax rate at that
      time; therefore, cutting
      taxes would reduce tax
      revenue.

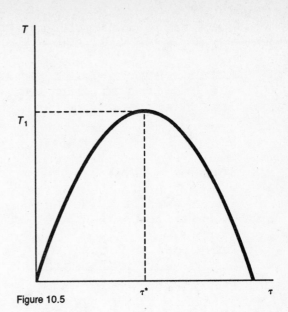

Figure 10.5

d)   The answer depends on
      whether the tax change is
      temporary or permanent.
      For a temporary cut in the
      marginal and average tax
      rate, the increase in the
      after-tax rate of return to
      labor would cause the
      equilibrium quantity of
      labor supplied to increase,
      given the usual assumption
      that the substitution effect is stronger than the income
      effect. The increase in tax revenue, however, is expected
      to be small. For a permanent tax rate reduction, the
      equilibrium quantity of labor supplied is more likely to
      decline, since the income effect becomes stronger. Based on
      the income and substitution effects analysis, we cannot
      unambiguously say what the net effect will be in either
      case, since the relative strengths of the two opposing
      effects are not known.

e)   The 1981-1984 marginal tax rate and average tax rate cuts
      had no significant effect on labor supply, as measured by
      the labor force participation rate. The 1986 marginal tax
      rate cut and average tax rate increase did increase labor
      supply by a small amount, in that it stopped the trend
      decline in the labor force participation by men. These
      results are consistent with the income and substitution
      effects analysis; they suggest that supply-side economists
      overstated the incentive effects of a tax cut.

6.   **The minimum wage law**

a)   The minimum wage law is a legal price support for labor,
      which may cause the real wage for low-skilled workers to
      exceed their market real wage.

b)   The minimum wage directly affects only low-skilled workers,
      whose market wage is lower than the minimum. Given that it
      affects only a small portion of labor, the minimum wage law
      has only small effects on the macroeconomic level of
      employment, rate of unemployment, wage rate, and labor

income. For the low-skilled workers directly affected,
however, a minimum wage that significantly exceeds their
market wage will have significant effects.

c)   A labor supply-labor demand diagram to illustrate the
     effects of a minimum wage
     law on the labor market.

     w_m = minimum wage

     (N_1, w_1) = equilibrium

     $(NS_m - ND_m)$ = unemployed
     low-skilled workers at w_m

     Principal effects:
     employment declines and
     real wage increases

d)   An *IS-LM* and *FE* line
     diagram to show the effects
     of a minimum wage law on
     the product market and
     money market.

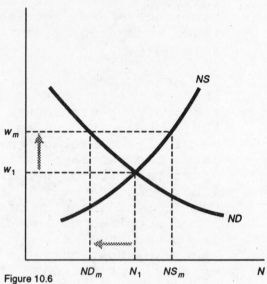

Figure 10.6

     Effects of minimum wage
     include: output declines,
     real interest rate
     increases, and price level
     increases.

e)   A minimum wage law may
     reduce the number of
     households living in
     poverty. This would occur
     most likely if most low-
     skilled workers lived in
     poverty at market wages,
     and if the minimum wage law
     created a percentage
     increase in the wage that
     exceeded the percentage
     decline in employment of
     low-skilled workers. The
     following market
     conditions, however,
     suggest that a minimum wage
     law may not be an efficient
     way to reduce the number of

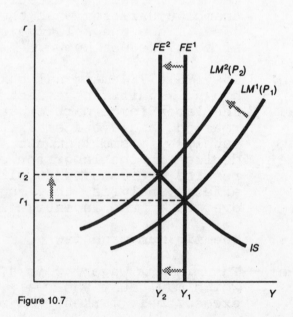

Figure 10.7

households living in poverty: 1) the household incomes of
most low-skilled workers already exceed the poverty income
level; 2) it increases the unemployment of low-skilled
workers, which reduces the income of those who

lose their jobs; and 3) the currently unemployed low-skilled workers will not benefit from the minimum wage unless they find a job.

CHAPTER 11

CLASSICAL BUSINESS CYCLE ANALYSIS: MARKET-CLEARING MACROECONOMICS

A Review of Chapter Highlights

Real business cycle (RBC) theory is a version of the classical model that contends that business cycle fluctuations in aggregate economic activity are principally caused by real shocks, especially productivity shocks. All shocks to the economy are either real shocks or nominal shocks. **Real shocks**, such as a change in aggregate labor supply or a change in aggregate saving, are changes that originate in the labor market or the goods market. **Nominal shocks**, such as a change in the aggregate money supply or money demand, are changes that originate in the asset market. There are many different kinds of adverse and beneficial **productivity shocks**, and any productivity shock will change the full-employment level of output.

One critique of the real business cycle model is that some business cycles are caused by changes in the money supply, which are nominal shocks. One business cycle fact that appears to support this critique is the fact that the money supply is a leading and procyclical variable. However, correlation does not prove causation; the fact that a decline in the money supply usually precedes a contraction in the business cycle does not prove that money supply reductions cause these contractions. RBC theorists believe that the leading, procyclical nature of the money supply illustrates **reverse causation**, which means that the anticipated change in the business cycle causes the Federal Reserve to change the money supply to maintain price level stability.

The classical aggregate demand-aggregate supply diagram illustrates general equilibrium. The **aggregate demand curve** shows that the level of real output demanded is negatively related to the price level. Each point on the aggregate demand curve represents equilibrium in both the goods market and the asset market at one price level, which corresponds to an equilibrium point in an *IS-LM* diagram. Since a decline in the price level shifts the *LM* to the right along a negatively sloped *IS* curve to a higher equilibrium level of real output, the aggregate demand curve is negatively sloped. The vertical **aggregate supply curve** shows that the level of employment and the level of real output in the macroeconomy are independent of the price level. Each point on the aggregate supply curve represents equilibrium in the labor market at one price level, which corresponds to a full-employment (*FE*) line at one level of real output. Because a decline in the price level does not shift the *FE* line to a different level of output, the aggregate supply curve is vertical.

The basic classical model assumes that market actors have perfect information. One implication of the perfect information assumption is that the general public, including producers, usually know the price level, even if the price level is frequently changing. An alternative way of stating that producers know the price level is to say that the actual price level (*P*) is the expected price level (P^e), so that producers' expectations are correct. The vertical aggregate supply curve is, in part, based on this assumption of perfect information; at any point on the vertical aggregate supply curve, producers' expectations are correct (i.e., [$P = P^e$] at each possible price level).

The **misperceptions theory** critiques the classical model assumption of perfect information by market actors. According to the misperceptions theory, producers' expectations do not quickly adjust to changes in the price level; therefore, there are short-run periods of time during which the price level does not equal the expected price level. During these short-run periods, firms misperceive a change in the price level as being a change in the price of their products relative to the price level, which causes them to change their output levels.

The extended classical model is an extension, based on the misperceptions theory, of the basic classical model. The positively sloped **short-run aggregate supply curve** of the extended classical model shows that firms will produce more than the full-employment level of output when ($P > P^e$), and they will produce less than the full-employment level of output when ($P < P^e$). The vertical **long-run aggregate supply curve** of the extended classical model, shows that firms will produce the full-employment level of aggregate output when their price level expectations are correct (i.e., $P = P^e$). The long-run aggregate supply curve in the extended classical model is identical to the aggregate supply curve in the basic classical model.

Although the basic classical model shows that money is neutral, this conclusion depends on the assumption that producers' anticipate any changes in the money supply and understand the price level effects of any changes in the money supply. In contrast, the extended classical model shows that money is not neutral in the short run, because producers do not anticipate changes in the money supply or do not understand the price level effects of changes in the money supply. In both models, however, money is neutral in the long run.

According to the **rational expectations** hypothesis, market actors are rational, which means that they will efficiently use all available information to form correct expectations about changes in the values of economic variables. One implication of the rational expectations hypothesis is that producers will anticipate any systematic changes in the money supply and they will understand the price level effects of these changes; only nonsystematic changes in the money supply (i.e., monetary surprises) will be unanticipated. Consequently, money is neutral, even in the short run, except in the unusual case of a monetary surprise. Therefore, a change in the money supply normally has no real economic effect, it simply moves us along the vertical long-run aggregate supply curve, in both the short run and the long run, to a different price level.

Although the misperceptions theory shows how aggregate output could deviate from the full-employment level of output during the short-run misperceptions period, it does not explain the persistence of these business cycle deviations. Since money supply data is published weekly and price level data is published monthly, producers' expected price level errors appear to be short-lived. However, short-lived expectations errors could have longer-term real economic effects, if there is one or more **propagation mechanisms** at work in the economy. The output effect of firms adjusting their inventory levels, after an expectations error has been corrected, provides one example of a propagation mechanism at work in the economy.

Questions

These questions test your understanding of the **key terms**, **key relationships**, and **key diagrams** highlighted in your text.

Multiple Choice Questions: Circle the letter corresponding to the correct answer to each question.

1. According to real business cycle theory, which of the following events is least likely to cause a recession?

    a.   a decline in the money supply.
    b.   a decline in investment.
    c.   a decline in productivity.
    d.   a decline in labor supply.
    e.   an increase in taxes.

2. Real shocks are disturbances in the:

    a.   labor market only.
    b.   asset market only.
    c.   goods market and asset market.
    d.   asset market and labor market.
    e.   labor market and goods market.

3.   According to the basic classical model, an increase in the
     money supply will cause:

     a.   employment to increase.
     b.   output to increase.
     c.   investment to increase.
     d.   the price level to increase.
     e.   saving to decline.

4.   Research on productivity shocks has shown that:

     a.   productivity shocks have only nominal effects.
     b.   there have been no identifiable productivity shocks in
          the U.S. economy since World War II.
     c.   small productivity shocks can explain large business
          cycle fluctuations.
     d.   large productivity shocks produce only small deviations
          in aggregate output.
     e.   productivity shocks have real effects but they don't
          have nominal effects.

5.   A decline in the money supply usually precedes a decline in
     business cycle activity; according to RBC theorists, this
     shows that the Federal Reserve:

     a.   intentionally causes most recessions.
     b.   should not be allowed to control the money supply.
     c.   does not know what it is doing.
     d.   often creates productivity shocks.
     e.   anticipates changes in business cycle activity, and
          efficiently changes the money supply to maintain price
          level stability.

6.   An increase in saving will shift the *IS* curve to the:

     a.   left, but will not shift the *AD* curve.
     b.   left, and shift the *AD* curve to the left.
     c.   left, and shift the *AD* curve to the right.
     d.   right, and shift the *AD* curve to the left.
     e.   right, and shift the *FE* line to the right.

7.   If aggregate supply declines, the aggregate supply curve:

     a.   shifts to the left, and the *IS* curve shifts to the
          left.
     b.   shifts to the left, and the *LM* curve shifts to the
          left.
     c.   does not shift, but the *FE* line shifts to the left.
     d.   shifts to right, and the *FE* line shifts to the right.
     e.   shifts to the right, and the *IS* curve shifts to the
          left.

8.   Misperceptions theory best explains why:

    a.   the aggregate demand curve is negatively sloped.
    b.   the aggregate supply curve is vertical.
    c.   the *SRAS* curve is positively sloped.
    d.   the *LM* curve is positively sloped.
    e.   money is neutral.

9.   In the extended classical model, a 5% decline in the money supply that is unanticipated will:

    a.   cause output to increase in the short run.
    b.   cause output to increase in the long run.
    c.   cause employment to decline in the long run.
    d.   not change employment in the short run or long run.
    e.   cause both output and employment to decline in the short run.

10.   In the extended classical model, the economy is operating on the long-run aggregate supply curve when:

    a.   output = employment.
    b.   the real wage = the real interest rate.
    c. $P = P^e$, at various price levels.
    d.   there is no frictional nor structural unemployment.
    e.   output exceeds the full-employment level of output.

11.   The misperceptions theory and the rational expectations hypothesis together suggest that systematic attempts by the Federal Reserve to increase aggregate output will:

    a.   cause ($P > P^e$) in the short run.
    b.   not have any real economic effects.
    c.   not increase the price level.
    d.   cause the *AD* curve to shift to the right along a fixed *SRAS* curve.
    e.   cause employment to increase more than the real wage.

12.   In the extended classical model, some kind of propagation mechanism is needed to explain:

    a.   the persistence of a recession.
    b.   imperfect information.
    c.   why money is neutral.
    d.   the difference between correlation and causation.
    e.   why producers are rational.

13.   A classical *IS-LM* diagram can be used to develop an *AD* curve by analyzing the effect of:

    a.   an increase in the price level on real output.
    b.   an increase in the real interest rate on the price level.

    c.   an increase in real output on the real interest rate.

    d.   a rightward shift in the *IS* curve on real output.

    e.   a leftward shift in the *IS* curve on the real interest rate.

14. If money is neutral, then a 5% decline in the money supply causes:

    a.   the price level to change, but does not change absolute product prices.

    b.   the price level to change, but does not change the nominal wage.

    c.   the price level to change, but does not change nominal income.

    d.   both the price level and nominal income to change.

    e.   the price level to increase by 5%, but has no real economic effects.

15. In the classical *IS-LM* and *FE* line diagram, a temporary increase in government purchases causes the:

    a.   *IS* curve to shift down to the left along a fixed *FE* line.

    b.   *IS* curve to shift up to the right along a fixed *FE* line.

    c.   *LM* curve to shift down to the right along a fixed *IS* curve.

    d.   *LM* curve to shift up to the left along a fixed *IS* curve.

    e.   *FE* line to shift to the right, the *IS* curve to shift up to the right, and the *LM* curve to shift up to the left.

16. In the extended classical model, an unexpected increase in the money supply causes the economy to:

    a.   move up the *LRAS* curve in the short run and long run.

    b.   move down the *LRAS* curve in the long run, but not in the short run.

    c.   move up the *SRAS* curve in the short run, and to shift the *SRAS* curve up along the *LRAS* curve in the long run.

    d.   shift the *SRAS* curve down along the *LRAS* curve in the short run, but not in the long run.

    e.   move down the *LRAS* curve in the short run and long run.

17. Equilibrium in the classical *AD-AS* diagram represents:

    a.   equilibrium in the goods market, but not in the labor market.

    b.   equilibrium in the goods market, but not in the asset market.

    c.   general equilibrium.

    d.   equilibrium in the labor market and goods market, but not in the asset market.

e.   equilibrium in the asset market and goods market, but not in the labor market.

Short-Answer Essay Questions

1.   **General equilibrium in the classical IS-LM and FE line model:** a) Draw a classical *IS-LM* and *FE* line diagram. Label the axes, curves, and equilibrium values. b) Identify and briefly explain the slope of each curve. c) Do classical economists believe that the economy usually operates in equilibrium? Briefly explain. d) Identify one variable that will cause each curve to shift, state the direction of the shift for a decline in each variable, and determine the effects on equilibrium values.

2.   **General equilibrium in the classical AD-AS model:** a) Show how to use an *IS-LM* and *FE* line diagram to construct an *AD-AS* diagram. b) Identify and explain the slopes of the *AD* curve and the *AS* curve. c) Draw an *AD-AS* diagram and use the diagram to show the effects of a decline in aggregate demand. d) Draw an *AD-AS* diagram and use the diagram to show the effects of a beneficial supply shock. e) Draw an *AD-AS* diagram and use the diagram to show the effects of a decline in the expected rate of inflation.

3.   **Real business cycle (RBC) theory:** a) According to the real business cycle theory, what is the principal cause of business cycle fluctuations? b) Define real shocks, define nominal shocks, and give an example of each. c) How do RBC theorists answer the objection that there have been few examples of large and easily measurable real shocks to the U.S. economy in recent decades? d) How do RBC theorists answer the objection that the money supply is a leading, procyclical variable? e) What problem does the empirical evidence of a steep labor supply curve pose for RBC theorists?

4.   **Fiscal and monetary policy in the classical model:** a) Draw a classical *IS-LM* and *FE* line diagram and a corresponding *AD-AS* diagram, then use the diagrams to show the effects of an increase in government purchases. b) During a recession, would classical economists propose that changes in government spending or taxes be used to improve economic conditions? Briefly explain. c) Draw a classical *IS-LM* and *FE* line diagram and a corresponding *AD-AS* diagram, then use the diagrams to show the effects of an increase in the money supply. d) During a recession, would classical economists propose that changes in the money supply be used to improve economic conditions? Briefly explain.

5. **The extended classical model:** a) State the short-run aggregate supply equation and use the equation to explain the slope of the *SRAS* curve. b) Draw an *AD-AS* diagram for the extended classical model and use the diagram to show the effects of an unanticipated decline in the money supply in the short run and long run. c) Draw an *AD-AS* diagram for the extended classical model and use the diagram to show the effects of an anticipated decline in the money supply in the short run and the long run. d) In the extended classical model is money neutral, and can nominal shocks create business cycle fluctuations? Briefly explain. e) Does the extended classical model explain the persistence of business cycle contractions and expansions? Briefly explain.

6. **Rational expectations hypothesis (REH):** a) Briefly state the rational expectations hypothesis. b) If producers are rational will they anticipate changes in the money supply? Briefly explain. c) Why do REH theorists believe that any monetary policy attempt to increase output during a recession will be systematic, rather than a monetary surprise? d) How do producers know how much the price level will increase when the money supply increases by 5%? e) What critique of the extended classical model does the rational expectations hypothesis make?

Answers to Multiple Choice Questions

1.	a	8.	c	15.	e
2.	e	9.	e	16.	c
3.	d	10.	c	17.	c
4.	c	11.	b		
5.	e	12.	a		
6.	b	13.	a		
7.	b	14.	d		

Answers to Short-Answer Essay Questions

1. **General equilibrium in the classical IS-LM and FE line model**

a) Classical *IS-LM* and *FE* line diagram. See Figure 11.1 on page 140.

b) Slopes of the curves:

   1) The *FE* line: is vertical at the full-employment level of output, indicating that output is independent of the real interest rate and independent of the price level.

   2) The *IS* curve: is negatively sloped, because an increase in output increases saving, creating an excess supply

of saving at the
initial interest rate;
therefore, the
interest rate must
decline to reduce
desired saving and
increase desired
investment, to restore
equilibrium at the
higher output level.

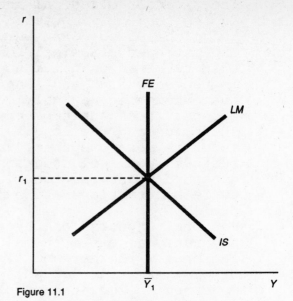

Figure 11.1

3. The *LM* curve: is
    positively sloped,
    because an increase in
    income increases the
    quantity of money
    demanded, creating
    excess demand for
    money at the initial
    interest rate;
    therefore, the
    interest rate must
    rise to reduce the amount demanded, to restore
    equilibrium at the higher output level.

c) Yes, classical economists believe that the economy normally
    operates in equilibrium in all markets, which it calls
    general equilibrium. Flexible prices quickly adjust to
    their equilibrium (i.e., market-clearing) values and, once
    there, there is no further tendency for these values to
    change. If there is some change in supply or demand in a
    market, flexible price adjustments quickly return the market
    and the economy to equilibrium.

d) Examples of shift variables:

    1) Productivity: A decline in productivity will shift the
        FE line to the left, causing output to decline,
        employment to decline, the real interest rate to
        increase, and the price level to increase.

    2) Government purchases: A decline in government
        purchases causes the *IS* curve to shift down to the left
        and causes the *FE* line to shift to the left, causing
        output to decline, employment to decline, the interest
        rate to decline, and the price level to decline.

    3) Expected rate of inflation: A decline in the expected
        rate of inflation causes the *LM* curve to shift up to
        the left. In the classical model, the price level
        falls, shifting the *LM* curve back to its initial
        position so that equilibrium output, employment, and
        the real interest rate are unchanged.

2.   General equilibrium in the classical AD-AS model

a)   Using an *IS-LM* and *FE* line diagram to construct an *AD-AS*
      diagram. The (*Y, P*) points labeled *A* and *B* are used to
      construct the *AD* curve. The (*Y, P*) points labeled *A* and *C*
      are used to construct the *AS* curve.

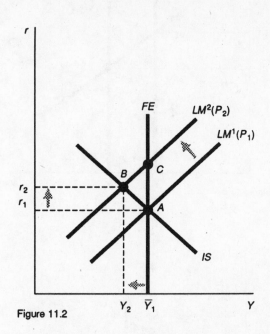
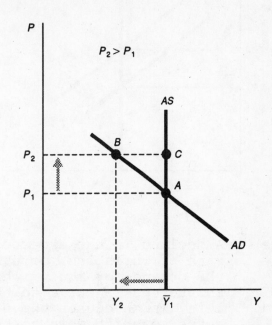

Figure 11.2

b)   The slopes of *AD* and *AS* curves:

    1)   The *AD* curve is negatively sloped, because a decline in
        price level shifts the *LM* curve down to the right along
        a negatively sloped *IS* curve, causing the amount of
        output demanded to increase. The negatively sloped
        aggregate demand curve reflects this increase in output
        demanded at a lower price level.

    2)   The *AS* curve is vertical, because a decline in the
        price level shifts the *LM* curve down to the right along
        the vertical *FE* line, which does not change the full-
        employment level of output supplied. The aggregate
        supply curve shows that the full-employment level of
        output is independent of the price level.

c)   In a classical *AD-AS* diagram, a decline in *AD* lowers the
      equilibrium price level (*P*). See Figure 11.3 on page 142.

d)   In a classical *AD-AS* diagram, a beneficial supply shock
      increases the level of output and lowers the price level.
      See Figure 11.4 on page 142.

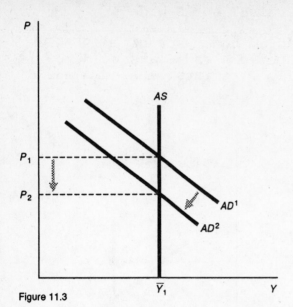

Figure 11.3

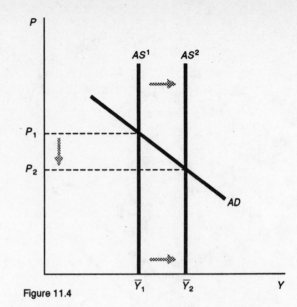

Figure 11.4

e)   A decline in the expected rate of inflation increases the demand for money, which shifts the *LM* curve to the left, which causes the *AD* curve to shift down to the left. In the classical *AD-AS* model, a decline in *AD* causes the price level to decline.

3.   **Real business cycle (RBC) theory**

a)   According to the real business cycle theory, real shocks, especially productivity shocks, are the principal cause of business cycle fluctuations in aggregate economic activity.

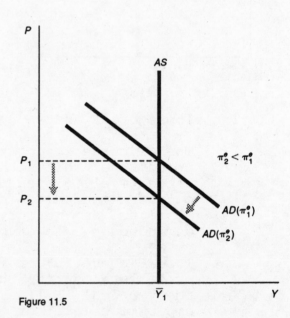

Figure 11.5

b)   Real shocks are changes that disturb labor market equilibrium or goods market equilibrium. Nominal shocks are changes that disturb the asset market. A change in aggregate saving is an example of a real shock. A change in the money supply is an example of a nominal shock.

c)   Computer simulations of RBC statistical models have shown
     that frequent, small, randomly generated productivity shocks
     can produce large business cycle fluctuations. Therefore,
     large business cycle fluctuations occur, even in the absence
     of large productivity shocks.

d)   The money supply is a leading, procyclical variable, but
     correlation does not prove causation. One plausible
     explanation is that the Federal Reserve anticipates changes
     in the business cycle, then reduces the money supply prior
     to a recession and increases it prior to an expansion to
     achieve its policy goal of maintaining price level
     stability.

e)   RBC theory suggests that productivity shocks are the
     principal cause of business cycle fluctuations. In the
     labor market, temporary productivity shocks shift the labor
     demand curve along a fixed labor supply curve. If the labor
     supply curve is steep, movements along the labor supply
     curve would create larger changes in the real wage than in
     employment levels. Therefore, a steep labor supply curve
     suggests that productivity shocks cannot create large
     fluctuations in employment and output; some other kind of
     shock is needed to explain these large fluctuations in
     employment and output. However, RBC theorists contend that
     the labor supply curve may be much flatter than previous
     research suggests, which means that productivity shocks
     could be the principal cause of most business cycles.

4.   **Fiscal and monetary policy in the classical model**

a)   In the classical *IS-LM* and *FE* diagram, a temporary increase
     in government purchases causes the *FE* line to shift to the
     right and the *IS* curve to shift up to the right. Price
     level adjustments cause the *LM* curve to shift up to the left
     to restore general equilibrium at a higher real interest
     rate, a higher level of output, and at a higher price level.
     In the classical *AD-AS* model, the *AD* curve shifts up to the
     right and the *AS* curve shifts to the right; equilibrium is
     restored at a higher output and price level. See Figure
     11.6 on page 144.

b)   No. Classical economists do not endorse changes in
     government spending or taxes designed to offset
     business cycle fluctuations; the classical model shows that
     such policy attempts are not likely to improve macroeconomic
     conditions. From a classical viewpoint, government spending
     and tax decisions should be long-run decisions, based on
     cost-benefit analysis.

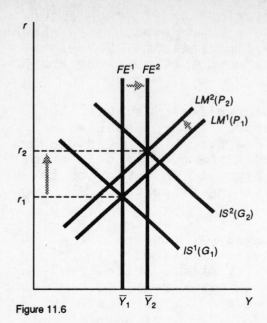

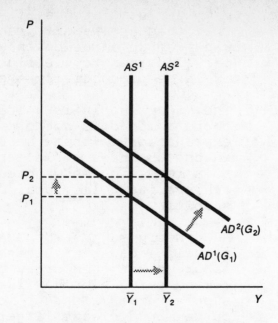

Figure 11.6

c)   In a classical *IS-LM* and *FE* line diagram, an increase in the
      money supply does not shift any curve, because the change in
      the nominal money supply creates a proportional change in
      the price level, so that the real money supply does not
      change; therefore, the *LM* does not shift.   In the classical
      AD-AS diagram, an increase in the money supply shifts the *AD*
      curve up to the right along the vertical *AS* curve, causing
      the price level to increase.

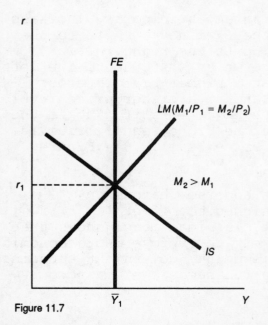

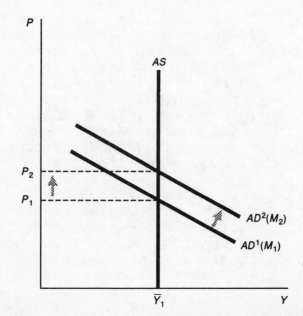

Figure 11.7

d)   No. In the classical model, an increase in the money supply
      cannot improve economic conditions, because it has no real
      economic effects. Money is neutral in the classical model.

5.   The extended classical model

a)   The short-run aggregate supply equation is:

$$Y = \bar{Y} + b(P - P^e), \text{ where } b > 0$$

This equation states the SRAS curve is a set of (Y, P) points
where: 1) Output equals the full-employment level of
output, when the actual price level equals the expected
price level. 2) Output exceeds the full-employment level of
output, when the price level exceeds the expected price
level. 3) Output is less than the full-employment level of
output, when the price level is less than the expected price
level.

b)   In the extended classical model, an unanticipated decline in
      the money supply causes the price level to decline and
      output to decline, as shown
      by the movement from A to
      B. In the long run, the
      price level declines
      further, as the expected
      price level declines, but
      there is no output effect
      in the long run, as shown
      by the movement from A to
      C.

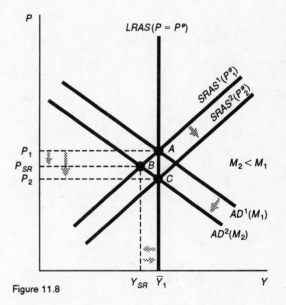

Figure 11.8

c)   In the extended classical
      model, an anticipated
      decline in the money supply
      causes the price level and
      the expected price level to
      immediately decline,
      without producing any
      change in real output. The
      neutrality of money is
      shown by the movement from
      A to B in the diagram. See
      Figure 11.9 on page 146.

d)   In the extended classical model, money is neutral in the
      long run. In the short run, anticipated changes in the money
      supply are neutral, but unanticipated changes in the money
      supply are nonneutral. Changes in the money supply are
      nominal shocks. Only unanticipated nominal shocks can
      create business cycle fluctuations in the extended classical
      model.

e)   No. Although the model shows that a monetary surprise can create short-run business cycle fluctuations in aggregate economic activity, the frequent publication of money supply data and price level data suggest that these errors will not persist. The persistence of a business cycle contraction requires some additional propagation mechanism to explain it. One such propagation mechanism is the process of adjusting inventories to their desired level, once misperceptions have been corrected.

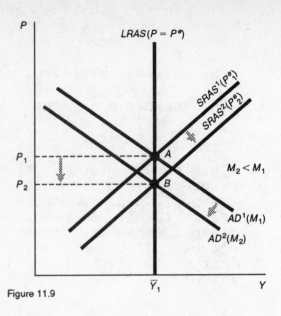

Figure 11.9

6.   **Rational expectations hypothesis (REH)**

a)   The rational expectations hypothesis states that market actors will use all available information in predicting the values of important economic variables, and they will learn to improve the accuracy of their predictions over time.

b)   Rational producers will learn to anticipate any systematic changes in the money supply, but they cannot anticipate nonsystematic monetary surprises.

c)   REH theorists argue that the public will learn to understand the Federal Reserve's behavior and will expect the Federal Reserve to increase the money supply when the economy is in a recession. But if the public anticipates the increase in the money supply, output will be unaffected by the increase in the money supply.

d)   Producers know that classical economic theory predicts that a 5% increase in the money supply will cause the price level to increase by 5%, because price level changes are proportional to money supply changes in the long run.

e)   Although the extended classical model, based on the misperceptions theory, suggests that any change in the money supply could have real economic effects in the short run, the rational expectations hypothesis suggests that only nonsystematic changes in the money supply could have short-run real effects. Because monetary policymakers do not use nonsystematic policies, money is neutral.

CHAPTER 12

KEYNESIANISM: THE MACROECONOMICS OF WAGE AND PRICE RIGIDITY

A Review of Chapter Highlights

Real wage rigidity, in the short run, is an important feature of the Keynesian model of the labor market. Real wage rigidity means that the real wage does not change when firms' aggregate demand for labor increases or declines. The assumption of real wage rigidity in the Keynesian model contrasts with the assumption of perfectly flexible real wages in the classical model.

The Keynesian model of the labor market is also an **efficiency wage model**, in which the point on the **effort curve** that maximizes each worker's effort per hour of real wage is the **efficiency wage**. In the Keynesian model of the labor market, firms can hire all the labor they want at the efficiency wage. At the efficiency wage, there is an excess supply of labor; changes in labor supply do not affect the efficiency wage or employment. The efficiency wage in the Keynesian model contrasts with the market-clearing wage in the classical model.

Price stickiness, in the short run, is another important feature of the Keynesian model. Price stickiness means that firms do not change the price at which they supply goods when the aggregate demand for goods either increases or declines. Given price stickiness, the short-run aggregate supply curve is horizontal at a fixed price level for all levels of output. The assumption of price stickiness in the Keynesian model contrasts with the assumption of perfectly flexible prices in the classical model.

Another contrast is that individual firms are **price takers** in the classical model, whereas individual firms are **price setters** in the Keynesian model. This difference is based on another contrast; the classical model assumes **perfect competition** among firms, but the Keynesian model assumes **monopolistic competition** among firms. A perfectly competitive firm is a price taker, which cannot increase its selling price without losing all its customers to competing firms. In contrast, a monopolistically competitive firm is a price setter, which can vary its price by a small margin without greatly affecting its market share.

The cost incurred by a firm in changing its price is called its **menu cost**. To maximize profits, a firm will only change its price if the change is large enough to create an increase in revenue minus production costs large enough to pay for the menu cost. Keynesians believe that, although menu costs are small, they are large enough for monopolistically competitive firms to prevent them from frequently changing their prices; therefore prices are sticky.

For the perfectly competitive firms of the classical model, operating under long-run, general equilibrium market conditions, price equals marginal cost. For an individual firm, the **marginal cost** is the cost of producing the last unit of output. In contrast, the monopolistically competitive firms of the Keynesian model, in the short run, may charge a price that exceeds marginal cost. The **markup** is the percentage by which price exceeds marginal cost (e.g., 10%).

In the Keynesian model, employment is independent of labor supply; labor demand depends on the quantity of goods demanded. Firms demand just enough labor to produce the level of output demanded.   The **effective labor demand curve** shows that more labor will be demanded and employed as output increases. In the short run, output may exceed or be less than the full-employment level of output.

The Keynesian model offers an explanation for the Great Depression. It shows how a short-run period of recession and high unemployment can continue for several years. Keynesians propose that national government policymakers attempt to pull the economy out of recessions by using expansionary **macroeconomic stabilization** policies, such as increasing the money supply or increasing government purchases. Macroeconomic stabilization policies attempt to maintain the level of aggregate demand at the full-employment level of output; they represent **aggregate demand management**, in that they are attempts to manage the level of aggregate demand.

The Keynesian model highlights the importance of aggregate demand in the determination of output and employment. Changes in the goods market and the asset market create changes in aggregate demand, called **aggregate demand shocks**. Aggregate demand shocks, in turn, create changes in output, employment, and unemployment. The early Keynesians believed that most recessions were caused by some aggregate demand shock.

Although the basic Keynesian model can explain many of the business cycle facts, it requires the additional assumption of **labor hoarding** to explain why the average productivity of labor is procyclical. Average labor productivity declines during recessions because the high cost of firing, hiring, and training labor causes firms to retain more labor than is needed to produce output during these short-run contractions.

Questions

These questions test your understanding of the **key terms**, **key relationships**, and **key diagrams** highlighted in your text.

Multiple Choice Questions: Circle the letter corresponding to the correct answer to each question.

1. Real wage rigidity in the Keynesian efficiency wage model diagram of the labor market is depicted by:

   a. a vertical labor supply curve at the efficient level of employment.
   b. a vertical labor demand curve at the efficient level of employment.
   c. a horizontal wage curve at the efficiency wage.
   d. a steep, positively sloped labor supply curve, depicting various efficiency wages at various employment levels.
   e. an equilibrium wage, where the quantity of labor demanded equals the quantity of labor supplied.

2. At full-employment in the Keynesian efficiency wage model:

   a. the real wage is the market-clearing wage.
   b. there is an excess demand for labor.
   c. $MPN^* < w^*$
   d. there is an excess supply of labor.
   e. there is no structural or frictional unemployment.

3. The effort curve is:

   a. horizontal, because work effort is independent of the real wage.
   b. negatively sloped, because of diminishing marginal returns to labor.
   c. positively sloped, because of the law of increasing cost.
   d. S-shaped, because a small increase in the real wage will increase work effort more at an intermediate wage than at a low wage or at a high wage.
   e. positively sloped at low wages, because of the substitution effect, but negatively sloped at high wages because of the income effect.

4. The efficiency wage is the real wage that:

   a. maximizes labor income.
   b. maximizes profits.
   c. maximizes employment.
   d. maximizes labor supply.
   e. clears the labor market.

5.   Because of price stickiness in the Keynesian model, a
      decline in investment demand will not cause the:

      a.   *LM* curve to shift down to the right in the short run.
      b.   *LM* curve to shift in the long run.
      c.   *IS* curve to shift down in the short run.
      d.   *IS* curve to shift in the long run.
      e.   *FE* line to shift to the left in the long run.

6.   A firm is a price taker if it:

      a.   always sells its output at the industry-determined
            price.
      b.   takes consumer demand into consideration in setting its
            price.
      c.   takes its production costs into consideration in
            setting its price.
      d.   uses a pricing strategy to gain market share.
      e.   sells its output at a fixed price despite short-run
            fluctuations in industry demand, but adjusts its price
            to the market-clearing price in the long run.

7.   If firms are price setters, a small decline in the demand
      for their outputs will cause them to:

      a.   reduce price and reduce the level of output produced.
      b.   reduce output in the short run, but reduce price in the
            long run.
      c.   reduce output and price in the short run, but only
            reduce output in the long run.
      d.   increase price in the short run to offset the effect on
            profits of a decline in output.
      e.   hold price and output constant in the short run, since
            price setters do not have to respond to changing market
            conditions in the short run.

8.   In an economy where firms in most industries are purely
      competitive firms, individual firms in each industry would
      produce:

      a.   differentiated products and a large share of industry
            output.
      b.   differentiated products and a small share of industry
            output.
      c.   standardized products and a large share of industry
            output.
      d.   standardized products, but a few firms would produce a
            large share of industry output, while most firms
            produced a small share.
      e.   standardized products and a small share of industry
            output.

9.   In the Keynesian model, firms are best characterized as:

     a.   perfectly competitive.
     b.   irrational.
     c.   small producers.
     d.   price takers.
     e.   monopolistically competitive.

10. In the Keynesian model, a firm's high menu cost causes:

     a.   real wage rigidity.
     b.   full employment.
     c.   price stickiness.
     d.   efficiency wages.
     e.   perfectly flexible price adjustments.

11. The cost to a firm of producing one more unit of output:

     a.   usually exceeds the firm's price.
     b.   is significantly less than the firm's price for purely
          competitive firms operating in long-run equilibrium.
     c.   usually equals the firm's price for monopolistically
          competitive firms.
     d.   is the firm's marginal cost.
     e.   declines as more output is produced in the short run.

12. Firms that charge a price for their output in excess of
     marginal cost in the short run:

     a.   are not maximizing profits.
     b.   cannot find buyers for their output.
     c.   are charging a markup.
     d.   will suffer huge losses.
     e.   are purely competitive firms.

13. As the economy moves down an effective labor demand curve:

     a.   output declines and employment declines.
     b.   the price level declines and employment increases.
     c.   the real wage declines and employment increases.
     d.   goods demand increases and employment declines.
     e.   the efficiency wage declines and employment increases.

14. During a severe and persistent recession, Keynesians would
     most likely propose:

     a.   tax increases.
     b.   a tight money policy.
     c.   annually balanced federal budgets.
     d.   no government intervention into the economy.
     e.   macroeconomic stabilization.

15. In practice, one of the principal problems with aggregate demand management is that:

   a.   changes in aggregate demand do not affect output.
   b.   changes in aggregate demand cannot reduce unemployment.
   c.   changes in aggregate demand are highly inflationary.
   d.   stabilization policies could increase aggregate demand too much and at the wrong times.
   e.   the price level is sticky in the short run.

16. In a short-run Keynesian *IS-LM-FE* diagram, an aggregate demand shock could not cause:

   a.   the real interest rate to change.
   b.   output to change.
   c.   the *IS* curve to shift.
   d.   the *FE* curve to shift.
   e.   the *LM* curve to shift.

17. The Keynesian model can be extended to explain why average labor productivity is procyclical by assuming:

   a.   labor hoarding by firms.
   b.   that the production function does not shift during the business cycle.
   c.   that the wage is procyclical.
   d.   that prices are perfectly flexible.
   e.   that firms are perfectly competitive.

18. In the Keynesian model, the full-employment level of output is the amount of output produced when:

   a.   the quantity of labor demanded equals the quantity of labor supplied.
   b.   the market wage exceeds the efficiency wage.
   c.   labor is paid an efficiency wage, and the real wage equals the marginal product of labor.
   d.   the real wage exceeds the nominal wage.
   e.   there are no productivity shocks.

19. In the Keynesian *IS-LM-FE* diagram, if aggregate demand is less than the full-employment level of output in the short run:

   a.   the price level will rise in the long run.
   b.   the price level will decline in the long run.
   c.   the *LM* curve will shift up to the right in the long run.
   d.   the *FE* line will shift to the left in the long run.
   e.   the *IS* curve will shift up to the right in the long run.

20. In the Keynesian *AD-AS* diagram, the short-run aggregate supply curve is:

    a. horizontal at one price level.
    b. horizontal at the full-employment level of output.
    c. horizontal at the efficiency wage.
    d. vertical at the full-employment level of output.
    e. negatively sloped, because of diminishing marginal returns to labor.

Short-Answer Essay Questions

1. **The efficiency wage model:** a) How do Keynesians explain real wage rigidity during a recession? b) Why might firms pay an efficiency wage, rather than a market-clearing wage? c) Draw a labor demand-labor supply diagram for the efficiency wage model and draw a corresponding effective labor demand curve diagram. Label the axes, curves, and equilibrium values. d) State the full-employment output equation for the efficiency wage model, and define the variables. e) Why might Keynesians want to specify also that the unemployment rate is a determinant of labor effort?

2. **Price stickiness:** a) Briefly define price stickiness. b) Briefly explain how monopolistic competition and high menu costs can explain price stickiness. c) Why does price stickiness not occur in the classical model? d) How is price stickiness illustrated in the Keynesian *IS-LM-FE* diagram and in the *AD-AS* diagram? e) Do the real effects of aggregate demand shocks differ in the short run and long run in the Keynesian sticky-price model from the effects of these shocks in the classical model of perfectly flexible prices? Briefly explain.

3. **Fiscal stabilization policy:** a) Draw a Keynesian *IS-LM-FE* diagram, an effective labor demand curve diagram, and a corresponding *AD-AS* diagram. Label the axes, curves, and equilibrium values. b) Use the diagrams to show the short-run effects and long-run effects of a temporary decline in investment spending. c) What is the principal goal of macroeconomic stabilization and how can fiscal policy be used to achieve this goal? d) Do Keynesians and classicals agree on the effectiveness and desirability of macroeconomic stabilization? Briefly explain.

4. **Monetary stabilization policy:** a) Draw a Keynesian *IS-LM-FE* diagram, an effective labor demand curve diagram, and a corresponding *AD-AS* diagram. Label the axes, curves, and equilibrium values. b) Use the diagrams to show the short-run effects and long-run effects of a temporary decline in consumption spending. c) Could monetary stabilization policy be used to reduce or offset the negative short-run

output effect of a temporary decline in consumption spending? Briefly explain. d) Is money neutral in both the classical model and the Keynesian model? Briefly explain. e) Do Keynesians believe that aggregate demand management policies should be used to "fine tune" the economy? Briefly explain.

5.   **Supply shocks and other critiques**: a) What critique does the real business cycle theory make of the Keynesian belief that most recessions are caused by aggregate demand shocks? b) What critique does the real business cycle theory make of macroeconomic stabilization? c) Draw a Keynesian *IS-LM-FE* diagram and a corresponding *AD-AS* diagram and use the diagrams to show the effects of an adverse productivity (i.e., aggregate supply) shock. d) Can macroeconomic stabilization policies effectively reduce the negative effects of a temporary supply shock? Briefly explain. e) Compare and contrast the effects of a tax cut on the positions of the *FE* line and the *IS* curve in the Keynesian and classical models.

6.   **Business cycle facts and other empirical evidence**: State and briefly explain whether or not the business cycle facts and other empirical evidence appear to support the following characteristics of the Keynesian model: a) efficiency wage; b) real wage rigidity; c) price stickiness; d) effective labor demand; and e) labor hoarding.

Answers to Multiple Choice Questions

1.	c	8.	e	15.	d
2.	d	9.	e	16.	d
3.	d	10.	c	17.	a
4.	b	11.	d	18.	c
5.	a	12.	c	19.	b
6.	a	13.	a	20.	a
7.	b	14.	e		

Answers to Short-Answer Essay Questions

1.   The efficiency wage model

a)   In the Keynesian efficiency wage model, firms pay each worker the efficiency wage. A recession reduces labor demand, which causes employment to decline, but firms do not lower the efficiency wage. Since the efficiency wage is the wage that maximizes effort per dollar of real wage paid to labor, reducing the real wage would reduce the productivity of labor, which would increase production cost. Another

problem with lowering the wage enough to induce the desired
number of workers to quit during a recession is that the
most productive workers are the most likely workers to quit.

b)   An efficiency wage is better than a market-clearing wage in
that it maximizes effort per dollar of wage income paid to
labor. This means that labor productivity per dollar spent
on labor is maximized; which means that labor cost per unit
of output is minimized. The "gift-exchange motive" and the
"shirking model" provide two explanations for why an
efficiency wage that is above the market-clearing wage may
increase productivity per wage dollar. The gift-exchange
motive views the higher wage as a gift to the worker who, in
exchange, gives the firm a gift of higher labor
productivity. The shirking model views the wage as the
reward that the worker risks losing if he is so unproductive
that he gets fired; a higher wage increases productivity by
increasing the expected cost of shirking (i.e., having low
productivity).

c)   A labor demand-labor supply diagram for the efficiency
wage model, and a corresponding effective labor demand curve
diagram.

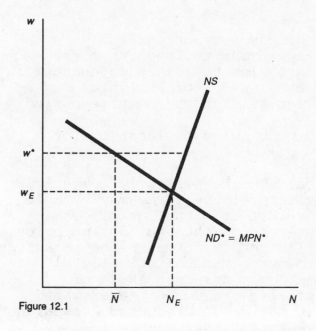
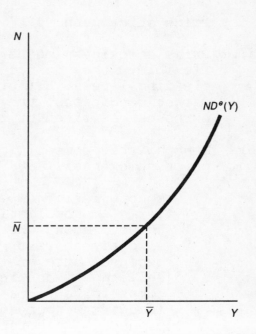

Figure 12.1

d)   The full-employment output equation for the efficiency wage
model:

$$\bar{Y} = AF(K, \; E^* \times \bar{N})$$

$E^* \times N$ = The quantity of effort-hours worked when labor is
paid the efficiency wage.

$\bar{N}$ =   The full-employment level of employment at which the efficiency wage (w^*) equals the marginal product of labor (MPN^*), with effort per effort-hour held constant at the maximum effort per real wage dollar (E^*).

$\bar{Y}$ =   full-employment level of output in the efficiency wage model.

A =   overall productivity.

K =   capital stock employed.

e)   The basic efficiency wage model suggests that the real wage is rigid over the business cycle; this is inconsistent with the business cycle fact that the real wage is mildly procyclical. By adding the unemployment rate as a determinant of labor effort, the extended model can explain this business cycle fact. The efficiency wage can be lower in a recession because a high unemployment rate already encourages workers to be productive, to avoid being fired. At a lower unemployment rate, in an expansion, the efficiency wage would need to be higher, to reduce shirking.

2.   **Price stickiness**

a)   Price stickiness means that prices are not perfectly flexible; they do not quickly adjust to long-run market-clearing levels. If prices are slow to adjust to changes in market conditions, they may be viewed, for analytic purposes, as fixed or rigid for some short-run time period.

b)   Monopolistic competition and menu costs explanations of price stickiness:

1)   Monopolistic competition: Unlike perfectly competitive firms, monopolistically competitive firms may be able to sell about the same volume of output at prices slightly above or slightly below the equilibrium price, because there are fewer competing firms in the market selling an identical product. Monopolistically competitive firms each produce a larger share of industry output and typically produce differentiated products, rather than standardized products. Compared to perfectly competitive firms, they engage in more nonprice competition (e.g., advertising) and less price competition. If all monopolistically competitive firms in each industry held their prices constant during a recession and reduced their output levels, the market share of each firm may not change. Therefore, prices can be sticky.

2)   Menu costs: To maximize profits a firm would not change its price unless the menu cost of changing the price were less than the expected benefit (i.e., the increase in revenue minus production cost) of the price change. Compared to perfectly competitive firms, monopolistically competitive firms obtain smaller benefits from price changes. Consequently, changes in market conditions tend to produce fewer price changes. Prices and the price level tend to be sticky.

c)   In the classical model, prices are perfectly flexible because firms are assumed to be perfectly competitive and because the model abstracts from the transactions cost (i.e., menu cost) of price changes. In the classical model, menu costs are assumed to be negligible.

d)   A change in prices create a change in the price level. A change in the price level shifts the *LM* curve. Price stickiness is illustrated in the Keynesian *IS-LM-FE* diagram by the absence of any price-induced shift in the *LM* curve. Price stickiness is illustrated in the Keynesian *AD-AS* diagram by a horizontal *SRAS* curve at one price level, with the position of the curve being fixed in the short run.

e)   Yes, in the short run. In the Keynesian model, aggregate demand shocks affect real output, employment, and unemployment in the short run. There is no short-run adjustment period in the classical model, since economic shocks cause prices to adjust immediately to their long-run, general equilibrium values. Keynesian and classical economists agree that aggregate demand shocks have no real output or employment effects in the long run.

3.   Fiscal stabilization policy

a)   A Keynesian *IS-LM-FE* diagram, an effective labor demand curve diagram, and a corresponding *AD-AS* diagram. See Figure 12.2 on page 158.

b)   The effects of a decline in investment spending, as shown in the diagrams are:

1)   short-run effects: Y declines, r declines, and N declines, as the economy moves from E to F.

2)   long-run effects: r declines and P declines, as the economy moves from E to H.

c)   The principal goal of macroeconomic stabilization is to maintain aggregate demand (*AD*) at the full-employment level of output. Countercyclical changes in government purchases, and possibly taxes, can be used to offset the output effects of private sector *AD* shocks, to maintain *AD* at the full-

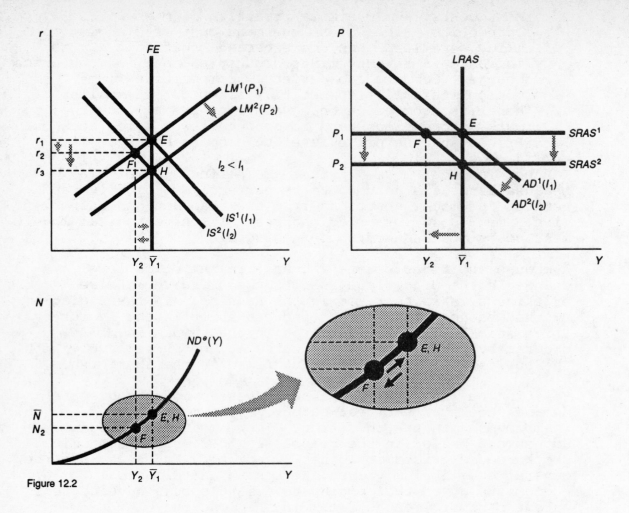

Figure 12.2

employment level of output. For example, the downward shift
in *IS* and *AD*, caused by a decline in investment spending,
can be offset by a temporary increase in government
purchases, causing *IS* and *AD* to shift back to their original
positions.

d)   No, Keynesians and classical economists disagree on the
     effectiveness and desirability of macroeconomic
     stabilization.

     1)   In the classical model: business cycles fluctuations
          are the optimal response of the economy to various
          shocks that hit the economy; thus they should not be
          offset by macroeconomic policy.

     2)   In the Keynesian model: large and persistent business
          cycle fluctuations are usually caused by aggregate
          demand shocks in the presence of price stickiness.
          Macroeconomic stabilization policies can effectively
          reduce business cycle fluctuations, so these policies

are desirable in that they can help the economy to
maintain output at the full-employment level.

4.   Monetary stabilization policy

a)   A Keynesian *IS-LM-FE* diagram, an effective labor demand
     curve diagram, and a corresponding *AD-AS* diagram.

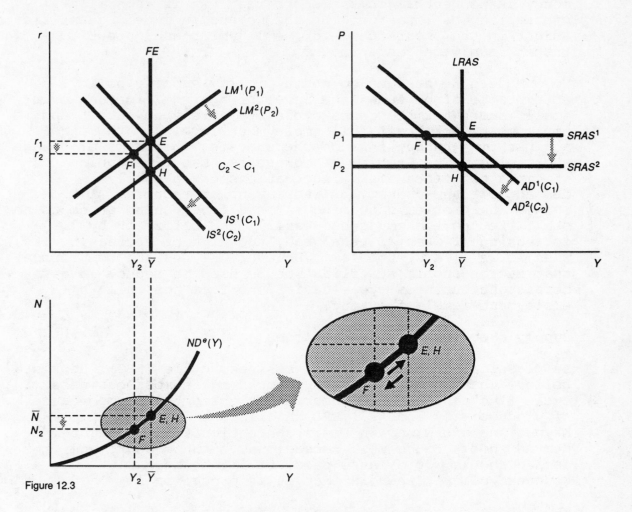

Figure 12.3

b)   As shown in the diagrams, the effects of a temporary decline
     in consumer spending are:

   1)   short-run effects: *Y* declines, *N* declines, *r* declines,
        as the economy moves from *E* to *F*.

   2)   long-run effects: *r* declines and *P* declines, as the
        economy moves from *E* to *H*.

c)   Yes, an increase in the money supply would shift the *LM*
     curve down to the right and shift *AD* up to the right, to

offset the output effect of a decline in consumer spending.
The increase in the money supply returns the *AD* curve to its
original position, at the full-employment level of output.

d)   Money is neutral in the classical model, which is a long-run
model with perfectly flexible wages and prices. In the
Keynesian model of imperfectly flexible wages and prices,
money is nonneutral in the short run, but it is still
neutral in the long run. In the Keynesian model, quantities
adjust in the short run (e.g., employment and output),
rather than wages and prices.

e)   No. Modern Keynesians do not typically endorse policy
attempts to "fine tune" the level of aggregate demand over
small, short-term business cycle deviations in output and
employment from their full-employment levels. Arguments
against fine-tuning include the practical problems of dosage
and timing. The problem of dosage is that fine-tuning
attempts to offset small fluctuations could easily
destabilize the economy by increasing or reducing *AD* too
much. The problem of timing is that fine-tuning attempts to
stabilize the economy could easily destabilize it by
increasing *AD* when *AD* is already too high or decreasing it
when *AD* is already too low. However, Keynesians do propose
that macroeconomic stabilization be used to reduce large,
persistent business cycle deviations from the full-
employment level of output.

5.   **Supply shocks and other critiques**

a)   As classical economists, real business cycle (RBC) theorists
believe that aggregate supply shocks cause most business
cycle fluctuations. RBC theorists highlight the importance
of productivity shocks. RBC theorists believe that
Keynesians are wrong in their contention that aggregate
demand shocks cause most recessions, because aggregate
demand shocks would cause productivity to be
countercyclical, when in fact, it is procyclical.

b)   RBC theory suggests that small, random productivity shocks
create business cycle fluctuations in aggregate economic
activity, which represent the economy's best response to
these unpredictable supply shocks. Macroeconomic
stabilization policies are ineffective in offsetting
aggregate supply shocks and, therefore, these policies are
undesirable.

c)   Keynesian *IS-LM-FE* diagram and corresponding *AD-AS* diagram,
showing the effects of a temporary adverse productivity
shock: The short-run effects: output and employment
decline; the interest rate and the price level increase.
The long-run effects: the interest rate and the price level
increase. See Figure 12.4 on page 161.

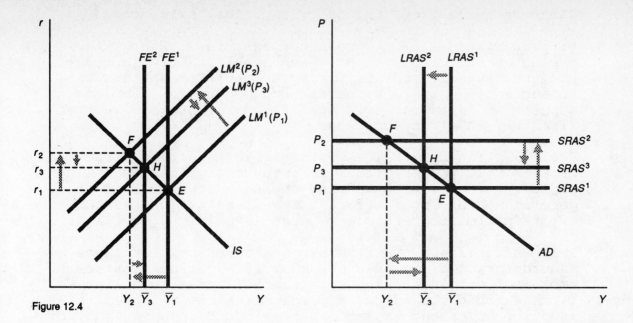

Figure 12.4

d)   No, Keynesian macroeconomic stabilization policies cannot
     effectively reduce the effects of a temporary supply shock.
     Stabilization policies are attempts to offset undesirable
     shifts in the aggregate demand curve, but they cannot offset
     undesirable supply-side shifts in the FE line and in the
     aggregate supply curves. In the short run, expansionary
     macroeconomic stabilization policies could offset the
     negative output effect of an adverse supply shock; in the
     long run, however, this would increase the price level.

e)   The effects of a lump-sum, temporary tax cut on:

     1)   the FE line: It will not affect the FE line in the
          classical model, because the present value of taxes is
          unchanged. Keynesians do not believe that a tax cut
          will significantly increase labor supply, but, even if
          it did, it would not increase employment nor shift the
          FE line, since employment is determined by output along
          the effective demand curve for labor.

     2)   the IS curve: Classical economists, relying on the
          Ricardian Equivalence Proposition, do not believe that
          a temporary tax cut will shift the IS curve, in the
          absence of borrowing constraints. If a sufficiently
          large share of the population does face borrowing
          constraints, then a tax cut could increase consumption
          spending, causing the IS curve to shift to the right.
          Keynesians believe that a temporary tax cut will
          significantly increase consumption spending, causing
          the IS curve to shift up to the right.

6. **Business cycle facts and other empirical evidence**

a) Efficiency wage: The case study example of Henry Ford
    paying an efficiency wage (which significantly increased
    productivity and profits for Ford Motor Company and was
    subsequently adopted by other auto producers) provides
    supporting empirical evidence of the Keynesian view that
    firms pay an efficiency wage.

b) Real wage rigidity: The business cycle fact that the real
    wage is mildly procyclical is evidence against real wage
    rigidity. However, by adding the unemployment rate as a
    determinant of labor effort, Keynesians can explain why the
    effort-maximizing efficiency wage is mildly procyclical.

c) Price stickiness: Carlton's research on price changes by
    manufacturing firms over the 1957-1966 period provides
    empirical evidence that supports the Keynesian belief that
    firms exhibit considerable price stickiness. Cecchetti's
    study of newsstand magazine prices and Kashyap's study of
    catalogue prices also found considerable price stickiness.

d) Effective labor demand: Empirical evidence in support of
    the efficiency wage and in support of real wage rigidity
    also supports the Keynesian view that effective labor demand
    determines employment. Evidence in favor of price
    stickiness also supports the Keynesian view that the amount
    of labor effectively demanded depends on the amount of
    aggregate output demanded.

e) Labor hoarding: Empirical research by Fay and Medoff found
    that manufacturing firms do retain a significant amount of
    redundant labor during recessions; this empirical evidence
    supports the Keynesian assumption of labor hoarding. The
    assumption of labor hoarding also enables the Keynesian
    model to explain the business cycle fact that the average
    productivity of labor is procyclical.

CHAPTER 13

BUSINESS CYCLES AND MACROECONOMIC POLICY IN THE OPEN ECONOMY

A Review of Chapter Highlights

The **nominal exchange rate** is the number of units of foreign currency that exchange for one unit of domestic currency; it is the foreign currency price of the domestic currency. For example, in a two-country model, a nominal exchange rate of 135 yen per dollar would mean that a dollar costs 135 yen or, alternatively, a dollar buys 135 yen. The nominal exchange rate is also called the **exchange rate**.

In international markets, the currency of a country is called its foreign exchange. The currencies of different countries are traded internationally in the **foreign exchange market**. Each country prices its goods and assets in units of its own currency. Buyers of foreign goods or foreign assets must first buy the foreign exchange and then use the foreign exchange to buy the foreign good or foreign asset. Therefore, the real domestic currency price of a foreign good depends on both the foreign exchange price of domestic currency and on the foreign exchange price of the foreign good. In a two-country model of two goods, the real exchange rate is the nominal exchange rate multiplied by the domestic currency price of the domestic good divided by the foreign currency price of the foreign good ($e = e_{nom}P/P_{FOR}$). For example, 100 cameras per car = (135 yen per dollar x \$20,000 per car/27,000 yen per camera). Since a dollar buys 135 yen, an American could buy an imported Japanese camera for \$200 = (27,000 yen per camera/135 yen per dollar).

There are two principal international monetary payment systems for determining exchange rates. In a **flexible exchange rate system**, a country's exchange rate is determined by the international forces of supply and demand in the foreign exchange market. In a **fixed exchange rate system**, a country's exchange rate is fixed at some particular rate, as determined by an international agreement among major trading countries; the central bank of a country maintains its fixed exchange rate by agreeing to buy and sell its currency at that particular exchange rate in the foreign exchange market.

The **real exchange rate** is the number of units of the foreign good that exchange for one unit of the domestic good; it is the foreign goods price of a domestic good. For example, a real exchange rate of 100 Japanese cameras per U.S. car would mean that it costs the Japanese 100 cameras for each American car they buy. The real exchange rate is also called the **terms of trade**.

In a flexible exchange rate system, a **nominal depreciation** is a decline in the exchange rate. For example, if the yen price of the dollar declined from 135 yen per dollar to 125, this would be a nominal depreciation of the dollar. After a nominal depreciation, it takes fewer yen to buy a dollar. A **nominal appreciation** is an increase in the exchange rate. In a fixed exchange rate system, a decline in the exchange rate is called a **devaluation**, whereas an increase in the exchange rate is called a **revaluation**.

In a flexible exchange rate system, a **real appreciation** is an increase in the real exchange rate. For example, if the real exchange rate increased from 100 Japanese cameras per U.S. car to 110, this would be a real appreciation. A **real depreciation** is a decline in the real exchange rate. After a real depreciation, it takes fewer units of the foreign good to buy a unit of the domestic good; alternatively, it takes more units of the domestic good to buy a unit of the foreign good.

A real depreciation makes the domestic economy's exported good cheaper, in terms of the imported good, to both domestic buyers and to foreigners, which causes people to buy more of the exported good and to buy less of the imported good. However, a real depreciation increases the value of the imported good, in terms of the exported good, such that the real value of imports may increase after a depreciation, even though the volume of imports declines. According to the **Marshall-Lerner condition**, a real depreciation increases only net exports if buyers of exports and imports are sufficiently sensitive to the change in the terms of trade to reduce their purchases of imports, and to increase their purchases of exports enough to more than offset the increase in the price of imports in terms of the exported goods.

The **J-curve** shows that a real exchange rate depreciation initially reduces net exports, but will increase net exports after some adjustment period. The J-curve pattern of changes in the value of net exports occurs because people are slow to adjust their buying decisions to a change in the real exchange rate. Although buyers are not sufficiently sensitive to a change in the real exchange rate to satisfy the Marshall-Lerner condition immediately after a decline in the real exchange rate; usually they are sufficiently sensitive to satisfy the Marshall-Lerner condition after a longer adjustment period.

If the real value of exports is just equal to the real value of imports, the country has achieved external balance. External balance means that net exports have neither a negative value nor a positive value; net exports have a value of zero. For given values of domestic income, foreign income, and demand for exports relative to imports, a country's current real exchange rate determines whether or not a country achieves external balance in the current period. Although a country can incur negative net exports in any year, the **intertemporal external balance** condition states that its current real exchange rate and future real exchange rate (e, e^f) must ensure that deficits in some years will be offset by surpluses in other years, so that the country will achieve external balance over a sufficiently large number of years. In a two-period model, negative net exports in the current period must be offset by positive net exports in the future time period.

Negative net exports in the current period must be financed in the current period by borrowing from foreigners; the net export deficit equals the amount of domestic borrowing from the foreign country. If the domestic economy borrows from foreigners to enable it to import a greater real value of goods than it exports in the current period, then it must achieve positive net exports in the future period, equal to the principal and interest accrued on the loan, to achieve intertemporal external balance. Given that each economy will repay its debt, this means that a current trade deficit must be financed by a future trade surplus. Therefore, intertemporal external balance means that the **present value of net exports** equals zero (i.e., $NX + [NX^f/(1 + r)] = 0$). The intertemporal external balance (*IEB*) curve is the set of possible (e, e^f) points at which the present value of net exports is zero, assuming domestic income, foreign income, and the demand for exports relative to imports remain constant.

Assets are traded in the international asset market. Domestic residents buy some foreign assets and foreigners buy some domestic assets to achieve their most preferred combination of risk and return on their assets. For an asset that matures in one year, the nominal interest rate is the nominal rate of return on an asset in units of a country's currency. The real interest rate is the rate of return on an asset in units of a country's good.

The international asset market is in equilibrium when the interest rate parity condition is achieved. **Nominal interest rate parity** is achieved when the gross nominal rates of return on foreign and domestic assets of comparable risk and liquidity are equal, when measured in terms of one currency. The interest rate parity condition does not require that the interest rates be equal in the two countries, but it does require that any interest rate difference be offset by an appreciation of the currency of the country whose interest rate is lower. In notation form, the nominal interest rate parity condition is that: (e_{nom}/e^f_{nom})(1 + i_{FOR}) = 1 + i. For example, in a two-country model with each country issuing a comparable government bond, if the U.S. bond pays 6% interest and the Japanese bond pays 9% interest, interest rate parity requires that the dollar appreciate by approximately 3% over the next year. If the initial exchange rate is 135 yen per dollar, the future exchange rate would be approximately 139 yen per dollar.

In terms of real interest rates, the **real interest rate parity** condition is the equilibrium condition for the international asset market. In notation form, the real interest rate parity condition is that: $(e/e^f)(1 + r_{FOR}) = 1 + r$. Like the nominal interest rate parity condition, the real interest rate parity condition requires that any difference in the real interest rates, measured in units of a country's good, will be offset by an appreciation of the currency of the country whose real interest rate is lower.

Questions

These questions test your understanding of the **key terms**, **key relationships**, and **key diagrams** highlighted in your text.

Multiple Choice Questions: Circle the letter corresponding to the correct answer to each question.

1. The nominal exchange rate of the dollar is best defined as the number of units of the:

    a. foreign currency that it takes to buy a dollar.
    b. foreign currency that it takes to buy a unit of U.S. goods.
    c. foreign currency that it takes to buy a unit of U.S. assets.
    d. foreign goods that it takes to buy a unit of U.S. goods.
    e. foreign asset that it takes to buy a unit of the U.S. asset.

2. In the long run, a 5% increase in the domestic money supply will:

    a. reduce both the exchange rate and the real exchange rate by 5%.
    b. reduce the real exchange rate by 5% and increase net exports.
    c. reduce the exchange rate by 5%, but have no real economic effects.
    d. increase the exchange rate by 5% and reduce net exports.
    e. increase the real exchange rate by 5%, but have no nominal effects.

3. In the foreign exchange market:

    a. exports and imports are exchanged.
    b. domestic bonds are traded for foreign bonds.
    c. exported domestic goods are traded for imported assets.
    d. exports and imports are purchased and sold.
    e. domestic currency is traded for foreign currencies.

4. The international monetary payments system in which the exchange rate is determined by the international market forces of supply and demand is called:

    a. a managed float.
    b. a dirty float.
    c. an adjustable-peg system.
    d. a fixed exchange rate system.
    e. a flexible exchange rate system.

5. In the post-World War II period, prior to the collapse of the Bretton Woods system in the early 1970s, the exchange rate of the dollar was:

    a. determined in a flexible exchange rate system.
    b. determined by the market forces of supply and demand.
    c. fixed at $35 per ounce of gold.
    d. determined by a managed float.
    e. fixed in terms of the Japanese yen.

6. For a given nominal exchange rate, an increase in the price of the foreign good relative to the price of the domestic good causes:

    a. domestic residents to buy more units of the foreign good.
    b. domestic residents to buy less of the domestic good.
    c. the real exchange rate to decline.
    d. the number of units of the foreign good needed to buy a unit of the domestic good to increase.
    e. foreign residents to buy less of the domestic good.

7. If four Saudi Arabian barrels of oil exchange for one Japanese camera, this is a measure of Japan's:

    a. nominal exchange rate.
    b. terms of trade.
    c. exchange rate.
    d. price level in terms of the foreign price level.
    e. trade deficit.

8. In a flexible exchange rate system, a decline in the number of units of the foreign currency per unit of the domestic currency is a:

    a. nominal appreciation of the domestic currency.
    b. nominal depreciation of the domestic currency.
    c. real appreciation of the domestic currency.
    d. real depreciation of the domestic currency.
    e. nominal appreciation, but a real depreciation of the domestic currency.

9.   For a given real exchange rate, a nominal appreciation will
     result from:

     a.   a decline in the terms of trade.
     b.   an increase in the price of the foreign good.
     c.   an increase in the price of the domestic good.
     d.   an increase in the domestic rate of inflation.
     e.   a decline in the foreign rate of inflation.

10. In a fixed exchange rate system, a decline in the value of
     the dollar would be called a:

     a.   depreciation.
     b.   appreciation.
     c.   revaluation.
     d.   devaluation.
     e.   market adjustment.

11. During the period of the Bretton Woods system, the U.S.
     government prevented a revaluation of the dollar by:

     a.   offering to sell dollars at the fixed exchange rate.
     b.   allowing the dollar to appreciate.
     c.   liberalizing its trade policies.
     d.   increasing the money supply.
     e.   increasing government purchases.

12. In a flexible exchange rate system, an increase in foreign
     income will cause the:

     a.   *IRP* line to pivot clockwise, creating a real
          appreciation in the current exchange exchange.
     b.   *IRP* line to pivot clockwise, creating a real
          depreciation in the current exchange rate.
     c.   *IRP* line to pivot counterclockwise, creating a real
          depreciation in the current exchange rate.
     d.   *IEB* curve to shift down to the left, creating a real
          depreciation in the current exchange rate.
     e.   *IEB* curve to shift up to the right, creating a real
          appreciation in the current exchange rate.

13. In a flexible exchange rate system, an increase in the real
     interest rate on the foreign asset will cause the:

     a.   *IRP* line to pivot clockwise, creating a real
          appreciation of the future exchange rate.
     b.   *IRP* line to pivot clockwise, creating a real
          depreciation of the future exchange rate.
     c.   *IRP* line to pivot counterclockwise, creating a real
          appreciation of the future exchange rate.
     d.   *IEB* curve to shift up to the right, creating a real
          appreciation of the future exchange rate.

e.   *IEB* curve to shift up to the right, creating a real
     depreciation of the future exchange rate.

14. If the Marshall-Lerner condition is met, a real exchange
     rate depreciation will increase:

a.   net exports.
b.   foreign net exports.
c.   the number of units of the foreign good needed to buy a
     unit of the domestic good.
d.   the quantity of domestic imports.
e.   the foreign exchange price of the domestic currency.

15. The J-curve illustrates that a decline in the real exchange
     rate of the dollar will cause net exports to:

a.   increase immediately, because prices are perfectly
     flexible.
b.   increase after some adjustment period, because it takes
     some time for people to adjust their buying decisions
     to a change in the terms of trade.
c.   decrease immediately, because prices are perfectly
     flexible.
d.   decrease after some adjustment period, because it takes
     some time for people to adjust their buying decisions
     to a change in the real exchange rate.
e.   decline, which will cause the future real exchange rate
     to appreciate.

16. The intertemporal external balance curve is the set of
     possible (e, e^f) points at which:

a.   the asset market is in equilibrium.
b.   the money market is in equilibrium.
c.   output equals the full-employment level of output.
d.   the present value of net exports is zero.
e. $S^d + NX = I^d$.

17. An increase in the foreign demand for domestic goods, before
     adjustment of real exchange rates, causes the:

a.   present value of domestic net exports to increase.
b.   domestic *IS* curve to shift down to the left.
c.   domestic *LM* curve to shift down to the right.
e.   *IRP* line to pivot clockwise.
e.   foreign *IS* curve to shift up to the right.

18. Given a 6% nominal interest rate in the foreign country and
     an 8% nominal interest rate in the domestic economy, on
     one-year bonds of comparable risk and liquidity, the nominal
     interest rate parity condition suggests that:

    a.   the domestic interest rate will decline.
    b.   the exchange rate will depreciate over the next year.
    c.   the future exchange rate will exceed the current
         exchange rate.
    d.   the *IRP* line will pivot counterclockwise.
    e.   the *IEB* curve will shift up along the *IRP* line.

19. The real interest rate parity condition is:

     a. $r = r_{FOR}$
     b. $1 + r = 1 + r_{FOR}$
     c. $er = r_{FOR}$
     d. $(e/e^f)(1 + r_{FOR}) = 1 + r$
     e. $(e/e_{FOR})(1 + r_{FOR}) = 1 + r$

20. If the world economy is in a recession, an increase in the
     money supply in the domestic economy is:

     a.   neutral in the Keynesian model in the short run and
          long run, but not in the classical model.
     b.   expansionary in the Keynesian model and classical
          model in the short run, but not in the long run.
     c.   contractionary in the Keynesian and classical models
          in the short run, but not in the long run.
     d.   contractionary in the Keynesian and classical models
          in both the short run and long run.
     e.   expansionary in the Keynesian model in the short run,
          but is neutral in the long run in both the Keynesian
          and classical models.

Short-Answer Essay Questions

1.   **Exchange rates and net exports**: a) Define the nominal
     exchange rate. b) Define the real exchange rate. c) State
     the real exchange rate equation and use it to develop an
     equation for the nominal exchange rate in terms of the real
     exchange rate. d) State the net export equation, measured
     in terms of the domestic good. e) Briefly explain the
     difference between a nominal revaluation and a real
     depreciation of the exchange rate.

2.   **Intertemporal external balance**: a) Define intertemporal
     external balance (*IEB*). b) Briefly explain why a country
     will achieve intertemporal external balance. c) Briefly
     explain why the *IEB* curve is negatively sloped. d) Identify
     changes in two variables that will cause the *IEB* curve to
     shift up to the right. e) What does the Marshall-Lerner
     condition tell us about the effects of a decline in the real
     exchange rate?

3. **Interest rate parity**: a) Define interest rate parity. b) State the nominal interest rate parity equation and the real interest rate parity equation. c) Give an example of interest rate parity when the nominal interest rates, on otherwise comparable bonds, differ in a two-country model. d) Briefly explain why the *IRP* line is positively sloped. e) Identify changes in two variables that would cause the *IRP* line to pivot clockwise.

4. **The IS-LM model of an open economy**: a) Use a saving-investment diagram to construct an open economy *IS* curve. b) Compare and contrast the shift variables for a closed-economy *IS* curve and an open-economy *IS* curve. c) Why is the *IS* curve negatively sloped? d) Briefly explain how a change in the domestic economy is transmitted to the foreign country in a two-country model of the world. e) In the world economy, compare and contrast the Keynesian and classical output effects of an increase in domestic aggregate demand.

5. **Domestic fiscal policy in the world economy**: a) Define the term expansionary fiscal policy. b) Briefly explain why Keynesians propose using expansionary fiscal policy during a recession, and explain why the classical economists disagree with this proposal. c) Draw a domestic *IS-LM-FE* diagram, an *IEB-IRP* diagram, and a foreign *IS-LM-FE* diagram. Label the axes, curves, and equilibrium values. d) Use the diagrams to show a Keynesian analysis of the short-run effects on the world economy of a decline in investment. e) In the Keynesian model, could an expansionary fiscal policy offset these short-run effects? Briefly explain.

6. **Domestic monetary policy in the world economy**: a) Define the term expansionary monetary policy. b) Briefly explain why Keynesians propose expansionary monetary policy, and why the classical economists disagree with this proposal. c) Draw a domestic *IS-LM-FE* diagram, an *IEB-IRP* diagram, and a foreign *IS-LM-FE* diagram for the world economy. Label the axes, curves, and equilibrium values. d) Use the diagrams to show a Keynesian analysis of the short-run effects on the world economy of a decline in foreign demand for domestic goods. e) In the Keynesian model, could an expansionary monetary policy offset these short-run effects? Briefly explain.

Answers to Multiple Choice Questions

1.	a	8.	b	15.	b
2.	c	9.	b	16.	d
3.	e	10.	d	17.	a
4.	e	11.	a	18.	b
5.	c	12.	e	19.	d

6. c   13. c   20. e
7. b   14. a

Answers to Short-Answer Essay Questions

1.   Exchange rates and net exports

a)   The nominal exchange rate: is the number of units of the
     foreign currency that exchange for one unit of the domestic
     currency. For example, 135 yen per dollar.

b)   The real exchange rate: is the number of units of a foreign
     good that exchange for one unit of a domestic good. For
     example, in a two-good model, 100 Japanese cameras per U.S.
     car.

c)   The real exchange rate equation is:

$$e = e_{nom}P/P_{FOR}$$

     Therefore, the nominal exchange rate is:

$$e_{nom} = eP_{FOR}/P$$

     In a two-good model, the price of the domestic good is the
     macroeconomic price level; the price of the foreign good is
     the foreign macroeconomic price level. In a multigood
     model, P and P_{FOR} would still be the domestic and foreign
     macroeconomic price levels—the average price of products.
     Given the price level in each country, the equilibrium
     nominal exchange rate provides for purchasing power parity
     between the two countries, so that the dollar price of a
     camera is the same in the U.S.and Japan, and the yen price
     of a car is the same in Japan and the U.S.

d)   The net exports equation is: $NX = X - X_{FOR}/e$. X is the
     quantity of the exported good, which is the real value of
     exports. X_{FOR}/e is the quantity of the imported good
     measured in units of the exported good, which is the real
     value of imports. NX is the net amount of the domestic good
     exported, which is the real value of net exports.

e)   A nominal revaluation is an increase in the exchange rate in
     a fixed exchange rate system. A real depreciation is a
     decline in the terms of trade.

2.   Intertemporal external balance

a)   Intertemporal external balance: is goods market equilibrium
     for an open economy. It exists when the present value of
     net exports is zero, so that the present discounted value of
     net exports in one time period equals minus the present

discounted value of net exports in the other period. In equation form, this means that $NX(1 + r) = - NX^f$. Likewise, $NX = - NX^f/(1 + r)$. Note that the present discounted (i.e., current) value of current net exports is NX.

b)   When domestic net exports are negative, the domestic economy is paying more for imports than it is receiving in export earnings; this excess spending can be achieved only by borrowing enough from foreigners to pay for it. Assuming that foreign loans have to be paid back with interest in the future, the domestic economy must have positive net exports in the future that are sufficient to repay the previous loans. When future export surpluses are just large enough to finance (i.e., pay for) the principal and interest on foreign loans, then intertemporal external balance is achieved.

c)   For a given *IEB* curve, domestic income, foreign income, and the demand for domestic goods relative to foreign goods are held constant. The negative slope of the *IEB* curve shows that the future real exchange rate is negatively related to the current real exchange rate, when these other variables remain constant. An increase in the current real exchange rate causes net exports to become negative. To increase future net exports enough to achieve a future net export surplus sufficient to pay for the current net export deficit, the future real exchange rate must decline.

d)   An increase in foreign income (Y_{FOR}) or a decline in domestic income increases net exports at the current exchange rate, thereby causing the *IEB* curve to shift up to the right.

e)   According to the Marshall-Lerner condition, a real depreciation increases net exports if buyers of exports and imports are sufficiently sensitive to the change in the real exchange rate. Usually, buyers are not sufficiently sensitive immediately after a real depreciation to satisfy the Marshall-Lerner condition. Therefore, the immediate effect of a decline in the real exchange rate is a decline in net exports, measured in terms of the exported good. After a while, however, net exports increase as buyers adjust their purchases.

3.   **Interest rate parity**

a)   Interest rate parity: is asset market equilibrium for an open economy. It exists when the rates of return on assets of comparable maturity, risk, and liquidity are equal in different countries, measured in either a common currency or a common good.

b)   The nominal interest rate parity equation is:

$$(e_{nom}/e^f_{nom})(1 + i_{FOR}) = 1 + i$$

The real interest rate parity equation is:

$$(e/e^f)(1 + r_{FOR}) = 1 + r$$

c)   For one-year bonds of comparable risk and liquidity in a a two-country model of the world economy, nominal interest rate parity exists if a domestic bond pays 10% and the foreign bond pays 8% interest, and the dollar depreciates by approximately 2% over the next year. The currency of the country paying the lower nominal interest rate appreciates. Note that this calculation is based on the approximation equation for interest rate parity: 10% - 2% = 8%

d)   The positive slope of the *IRP* line shows that international asset market equilibrium requires that the future exchange rate is positively related to the current exchange rate. For given values of r and r_{FOR}, an increase in the current exchange rate causes the rate of return on foreign assets to exceed the rate of return on comparable domestic assets, measured in terms of one currency; the future exchange rate must appreciate to restore interest rate parity.

e)   The form of the interest rate parity equation that identifies the slope of the *IRP* line is:

$$e^f = [(1 + r_{FOR})/(1 + r)]e$$

The bracketed term is the slope of the *IRP* line. We can see from this equation that a decline in the foreign real interest rate or an increase in the domestic real interest rate would reduce the slope of the *IRP* line, causing the line to pivot clockwise.

4.   **The IS-LM model of an open economy**

a)   A saving-investment diagram and a corresponding *IS* curve for an open-economy. See Figure 13.1 on page 175.

b)   The shift variables (i.e., factors) for the *IS* curve in a closed economy also shift the open-economy *IS* curve. In addition, the open-economy *IS* curve shifts if net exports change, at a given income level and a given real interest rate.

c)   The negative slope of the open-economy *IS* curve shows that real output and the real interest rate are negatively related variables. Each point on the *IS* curve is an equilibrium (Y, r) point at which $S^d - I^d = NX$. An increase in output increases, $S^d - I^d$, while reducing NX. Now, at

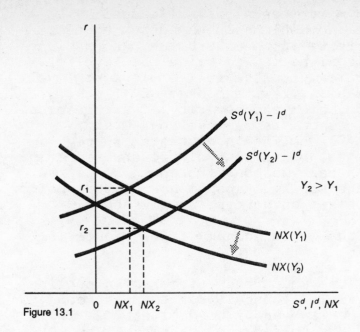
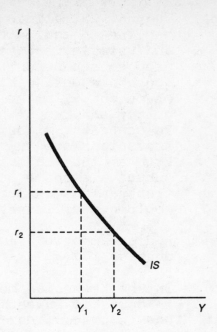

Figure 13.1

the initial interest rate, $S^d - I^d > NX$. Therefore, the
interest rate must decline enough to achieve a new
equilibrium in the goods market, at the higher output level.

d)   Domestic economy changes are transmitted to the foreign
     economy through changes in the exchange rate and through
     changes in net exports. An economic change in the domestic
     economy that changes net exports shifts the *IS* curve in the
     foreign country. In a two-country model, the exports of one
     country are the imports of the other; an increase in
     domestic net exports is also an increase in foreign net
     imports.

e)   In the classical model, there is no real output effect of an
     increase in aggregate demand, if government purchases are
     held constant, since the price level fully adjusts
     immediately. Likewise, in the Keynesian model, in the long
     run, there is no real output effect of an increase in
     aggregate demand. However, in the short run, in the open-
     economy Keynesian model, an increase in aggregate demand
     increases domestic output, which causes domestic economy
     imports to increase, which causes foreign output to
     increase.

5.   **Domestic fiscal policy in the world economy**

a)   Expansionary fiscal policy is an increase in government
     purchases or a reduction in taxes that causes the *IS* curve
     to shift up to the right.

b)   Keynesians believe that most recessions are caused by a
     decline in aggregate demand, which causes output to decline
     and unemployment to increase in the short run. Keynesians
     propose expansionary fiscal policy to raise the level of
     aggregate demand back quickly to the full-employment level
     of output. In the Keynesian view, expansionary fiscal
     policy can reduce the duration and severity of a recession.
     In contrast, classical economists believe that most
     recessions are caused by a decline in aggregate supply.
     From a classical viewpoint, business cycle fluctuations in
     output are the economy's best response to these small
     fluctuations in aggregate supply. Expansionary fiscal policy
     would not efficiently offset an adverse supply shock.

c)   A diagrammatic view of the world economy. See Figure 13.2
     on page 177.

d)   In the Keynesian model, the short-run effects of a decline
     in domestic investment are: 1) The IS curve shifts down to
     the left, causing Y to decline and r to decline. 2) The
     decline in Y causes imports to decline, causing NX to
     increase, causing the IEB curve to shift to the right. The
     decline in r causes the IRP curve to pivot counterclockwise.
     The combined effect of the change in IEB and the change in
     IRP on e is ambiguous, but e^f unambiguously increases. 3)
     The decline in domestic imports is a decline in foreign
     exports, which causes the foreign IS curve to shift down to
     the left, causing Y_{FOR} and r_{FOR} to decline.

e)   An expansionary fiscal policy could offset these short-run
     effects by offsetting the initial shift to the left in the
     domestic IS curve. Counter cyclical expansionary fiscal
     policy attempts to stabilize the IS curve at the full-
     employment level of domestic output.

6.   Domestic monetary policy in the world economy

a)   Expansionary monetary policy is an increase in the money
     supply that shifts the LM curve down to the right.

b)   Keynesians believe that most recessions are caused by a
     decline in aggregate demand, which causes output to decline
     and the unemployment rate to increase. Expansionary
     monetary policy can reduce or offset the decline in
     aggregate demand, thereby reducing the duration and severity
     of a recession. During a recession, expansionary monetary
     policy can be used to stabilize aggregate demand at the
     full-employment level of output. In contrast, classical
     economists believe that most business cycles are caused by
     adverse supply shocks that cannot be offset by expansionary
     monetary policy. In the classical model of perfectly

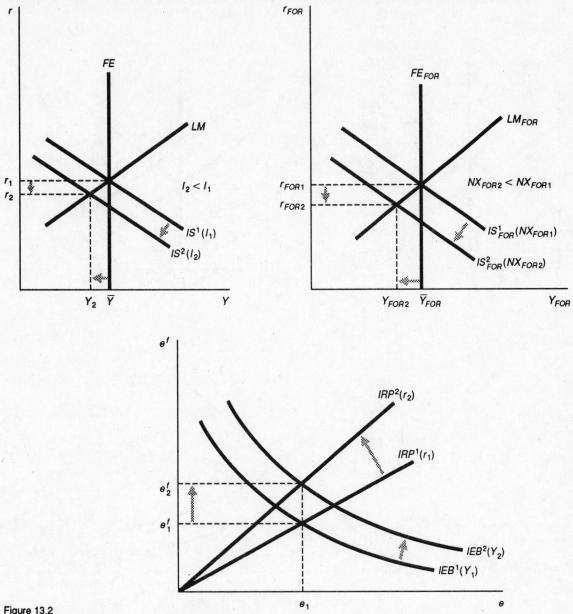

Figure 13.2

flexible price adjustments, money is neutral; therefore, expansionary monetary policy has no real output effect.

c)   A diagrammatic view of the world economy.   See Figure 13.3 on page 178.

d)   In the Keynesian model, the short-run effects of a decline in foreign demand for domestic goods are: 1)   The decline in foreign imports causes NX_{FOR} to increase, causing the foreign IS curve to shift up to the right, causing Y_{FOR} and

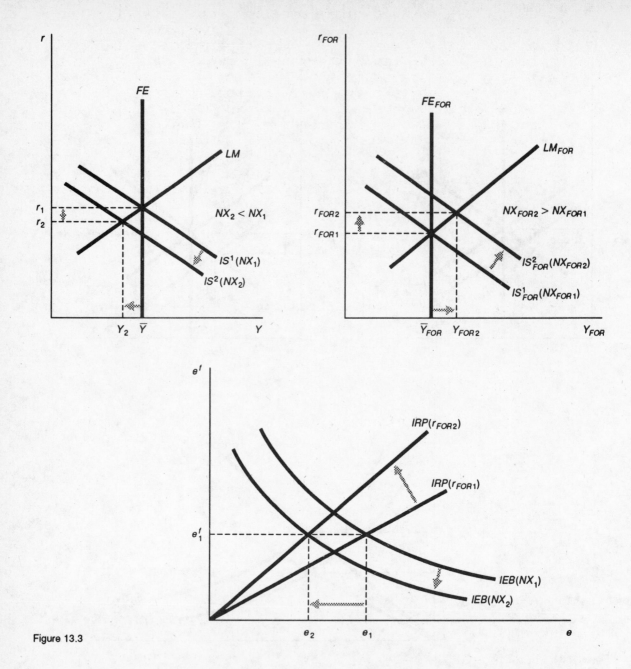

Figure 13.3

r_{FOR} to increase.   2)   The decline in NX causes the IEB curve
to shift down to the left.   The increase in r_{FOR} causes the
IRP line to pivot counterclockwise.   The combination of the
changes in the IEB curve and the IRP line causes e to
decline, but the effect on e^f is ambiguous.   3) The decline
in NX causes the domestic IS curve to shift to the left,
causing Y and r to decline.

e)   In the Keynesian model, an expansionary monetary policy
could reduce or offset the short-run decline in output, but

it would cause the real interest rate to decline further in the short run. The increase in domestic output would increase imports, causing net exports to decline further. The decline in the real interest rate would increase the counterclockwise pivot in the IRP line. The decline in net exports would increase the leftward shift in the IEB curve. The combination of the additional changes in the IEB curve and the IRP line would further reduce e, but the effect on e^f would be ambiguous. The increase in domestic imports would increase NX_{FOR}, causing the foreign IS curve to shift further to the right. Although some of the effects of expansionary monetary policy may be undesirable, Keynesians would argue that, most importantly, it could pull the domestic economy out of the recession quickly by quickly returning the level of aggregate demand in the domestic economy to the full-employment level of output.

CHAPTER 14

UNEMPLOYMENT AND INFLATION

A Review of Chapter Highlights

The **natural rate of unemployment** is the rate of unemployment
when the economy is at full employment, after complete wage and
price adjustment. Any policy attempt to reduce unemployment
below the natural rate of unemployment will cause the price level
to rise and inflation to rise. The natural rate of unemployment
is some positive percentage rate (e.g., 6%) because there is some
frictional unemployment and structural unemployment at the full-
employment level of output, but there is no **cyclical unemployment**
at the natural rate of unemployment. At the natural rate of
unemployment, there is no need for countercyclical stabilization
policies, because there is no cyclical unemployment.
    Okun's Law specifies the relationship between cyclical
unemployment and output. According to the levels form of Okun's
Law, each 1% decline in unemployment below the natural rate
causes output to rise by 2.5% above the full-employment level of
output. According to the growth rate form of Okun's Law, each 1%
increase in cyclical unemployment causes the growth rate of
output to fall by 2.5% below the growth rate of full-employment
output. If the growth rate of full-employment output is 3%, for
example, then a two percentage point increase in cyclical
unemployment would cause the growth rate of output to be -2%.
    The **simple Phillips curve** depicts a fixed tradeoff between
the unemployment rate and the inflation rate. As we move down
the simple Phillips curve to a higher unemployment rate, the
inflation rate declines. According to the simple Phillips curve,
the rate of inflation is zero at the natural rate of
unemployment. The simple Phillips curve has been replaced by the
expectations-augmented Phillips curve, which relates
unanticipated inflation to the unemployment rate. The **short-run
Phillips curve** shows the tradeoff between the unemployment rate
and the inflation rate during the short-run period, in which the
expected rate of inflation is fixed. For each possible expected
rate of inflation there exists a negatively sloped short-run

Phillips curve. On any short-run Phillips curve, the actual rate
of inflation equals the expected rate of inflation at the natural
rate of unemployment.

The **long-run Phillips curve** is vertical at the natural rate
of unemployment. At each point on the long-run Phillips curve,
the actual rate of inflation equals the expected rate of
inflation; actual and expected inflation rates increase together
as we move up the curve. The vertical long-run Phillips curve
illustrates that the level of output and the rate of unemployment
are independent of the rate of inflation in the long run and
independent of the expected rate of inflation in the long run.

In the long run, by definition, the macroeconomy is
operating in general equilibrium, at the natural rate of
unemployment, and at the full-employment level of output. In the
long run, there are no misperceptions, so expectations are
correct; the actual price level equals the expected price level,
and the actual rate of inflation equals the expected rate of
inflation.

The **misery index** is the sum of the unemployment rate and
the inflation rate. For a given unemployment rate, an increase
in the inflation rate makes us more miserable.

The theory of **hysteresis** tells us that an increase in the
unemployment rate causes the natural rate of unemployment to
increase. Alternatively, a decline in the unemployment rate
causes the natural rate of unemployment to decline. Therefore,
the natural rate of unemployment is positively related to the
actual rate of unemployment. The theory of hysteresis explains
why a recession-induced increase in the unemployment rate does
not quickly decline to the prerecession rate of unemployment as
soon as the recession is over. **Insider-outsider theory** shows
that hysteresis could be an economic effect of labor union
attempts to maximize wages for inside labor (i.e., current
employees) during recessions, without regard to outside labor
(i.e., potential future employees). When the recession ends,
firms will be reluctant to hire more labor at the high union
wage.

The principal costs of anticipated inflation are menu costs
and shoe-leather costs. If people expect the rate of inflation
to increase, they will reduce their demand for money because
inflation reduces the exchange value (i.e., purchasing power) of
money. **Shoe-leather costs** are the transactions costs incurred in
trading some of their money for other goods or assets.

Unanticipated inflation is the difference between the actual
rate of inflation and the expected rate of inflation. If the
actual rate of inflation is less than the expected rate of
inflation, the unanticipated rate of inflation is negative. The
principal costs of unanticipated inflation are the risk of
redistribution of wealth and relative price distortions.

Hyperinflation is an extremely high rate of inflation (e.g.,
above 50% per month) over a sustained period of time (e.g., a
year or more). When hyperinflation is unanticipated, the costs
of hyperinflation include the costs of both anticipated and

unanticipated inflation, and these economic costs may be enormous at very high rates of inflation.

Economists agree that persistently high rates of inflation are caused by excess money supply growth; reducing the rate of money supply growth will reduce the inflation rate in the long run. A decline in the rate of inflation is called **disinflation**. In the 1980-1983 period, for example, the U.S. experienced disinflation; inflation declined from 13.5% to 3.2%.

If the inflation rate is unacceptably high, classical economists propose that it be reduced quickly to an acceptable inflation rate; this approach to achieving disinflation is the **cold turkey** approach. Keynesians believe that the cold turkey approach will produce high unemployment in the short run. The Keynesian proposal for achieving disinflation is to reduce it gradually over several years; this is called **gradualism**.

The difference in the classical and Keynesian approaches to achieving disinflation is explained by differences in their views about the price-adjustment process. Classical economists believe that wages, prices, and expectations quickly adjust to changes in the inflation rate; Keynesians believe that wages, prices, and expectations slowly adjust to changes in the inflation rate. The longer the short-run adjustment period, the larger the output and unemployment costs of disinflation will be.

Questions

These questions test your understanding of the **key terms**, **key relationships**, and **key diagrams** highlighted in your text.

Multiple Choice questions: Circle the letter corresponding to the correct answer to each question.

1.   Over the 1955-1990 period in the United States, the natural rate of unemployment:

   a.   declined dramatically.
   b.   declined gradually.
   c.   increased gradually until the early 1970s, then declined gradually.
   d.   increased dramatically.
   e.   increased gradually.

2.   Cyclical unemployment is caused by:

   a.   people entering the labor force to search for jobs.
   b.   technological progress, which causes some industries to expand employment and others to reduce employment.
   c.   reducing international trade barriers, which causes some industries to expand employment and others to reduce employment.
   d.   the deindustrialization of America.
   e.   business cycle fluctuations.

3. Assuming that the natural rate of unemployment is 6%, that
    the full-employment growth rate is 3%, and that the actual
    unemployment rate is 8%, Okun's law predicts that the actual
    output growth rate is:

    a. 3%
    b. -3%
    c. 0%
    d. -2%
    e. 2.5%

4. The simple Phillips curve suggests that monetary
    policymakers could use monetary policy to:

    a. reduce the unemployment rate at the expense of higher
        inflation.
    b. reduce the unemployment rate while reducing inflation.
    c. reduce the unemployment rate without affecting the
        inflation rate.
    d. reduce inflation without affecting the unemployment
        rate.
    e. increase the inflation rate while increasing the
        unemployment rate.

5. Which of the following changes will cause the expectations-
    augmented Phillips curve to shift down to the left?

    a. a decline in the price level.
    b. a decline in the unemployment rate.
    c. a decline in the expected rate of inflation.
    d. a decline in the money supply.
    e. a decline in taxes.

6. If the expected rate of inflation is 15%, the short-run
    Phillips curve will:

    a. be the same as the simple Phillips curve.
    b. be the same as the long-run Phillips curve.
    c. intersect the long-run Phillips curve at the natural
        rate of unemployment, when the expected rate of
        inflation is 15%.
    d. be parallel to the long-run Phillips curve.
    e. be horizontal at an expected rate of inflation of 15%.

7. The long-run Phillips curve:

    a. will shift down to the left, as a result of
        expansionary monetary policy.
    b. will shift to a lower natural rate of unemployment, as
        a result of expansionary monetary policy.
    c. will shift down to the right to a lower inflation rate,
        as a result of expansionary monetary policy.
    d. will shift vertically to a higher rate of inflation and

expected inflation, as a result of expansionary monetary policy.

e.   is vertical at the natural rate of unemployment, and its position is independent of monetary policy.

8.   In the 1980-82 period in the United States, the decline in the inflation rate exceeded the increase in the unemployment rate, therefore the:

a.   economy was at the full-employment level of output.
b.   economic growth rate was rising.
c.   economy was experiencing deflation.
d.   misery index was declining.
e.   economy was adjusting to a beneficial supply shock.

9.   The theory of hysteresis explains why:

a.   inflationary expectations do not adjust quickly to changes in the inflation rate.
b.   the long-run Phillips curve is vertical at the natural rate of unemployment.
c.   a recession increases the natural rate of unemployment.
d.   a change in the demographics of the labor force can cause the natural rate of unemployment to change.
e.   cyclical unemployment has trivial output costs.

10.   According to the insider-outsider theory of labor markets:

a.   firms prefer to hire workers who can give them inside information about the plans of competing firms.
b.   firms prefer to promote workers inside their organization rather than hire more productive people from outside.
c.   within each firm, each level in the hierarchy of managers has insiders and outsiders.
d.   labor unions attempt to maximize the wage of currently employed workers while ignoring outsiders.
e.   firms will replace striking workers with nonunion outsiders quickly.

11.   The costs of quickly trading money for nonmonetary assets to reduce one's holdings of money are the:

a.   menu costs of anticipated inflation.
b.   menu costs of unanticipated inflation.
c.   shoe-leather costs of anticipated inflation.
d.   shoe-leather costs of unanticipated inflation.
e.   relative price distortion costs of unanticipated inflation.

12.   If the inflationary effect of an increase in the money supply is anticipated, money is neutral in the short run:

a.   in the basic classical model, but not in the extended classical model.
b.   in both the classical and Keynesian models.
c.   in the extended classical model, but not in the basic classical model.
d.   in both the basic classical and extended classical model, but not in the Keynesian model.
e.   in the Keynesian model, but not in the classical model.

13.   Most economists would agree that the best way to reduce hyperinflation is to:

a.   wipe out labor unions.
b.   reduce the government deficit.
c.   institute wage-price controls.
d.   reduce taxes.
e.   reduce the rate of money supply growth.

14.   If disinflation is unanticipated, it causes:

a.   inflation to initially decline along a short-run Phillips curve, followed by a decline in inflationary expectations.
b.   inflation to rise along a short-run Phillips curve, followed by an increase in inflationary expectations.
c.   no short-run real economic effects, because money is neutral in the extended classical model.
d.   inflationary expectations to fall immediately, with no real economic effects.
e.   unemployment and output to fall in the short run, with no long-run price level effect, in the Keynesian model.

15.   In analyzing the disinflationary period of the early 1980s in the United States, the Keynesians conclude that:

a.   political business cycle theory best explains this monetary policy attempt to reduce unemployment just prior to the 1980 Presidential election.
b.   the rational expectations hypothesis correctly predicts that systematic monetary policies are anticipated and are neutral.
c.   the basic classical model is correct in showing that changes in the money supply have only price effects.
d.   real business cycle theory correctly predicted that the disinflation resulted from small, random beneficial supply shocks.
e.   the cold turkey approach creates recessions.

16.   Which of the following disinflationary monetary policies would classical economists prefer?

a.   a dramatic monetary surprise.
b.   a cold turkey approach that is announced and credible.

   c.   a cold turkey approach that is announced, but not credible.

   d.   a gradualism approach that is announced and credible.

   e.   a gradualism approach that is unannounced.

17.   An unanticipated increase in the money supply causes the aggregate demand curve to shift to the right along:

   a.   the positively sloped *SRAS* curve in the extended classical model in the short run, and causes the *SRAS* to shift up the *LRAS* curve in the long run.

   b.   the horizontal *SRAS* curve in the extended classical model in the short run, and causes the *SRAS* to shift up the *LRAS* curve in the long run.

   c.   the negatively sloped *SRAS* curve in the extended classical model in the short run, and causes the aggregate demand curve to shift back to the left in the long run.

   d.   the positively sloped *SRAS* curve in Keynesian model of sticky prices and real wage rigidity in the short run, and causes the *SRAS* curve to shift up the *LRAS* curve in the long run.

   e.   the horizontal *SRAS* curve in the Keynesian model of nominal wage rigidity in the short run, and causes the aggregate demand curve to shift back to the left in the long run.

Short-Answer Essay Questions

1.   **Okun's Law and the natural rate of unemployment:** a) State the growth rate form of Okun's Law and define the variables. b) Briefly explain Okun's law, in terms of changes in labor market conditions during a recession. c) Assuming that the growth rate of full-employment output is 3%, the natural rate of unemployment is 6%, and the unemployment rate is 5%, use Okun's law to calculate the growth rate of output. d) Why is the natural rate of unemployment not equal to zero, and why did it increase over the last several decades in the United States? e) Briefly state the hysteresis theory critique and the classical model critique of Okun's Law.

2.   **Phillips curves and the price-adjustment process:** a) What tradeoff is demonstrated by the simple Phillips curve? b) Briefly explain the expectations-augmented Phillips curve critique of the simple Phillips curve. c) Assuming that the natural rate of unemployment is 6% and that the expected rate of inflation is 5%, draw a Phillips curve diagram with a short-run Phillips curve and a long-run Phillips curve. Label the axes, curves, and equilibrium values. d) Use the diagram to compare and contrast the effects of a 3%

unanticipated and anticipated increase in money supply growth rate. e) State the rational expectations theory critique and the political business cycles critique of monetary stabilization policy.

3.   **Supply shocks**: a) Draw the following diagrams and use them to show the effects of the OPEC oil price increase in the mid-1970s in the United States: 1) a Phillips curve diagram; 2) an extended classical model diagram; 3) a Keynesian model diagram. b) Define stagflation and explain how an oil price shock can create stagflation. c) Why did the government use expansionary monetary policies in the late 1970s, and what was the principal negative macroeconomic effect of these policies?

4.   **Demand shocks and disinflation**: a) Draw the following diagrams and use them to show the short-run and long-run effects of an unanticipated disinflationary monetary policy: 1) a Phillips curve diagram; 2) an extended classical model diagram; and 3) a Keynesian model diagram. b) Do these diagrams show the same effect on the misery index? Briefly explain. c) Were wage and price controls effective in reducing inflation in the United States in the early 1970s? Briefly explain.

5.   **The costs of unemployment and inflation**: a) Compare and contrast the costs of frictional, structural, and cyclical unemployment. Briefly explain any differences. b) Does unemployment insurance reduce the unemployment rate or reduce the costs of unemployment? Briefly explain. c) Identify and briefly explain the two principal costs of anticipated inflation. d) Identify and briefly explain the two principal costs of unanticipated inflation. e) Compare and contrast the classical cold turkey approach and the Keynesian gradualism approach to reducing inflation, under conditions of moderate inflation and under conditions of hyperinflation.

Answers to Multiple Choice Questions

1.	e	8.	d	15.	e
2.	e	9.	c	16.	b
3.	d	10.	d	17.	a
4.	a	11.	c		
5.	c	12.	d		
6.	c	13.	e		
7.	e	14.	a		

Answers to Short-Answer Essay Questions

1.   **Okun's Law and the natural rate of unemployment**

a)   Okun's Law is: $\dfrac{\Delta Y}{Y} = \dfrac{\Delta \bar{Y}}{\bar{Y}} - 2.5\Delta U$

$\dfrac{\Delta Y}{Y}$ = growth rate of output

$\dfrac{\Delta \bar{Y}}{\bar{Y}}$ = growth rate of full-employment output

ΔU = the change in the unemployment rate.

b)   An explanation of Okun's law: Since 100% of employed labor produces 100% of output, we might expect that a 1% increase in cyclical employment would only lower output by 1%. In a recession, however, an increase in cyclical unemployment is highly correlated with a decline in the size of the labor force, a decline in the average number of hours worked per week by workers, and a decline in labor productivity. The 2.5% decline in the growth rate of output for each 1% increase in unemployment is the combined effect of all these changes.

c)   Per Okun's law, the calculated growth rate of output is 5.5%.

5.5% = 3.0% - 2.5 x (5% - 6%) = 3.0% + 2.5%

d)   The natural rate of unemployment exceeds zero, because there is always some frictional and structural unemployment at the full-employment level of output. Two reasons why the natural rate of unemployment increased over the last several decades in the United States are:

1)   changes in the demographics of the labor force: During this period, labor force participation by women and teenagers increased dramatically; this especially tends to especially increase frictional unemployment.

2)   structural changes in the economy: During this period, increased foreign competition, technological progress (e.g., in computer technology), a reduction in employment in manufacturing industries, and employment growth in service industries all contributed to an increase in structural unemployment.

e)   Critiques of Okun's Law:

1)   hysteresis critique: An increase in cyclical unemployment causes the natural rate of unemployment to increase. A decline in cyclical unemployment causes the natural rate to decline. Therefore, the natural rate of unemployment is not independent of the rate of

cyclical unemployment. This explains why recessions may create longer periods of high unemployment than suggested by the natural rate theory.

2)   classical critique: Most recessions are caused by adverse supply shocks. Assuming that wages and prices are flexible, and that there are no misperceptions about the rate of inflation, a temporary adverse supply shock increases the natural rate of unemployment but creates little, if any, cyclical unemployment. Even allowing for some decline in aggregate demand and some misperceptions, any increase in cyclical unemployment will be short lived. In the classical model, expectations, wages, and prices quickly adjust to return the economy to the natural rate of unemployment quickly.

2.   Phillips curves and the price-adjustment process

a)   The simple Phillips curve depicts various possible combinations of unemployment and inflation that could exist in the economy. The negative slope of the simple Phillips curve shows that these variables are negatively related. Therefore, a tradeoff exists between them; any decline in the rate of unemployment increases the rate of inflation. Any decline in the rate of inflation increases the rate of unemployment. The simple Phillips curve suggests that policymakers could choose the particular combination of unemployment and inflation that they prefer, and that they could use monetary policy to move the economy to that preferred point on the simple Phillips curve.

b)   The expectations-augmented Phillips curve critique is that the simple Phillips curve fails to include the expected rate of inflation as a determinant of the actual rate of inflation. The simple Phillips curve suggests that there is a stable relationship between unemployment and inflation that policymakers can exploit, but the expectations-augmented Phillips curve shows that this relationship is not stable and, therefore, not exploitable. Any attempt to reduce the unemployment rate below the natural rate of unemployment will be effective only if unanticipated and, even then, only during the short-run period of misperceptions or wage-price rigidities. Once expectations, wages, and prices have adjusted, the short-run Phillips curve will shift up to the right and unemployment will return to the natural rate of unemployment at a higher rate of inflation.

c)   A Phillips curve diagram. See Figure 14.1 on page 190.

$$\bar{U} = 6\%$$

d)   The economic effects of a
     3% increase in money supply
     growth depend on whether
     the increase is anticipated
     or unanticipated:

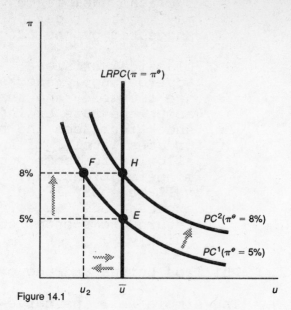

Figure 14.1

1)   anticipated: If the
     increase in money
     supply growth is
     anticipated, then
     money is neutral. In
     the diagram, the
     economy moves quickly
     from point E to H.
     There is no
     unemployment effect or
     output effect. Wages,
     prices, and
     expectations quickly
     adjust to general
     equilibrium.

2)   unanticipated: In the short run, the 3% increase in
     money supply growth causes the growth rate of output to
     increase, the unemployment rate to decline, and the
     inflation rate to increase, as we move from point E to
     F in the diagram along a fixed short run Phillips curve
     with the expected rate of inflation equal to 5%. In
     the long run, the expected rate of inflation rises to
     8%, causing the short-run Phillips curve to shift up to
     the right. In the diagram, we move from point E to H
     in the long run. At point H, the rate of inflation has
     increased to 8%, the expected rate of inflation has
     increased to 8%, and unemployment is at the natural
     rate of 6%.

e)   Critiques of monetary stabilization policy:

1)   rational expectations critique: Monetary stabilization
     policies are usually neutral, since most policies are
     systematic, systematic policies are anticipated, and
     anticipated monetary policies are neutral. Therefore,
     monetary stabilization policy is completely ineffective
     in lowering the rate of unemployment, even in the short
     run.

2)   political business cycles critique: Monetary
     stabilization policies could be effective in the short
     run, in stabilizing the economy or in destabilizing it;

yet they are more likely to create business cycles than
to offset them. Monetary policymakers use expansionary
monetary policies before Presidential elections to get
the incumbent U.S. President reelected. An increase in
money supply growth reduces the rate of unemployment
and increases the growth rate of output before an
election. After the election, monetary policymakers use
contractionary monetary policy to offset the
inflationary effects of the previously expansionary
policy. In effect, monetary policy is inefficiently
used to achieve partisan political goals, rather than
being used to efficiently achieve the economic goal of
stabilizing the economy. The primary objective of
monetary policy is not to stabilize output at the full-
employment level of output.

3.   **Supply shocks**

a)   The following diagrams show the stagflation effects of the
      mid-1970s oil price increase in the United States. The oil
      price increase is an adverse supply shock. The oil price
      increase causes all of the following to increase: the price
      level, the expected price level, the inflation rate, the
      expected inflation rate, the unemployment rate, and the
      natural rate of unemployment. The oil price increase causes
      the following to decline: the level of employment, the
      level of output, the full-employment level of output, the
      growth rate of output, and the growth rate of full-
      employment output.

      1)   Phillips curve
            diagram.

      2)   Extended classical
            model diagram. See
            Figure 14.3 on page
            192.

      3)   Keynesian model
            diagram. See Figure
            14.4 on page 192.

b)   Stagflation is an increase
      in unemployment,
      accompanied by an increase
      in inflation. The increase
      in unemployment reduces
      output, creating stagnation
      in the growth rate of
      output. For a given level
      of aggregate demand,
      anything that reduces
      aggregate supply causes stagflation. Since oil and its

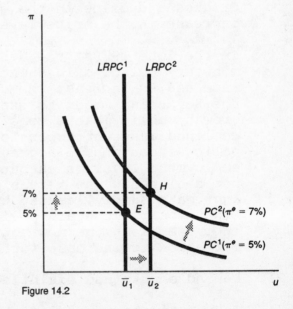

Figure 14.2

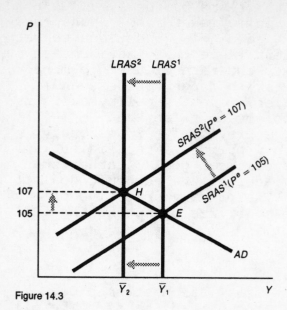

Figure 14.3

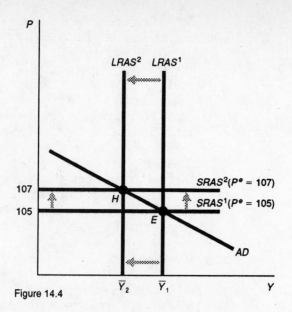

Figure 14.4

close energy substitutes are important factors of production, an increase in the price of oil increases production cost, causing firms to increase prices at each possible level of aggregate output, which is a decline in aggregate supply. A decline in the short-run aggregate supply curve is consistent with an increase in the short-run Phillips curve. A decline in long-run aggregate supply is consistent with a rightward shift of the long-run Phillips curve. Note that an increase in the unemployment rate creates a decline in the growth rate of output, and that an increase in the price level is an increase in inflation.

c)   In the late 1970s, the U.S. government used expansionary monetary policies in an attempt to reduce the unemployment rate and to increase the growth rate of output. Relying on the Keynesian model to explain the slowdown in economic growth, policymakers concluded that aggregate demand had declined and that expansionary monetary stabilization policies could pull aggregate demand back to the full-employment level of output. However, aggregate demand had not declined. The recession as created by a decline in aggregate supply, caused by an increase in the price of oil. Expansionary monetary policies caused aggregate demand to increase along the new aggregate supply curve, which caused inflation to increase further.

4.   Demand shocks and disinflation

a)   An unanticipated disinflationary monetary policy has both short-run and long-run effects. In the diagrams, the economy moves from point E to F in the short run.   The following variables decline in value: output, employment, the price level, and the rate of inflation.   The unemployment rate increases. The natural rate of unemployment and the full-employment level of output are unaffected. In the long run, the economy moves from point E to H. The price level declines, the rate of inflation declines, and the expected rate of inflation declines, but output returns to the full-employment level of output and unemployment returns to the natural rate of unemployment.

1)   Phillips curve
     diagram.

     $H = (\bar{U}, 5\%)$

2)   Extended classical
     model diagram.

3)   Keynesian model
     diagram. See Figure
     14.7 on page 194.

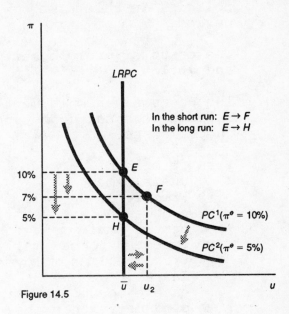

Figure 14.5

b)   In the short run, changes in the Keynesian model diagram unambiguously increase the misery index, because unemployment increases, while inflation is unchanged by the unanticipated disinflationary monetary policy. In the short run, in the extended classical model diagram and in the Phillips curve diagram, the effect on the misery index is ambiguous, because unemployment increases but inflation declines. In the long run, in all models, the misery index declines, because unemployment is unchanged, while inflation has declined.

c)   In the early 1970s in the United States, the imposition of wage and price controls reduced wage increases and reduced price increases during the period of controls, but wages and

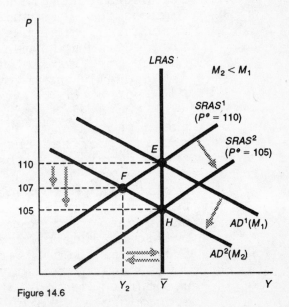

Figure 14.6

prices quickly increased, once controls were lifted. The 1971-1974 period of wage-price controls had no long-run effects, by 1975. Wages and prices were driven up by the oil price increase, by expansionary monetary policies, and by expansionary fiscal policies in this time period.

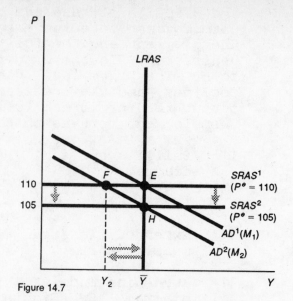

Figure 14.7

5. **The costs of unemployment and inflation**

a) The costs of unemployment include personal costs and output costs.

   1) frictional unemployment:
      Frictional unemployment is temporary unemployment by people who are readily employable but are searching for better employment positions. Personal costs are expected to be small, because the duration of a typical frictional unemployment spell is short for most people. There is no output cost, since frictional unemployment enables people to find new jobs where they become more productive than they were in their previous jobs.

   2) structural unemployment: Personal costs are the highest for structural unemployment, because structurally unemployed individuals typically suffer frequent unemployment spells of long duration. The output cost may be relatively small, because the structurally unemployed are not currently employable. Some output costs will be incurred in the form of skills training, education, or relocation costs to get these people back to work; these output costs will partially offset the increase in output produced by these people once they become employed.

   3) cyclical unemployment: Personal costs may be relatively small, particularly if the duration of individual unemployment spells are typically short, if cyclically unemployed workers receive reduced paychecks from firms, receive unemployment insurance compensation, and have sufficient personal savings to use during periods of unemployment. Classical economists also argue that unemployed workers receive the personal benefit of increased leisure, when they

are cyclically unemployed. The output cost is the highest for cyclical unemployment, since cyclically unemployed workers could, in the aggregate, produce a lot of output, if they were employed. Okun's Law predicts the aggregate output cost of cyclical unemployment. Note that output produced by the employed also declines during periods of cyclical unemployment.

b)   Unemployment insurance does reduce the personal cost of unemployment, by redistributing the cost to other time periods and to other people. Workers and firms pay the unemployment insurance premium all the time; not just when unemployment is high. Also, all workers and firms pay the insurance premium, while only a small percentage file for unemployment insurance income payments at any given time. Unemployment insurance increases the unemployment and output cost of unemployment by prolonging the duration of unemployment spells, since those receiving the income benefits have less incentive to return to work quickly. The output cost of unemployment insurance would increase with increases in the income payments provided by the insurance, increases in the number of months over which people could collect it, and increases in the eligibility of those unemployed. Supply-side economists believe that transfer programs, like the unemployment insurance program, increase unemployment and create large output costs in the United States.

c)   Costs of anticipated inflation:

1)   menu costs: The costs of changing prices are called menu costs. Classical economists believe these costs are small, assuming perfectly competitive market conditions. Keynesians believe these costs are large enough to create price stickiness, assuming monopolistically competitive market conditions.

2)   shoe-leather costs: The transactions costs incurred by households and firms in reducing the share of their assets they hold as money are called shoe-leather costs. These costs are likely to be larger than menu costs.

d)   Costs of unanticipated inflation:

1)   risk of redistribution of wealth cost: Unanticipated inflation creates a redistribution of wealth; what some people and firms lose, others gain. For example, creditors lose and debtors gain because unanticipated inflation lowers the real interest rate on existing loans. Although there is no aggregate income loss from redistribution, the costs incurred by market

participants trying to reduce their risk of losses may be large. For example, creditors may charge an inflation risk premium on all loans to cover their risk, even during periods when inflation is constant, thereby increasing the real interest rate in the long run.

2)   relative price distortions cost: Unanticipated inflation causes firms to misperceive a change in the price level as changes in the relative prices of their products. This misperception causes firms to charge inefficient prices for their products, produce inefficient levels of output, and employ inefficient amounts of labor at inefficient wages. These relative price distortions cause inefficiencies that are costly.

e)   With either approach, the short-run adjustment cost of reducing hyperinflation will be much higher than the cost of reducing moderate inflation.

1)   cold turkey approach: Classical economists propose a rapid reduction in money supply growth to achieve disinflation, assuming that prices, wages, and expectations adjust quickly. Unemployment costs and inflation costs are most likely to be small, if the classical assumptions about rapid market adjustments are correct, the policy is announced, and the announcement is credible. Both classical economists and Keynesians agree that the inflation costs would be smaller for a cold turkey approach than for gradualism, since inflation is being reduced more quickly. However, Keynesians believe that the unemployment costs could be very high.

2)   gradualism approach: Keynesians propose a gradualism approach of slowly reducing money supply growth over several years to achieve disinflation, assuming wages, prices, and expectations adjust slowly to changes in the inflation rate. Both classical economists and Keynesians believe that this approach would have small unemployment costs, but the inflation costs would be greater, since the rate of inflation would be higher for a long period of time. Classicals contend inflation costs could be much higher than for a cold turkey approach, since an announced gradualism approach is unlikely to be credible.

CHAPTER 15

MONETARY POLICY AND THE FEDERAL RESERVE

A Review of Chapter Highlights

In most countries, monetary policy is conducted by a **central bank**. The central bank of the United States is the Federal Reserve System. The Federal Reserve (i.e., the Fed) is one of the principal regulators of the banking industry. Private banks and thrifts, called **depository institutions**, are assisted by the central bank in providing banking services.

The Fed issues currency in the form of coins and paper money (i.e., Federal Reserve notes), based on the U.S. dollar monetary standard; this currency is **legal tender** in the United States. As legal tender, dollars are widely accepted in exchange for resources, products, and assets in the United States.

The Federal Reserve controls the money supply through its control over the **monetary base**, which is also called **high-powered money**. The monetary base equals **bank reserves** plus currency in circulation. In a **100% reserve banking** system, banks would hold all deposits on reserve, and they would charge fees to cover the cost of banking services. The **reserve-deposit ratio** in a **fractional reserve banking** system is less than 100%, and banks cover a large share of their operating costs with the interest earned on loans made with bank deposits.

In accepting deposits and lending out their excess reserves, banks and thrifts create money, with a **multiple expansion of loans and deposits**. The money supply includes currency in circulation plus deposits at these depository institutions. The public's demand for currency relative to deposits determines the **currency-deposit ratio**. An increase in the currency-deposit ratio reduces the amount of deposits created by a given amount of bank lending, which also reduces the **money multiplier**. The money multiplier is the increase in the money supply created by each dollar increase in the monetary base. In a fractional reserve banking system with currency in circulation, the money multiplier $= [(1 + cu)/(cu + res)]$.

The Federal Reserve controls the money supply indirectly through its control over the monetary base. Its principal monetary policy instrument for changing the size of the monetary base is open market operations. An **open market purchase** of government securities (e.g., U.S. Treasury bonds) by the Fed increases the monetary base. An **open market sale** of government securities by the Fed reduces the monetary base.

The seven members of the **Board of Governors of the Federal Reserve System** are nominated by the President of the United States and confirmed by the U.S. Senate for staggered terms of fourteen years. The Board of Governors proposes regulations and deregulations for the banking industry, sets reserve requirement ratios, and sets the discount rate. The Board of Governors, the president of the Federal Reserve Bank of New York, and the presidents of four other Federal Reserve regional banks make up the **Federal Open Market Committee (FOMC)** which controls monetary policy.

Private banks use **vault cash**, made up partly of daily deposits, to meet the daily withdrawal demands of depositors. On some occasion, if a bank does not have enough vault cash to satisfy withdrawal demands, the bank can draw down its deposits at the Fed or it can borrow the amount it needs from the Fed. The Fed serves as a **lender of last resort** in its **discount window lending** to private banks. The Fed charges banks an interest rate, called the **discount rate**, on these discount window loans. Banks also borrow and lend to each other at the **federal funds rate**. Unlike the discount rate, the federal funds rate is not a policy **instrument** of the Fed, but it is an **intermediate target** of the Fed. Although the Fed does not set the federal funds rate, it can use its policy instruments to cause the federal funds rate to rise or fall.

There are two opposing approaches to conducting monetary policy; **rules** versus **discretion**. Discretionary monetary policy is also called an **activist** approach, because it requires that policymakers continuously monitor the performance of the economy and actively use monetary policy to respond to economic events to achieve monetary policy goals. Keynesians propose that the Fed take an activist approach; monetarists propose that the Fed adopt a rules approach to conducting monetary policy.

Monetarism is an important school of macroeconomic thought. Although monetarists believe that changes in the money supply have even larger real economic effects than Keynesians contend, monetarists also believe that discretionary monetary policy attempts to stabilize the economy are likely to be destabilizing. From a monetarist viewpoint, the economy would be reasonably stable if the Fed would just stop destabilizing it.

A recently developed theoretical argument against discretionary monetary policy is the credibility argument. Some economists contend that discretionary policies lack **credibility**, which causes them to create different real economic effects than the effects intended by policymakers. From this viewpoint, only policy rules are credible, and only credible policies are effective. **Game theory** provides one way of analyzing why the effectiveness of monetary policy may depend on its credibility.

Questions

These questions test your understanding of the **key terms**, **key relationships**, and **key diagrams** highlighted in your text.

Multiple Choice Questions

1. Monetary policy in the United States is principally controlled by:

   a. the President of the United States.
   b. the U.S. Senate.
   c. the U.S. Congress.
   d. fiscal policymakers.
   e. the central bank.

2. Which of the following are depository institutions:

   a. the Federal Reserve Banks of New York and Chicago.
   b. the U.S. Treasury and the IRS.
   c. banks and thrifts.
   c. investment banks and finance companies.
   d. banks and insurance companies.

3. If a currency is legal tender in a country, then:

   a. the government will readily exchange it for gold.
   b. the government will not accept it in payment of taxes.
   c. it is the only legal form of wealth.
   d. it is widely accepted as a means of payment, and creditors are required to accept it in settlement of debts.
   e. it could not be used for illegal activities.

4. The monetary base (*BASE*) equals:

   a. $CU + RES$
   b. RES
   c. $CU + DEP$
   d. $M - CU$
   e. $M - RES$

5. Banks hold some deposits on reserve at the Fed because:

   a. the Fed pays a higher interest rate than banks can get in the private market.
   b. the Fed will insure those deposits, but will not insure regular bank deposits.
   c. these are membership dues for being a member bank.
   d. these deposits meet the reserve requirement of the Fed.
   e. the Fed will not allow them to hold all of bank deposits at the Fed; banks have to make some loans.

6.   In a fractional reserve banking system:

   a.   most deposits are used to make bank loans.
   b.   100% of deposits are held as reserves.
   c.   the money supply = high-powered money.
   d.   the money multiplier is less than one.
   e.   there has to be more than one bank, because one bank is allowed to hold only a fraction of all deposits.

7.   In a fractional reserves banking system with no currency, the money multiplier is:

   a. $[(cu + 1)/(cu + res)]$
   b. $1/(cu + res)$
   c. $1/res$
   d. $BASE/M$
   e. res

8.   If the public's demand for currency increased relative to its demand for deposits, the:

   a.   monetary base would decrease.
   b.   reserve requirement ratio would decrease.
   c.   currency-deposit ratio would decrease.
   d.   reserve-deposit ratio would increase.
   e.   money multiplier would decrease.

9.   If the Fed makes a large open market sale of bonds to the public, the:

   a.   money supply will increase.
   b.   money multiplier will increase.
   c.   federal funds rate will decrease.
   d.   unemployment rate will decrease.
   e.   money supply will decrease.

10.   Members of the Board of Governors are:

   a.   democratically elected by popular vote every four years.
   b.   appointed by the U.S. President and confirmed by the U.S. Senate, as relatively independent policymakers.
   c.   appointed by the U.S. President and serve as part of the executive branch of the federal government.
   d.   appointed by the U.S. Congress and serve as part of the legislative branch of the federal government.
   e.   appointed by the Supreme Court and serve as part of the judicial branch of the federal government.

11.   Within the Fed, the FOMC:

   a.   sets the discount rate.
   b.   controls monetary policy.

    c.   regulates securities markets.
    d.   sets reserve requirement ratios.
    e.   handles check clearance and settlement of bank
         balances.

12. By lending at the discount window, the Fed:

    a.   prevents banks from going bankrupt.
    b.   ensures that banks will make healthy profits.
    c.   eliminates the need for banks to pay market interest
         rates to attract deposits.
    d.   acts as a lender of last resort to enable banks to meet
         unexpectedly high withdrawal demands.
    e.   insures bank deposits.

13. The federal funds rate is:

    a.   the interest rate on federal government bonds.
    b.   the interest rate banks charge other banks for short-
         term loans.
    c.   the growth rate of the federal debt.
    d.   the interest rate penalty on late federal tax payments.
    e.   an intermediate monetary aggregate target of the Fed.

14. The dominant policy instrument typically used to change the
money supply is:

    a.   deregulation.
    b.   fiscal policy.
    c.   monetary policy announcements.
    d.   the discount rate.
    e.   open market operations.

15. If the principal source of instability in the economy is
instability in money demand, the best intermediate target of
monetary policy is:

    a.   the discount rate.
    b.   a monetary aggregate.
    c.   the short-term interest rate.
    d.   the monetary base.
    e.   government bonds.

16. The monetary policy rule proposed by monetarists is to:

    a.   follow political business cycles.
    b.   use long and variable policy lags.
    c.   reduce money supply growth quickly.
    d.   stabilize the domestic economy before stabilizing the
         exchange rate.
    e.   increase the money supply at a low, constant rate of
         growth every year.

17. The basic Keynesian argument for discretionary monetary policy is that:

   a. monetary policy is the principal cause of business cycles.
   b. monetary policy is more effective than fiscal policy.
   c. aggregate demand is unstable and monetary policy can help to stabilize it.
   d. reducing unemployment is much more important than reducing inflation.
   e. policy rules are likely to be destabilizing.

18. Money is neutral in the long run; this is the view of:

   a. classical economists, Keynesians, and monetarists.
   b. only classical economists.
   c. only monetarists.
   d. Keynesians and classical economists, but not monetarists.
   e. Keynesians and monetarists, but not classical economists.

19. In response to the credibility argument against discretionary monetary policies, Keynesians contend that:

   a. policies do not need to be credible to be effective.
   b. discretionary monetary policies pulled the economy out of the Great Depression.
   c. cold turkey policies are more credible than gradualism.
   d. policymakers need flexibility, even if it reduces their credibility.
   e. discretionary policies should be replaced by a rules-based approach.

20. According to game theory analysis of the game between firms and the Fed:

   a. the firms cannot determine the Fed's most preferred outcome.
   b. the Fed cannot determine the firms' least preferred outcome.
   c. The Fed and firms negotiate to reach a cooperative solution.
   d. The Fed and the firms act independently in their own rational self-interest.
   e. monetary policy has real effects in the short run, even when the firms anticipate the Fed's next move.

Short-Answer Essay Questions

1. **Federal Reserve control over the money supply:** a) Use the money supply and monetary base equations to develop an

equation for the money supply in terms of the monetary base.
b) Identify the market actors who control each of the
following variables and state whether the money supply is
positively related or negatively related to each variable:
the monetary base, the reserve-deposit ratio, and the
currency-deposit ratio. c) Was the money multiplier stable
during the Great Depression, and why would an unstable money
multiplier pose a problem for monetary policy? d) Why does
the U.S. use a fractional reserve banking system? e) Why
does the Fed impose a minimum reserve requirement ratio on
transactions?

2. **Monetary policy instruments of the Fed**: a) Identify the
most commonly used policy instrument for changing the money
supply, and explain how the Fed can use this policy
instrument to increase and to decrease the money supply. b)
What policy making body within the Fed controls monetary
policy and how are its members chosen? c) Identify two
other monetary policy instruments, and explain how each can
be used to increase the money supply. d) Explain why the
Fed typically does not use all its instruments together to
change the money supply. e) Given an economy with no
currency and a reserve-deposit ratio of 10%, explain how the
banking system creates money when the Fed buys a $1000 bond
from a bank.

3. **Monetary policy targets of the Fed**: a) Identify the two
principal intermediate targets of monetary policy and
explain why they are efficient targets. b) Why does the Fed
set a target range for its intermediate target? c) Why do
monetarists object to the Fed's use of multiple intermediate
targets? d) What is the optimal intermediate target of
monetary policy, when nominal shocks are the principal cause
of instability in the macroeconomy? e) What is the
intermediate target recommended by monetarists, and why do
they propose this target?

4. **Ultimate targets and monetary policy approaches**: a)
Identify the principal short-run ultimate target of monetary
policy in the Keynesian model, and explain why it is not a
long-run target. b) Identify the principal long-run
ultimate target of monetary policy in the Keynesian model,
and explain why it is not a short-run target. c) Compare
and contrast the classical and monetarist reasons for
opposing monetary stabilization policy. d) Explain why
monetarists believe their monetary policy rule will achieve
price level stability. e) From a Keynesian viewpoint, what
is wrong with the monetarist argument against an activist
monetary policy?

5. **Game theory, credibility, and monetary policy effects**: a)
Use game theory to explain why the Fed may not be able to
achieve its stabilization policy goal. b) Use game theory

to explain why the Fed may be able to achieve its goal under a policy rule approach. c) State the Keynesian critique of the credibility argument against discretionary monetary policy. d) State the empirical effects on unemployment and inflation of using a policy rule in West Germany, Japan, and the United States during the late 1970s and early 1980s. e) Evaluate the empirical evidence to determine whether it supports the credibility argument and the monetarist argument for using a policy rule.

Answers to Multiple Choice Questions

1.	e	8.	e	15.	c
2.	c	9.	e	16.	e
3.	d	10.	b	17.	c
4.	a	11.	b	18.	a
5.	d	12.	d	19.	d
6.	a	13.	b	20.	d
7.	c	14.	e		

Answers to Short-Answer Essay Questions

1.   **Federal Reserve control over the money supply**

a)   Using the money supply and monetary base equations to develop the money supply equation in terms of the monetary base:

1) $M = CU + DEP$
2) $BASE = CU + RES$
3) $res = RES/DEP$
4) $cu = cu/DEP$
5) $BASE = cu \times DEP + res \times DEP = (cu + res) \times DEP$
6) $DEP = [1/(cu + res)] \times BASE$
7) $CU + DEP = cu \times DEP + DEP$
8) $M = (cu + 1) \times DEP$
9) $M = [(cu + 1)/(cu + res)] \times BASE$

The money multiplier is $[(cu + 1)/(cu + res)] = M/BASE$.

b)   Determinants of the money supply:

1)   The monetary base ($BASE$): is positively related to the the money supply; an increase in the base increases the money supply. The Fed controls the monetary base.

2)   The reserve-deposit ratio (res): is negatively related to the money supply; an increase in the reserve-deposit ratio reduces the money multiplier and thus reduces the money supply. The Fed sets the minimum reserve

requirement ratio on transactions deposits, but the
private banks control the reserve-deposit ratio by
holding excess reserves (i.e., reserves in excess of
required reserves) on transactions deposits. Any
reserves on other deposits at banks and thrifts are
excess reserves, since there is no reserve requirement
for nontransactions deposits.

3)   The currency-deposit ratio (cu): is negatively related
to the money supply; an increase in the currency-
deposit ratio reduces the money multiplier and thus
reduces the money supply. The public (i.e., everyone
except banks, thrifts, and the Fed) controls the
currency-deposit ratio by deciding how much of their
money they want to retain as currency, rather than
deposit in a bank or thrift institution.

c)   No.   The money multiplier was not stable during the Great
Depression. In the 1931 to early 1933 period, the money
multiplier declined sharply, because the currency-deposit
ratio and the reserve-deposit ratio both rose dramatically.
Market actors increased their demand for currency and banks
increased their demand for excess reserves. Instability in
the money multiplier creates instability in the money
supply, for a given monetary base. The Fed could offset any
undesirable effect of a change in the money multiplier on
the money supply by changing the monetary base. However,
the Fed did not sufficiently compensate for the change in
the money multiplier, so the money supply declined by 35% in
this period. More than one third of the banks in the
country failed or were acquired by other banks in the
1930-1933 period. This financial crisis was stopped in
1933, when President Roosevelt temporarily shut down the
banking system, by declaring a "bank holiday."

d)   The U.S. uses a fractional reserve banking system to enable
banks to act as a financial intermediary between depositors
and borrowers. By bringing depositors and borrowers together
at a low transactions cost, banks greatly facilitate the
flow of money to its highest valued alternative uses. An
efficient banking system is, therefore, an important
institutional arrangement for promoting economic growth.
Under a 100% reserve banking system, banks could still
provide a low-cost checking account system for making
payments, but they would have to charge fees for these
checking account services because banks could not make loans
to help cover these expenses.

e)   The reserve requirement ratio is a monetary policy
instrument (i.e., tool) of the Fed. The Fed uses the
reserve requirement ratio, and the reserves that it creates,
to control the money supply. In a monetary system with no

currency, the money multiplier is (1/*res*) and the monetary base is *RES*. If banks keep the reserve-deposit ratio constant (e.g., by holding only required reserves), the Fed can use open market operations to increase the money supply [*M* = *DEP* = (1/*res*) × *RES* = (1/*res*) × *BASE*] by (1/*res*) for every dollar increase in the monetary base. The Fed could also increase the money supply by reducing the reserve requirement ratio. The Fed can also increase the money supply by lowering the discount rate, which encourages banks to borrow reserves from the Fed, so reserves (*RES*) increase. A decline in the discount rate also encourages banks to reduce their excess reserves, causing the reserve-deposit ratio to decline, which also increases the money supply.

2.   **Monetary policy instruments of the Fed**

a)   Open market operations is the most commonly used policy instrument for changing the money supply. The Fed can increase the money supply by making an open market purchase of government securities (i.e., bonds) from the public or banks. An open market purchase increases currency in circulation and bank reserves, which is an increase in the monetary base. An increase in the monetary base increases the money supply by the amount of the money multiplier times the increase in the money base. Alternatively, the Fed can reduce the monetary base and the money supply by making an open market sale of government securities.

b)   The Federal Open Market Committee (FOMC) controls monetary policy. There are twelve members of the FOMC, including the seven members of the Board of Governors, the President of the Federal Reserve Bank of New York, and the Presidents of four other Federal Reserve regional (i.e., district) banks. The members of the Board of Governors are nominated by the U.S. President and confirmed by the U.S. Senate. The Presidents of the Federal Reserve district banks are appointed by the nine-member directorate of each district bank.

c)   Two other monetary policy instruments (i.e., tools):

1)   reserve requirement ratio: The Fed could increase the money supply by reducing the reserve requirement ratio. If banks maintain a fixed ratio of excess reserves to deposits, a decline in required reserves will reduce the reserve-deposit ratio, which increases the money multiplier, which increases the money supply, for a given monetary base.

2)   discount rate: The Fed could increase the money supply by reducing the discount rate. A lower discount rate encourages banks to borrow more reserves from the Fed,

causing bank reserves and the monetary base to
increase. A lower discount rate also causes banks to
reduce their holdings of excess reserves, which reduces
the reserve-deposit ratio and increases the money
multiplier. The increase in the monetary base and
money multiplier both increase the money supply.

d) For several reasons, the Fed predominantly uses open market
operations (OMO) to change the money supply. First, OMO is
the best instrument for making small, controllable changes
in the money supply, in part because there is a large, well-
developed market for these securities. Second, the Fed does
not change the reserve requirement ratio frequently, in part
because a stable reserve requirement ratio helps to
stabilize the money multiplier, through which open market
operation work. Even small changes in the reserve
requirement ratio create large changes in the money supply
that are hard to control; this suggests that the reserve
requirement is a powerful but blunt instrument, rather than
a precision instrument. Third, the Fed may announce changes
in the discount rate when it is changing the money supply,
but this is a relatively "weak instrument" in itself for
changing the money supply. The principal effect of lowering
the discount rate is to give the public and banks a clear,
credible announcement that monetary policy is becoming
tighter or easier.

e) For an economy with no currency and a reserve-deposit ratio
of 10%, a $1000 open market purchase from a bank increases
the bank's excess reserves by $1000. The bank can make
loans up to the limit of its excess reserves, so it makes a
$1000 loan to some borrower. The borrower deposits the
amount of the loan in his bank account. The bank retains
10% of the $1000 deposit as reserves and now makes a $900
loan, using its excess reserves. The amount of the $900
loan is deposited in a second bank, which retains 10% as
reserves and makes a loan for the $810 balance. The
borrower deposits the amount of the $810 loan in a third
bank, which retains 10% as reserves and lends out the
balance. When all possible loans have been made by the
banking system, this multiple expansion of loans and
deposits will increase the money supply by $10,000 = (1/.10)
x $1000.

3.   Monetary policy targets of the Fed

a) The two principal intermediate targets of the Fed are a
monetary aggregate (e.g., M1) and a short-run interest rate
(e.g., the Federal funds rate). These intermediate targets
are efficient in the sense that the Fed can use its policy
instruments to create predictable changes in the values of
intermediate targets, and changes in the values of
intermediate target variables create predictable changes in

the values of the ultimate targets of monetary policy. In
trying to hit an ultimate policy target, the Fed can gauge
how well it is doing by observing changes in its
intermediate targets. Changes in the values of intermediate
targets are reported more frequently than changes in the
values of ultimate target variables. In brief, an
intermediate target is easier for the Fed to hit than an
ultimate target; also, the Fed gets earlier feedback on its
effectiveness (i.e., how close it came to hitting the
target) so intermediate targeting increases the overall
effectiveness of monetary policy in achieving its policy
goals.

b)   The Fed sets a target range rather than a target point for
its intermediate targets because generally, it cannot hit a
target point (e.g., the center of the target range), and
because it generally does not have to hit a target point to
achieve its ultimate target range. For example, a change in
the monetary base would not increase the money supply as
much as the Fed planned, if the Fed has overestimated the
size of the money multiplier.

c)   The Fed has often set multiple intermediate targets. For
example, it may set an interest rate target and targets for
M1, M2, and M3 in one policy period. The monetarists object
to multiple intermediate targets because the Fed can, at
best, hit only one target. With multiple targets, we don't
know which one they are committed to hit. For example, if
the Fed plans to reduce the interest rate and reduce the
money supply, its plans cannot be achieved. It could reduce
the interest rate by increasing the money supply. It could
reduce the money supply, but the interest rate would
increase. It cannot achieve both of these targets
simultaneously, but we don't know which one is the real
target. Therefore, a monetary policy directed at multiple
intermediate targets is not credible.

d)   When nominal shocks (e.g., changes in money demand) are the
principal cause of economic instability, the optimal
intermediate target of monetary policy is the short-run
interest rate (e.g., the Federal funds rate). Changes in
money demand primarily affect macroeconomic variables by
directly changing the market interest rate. Instability in
money demand creates instability in the interest rate, which
causes other macroeconomic effects. By trying to stabilize
the Federal funds rate, monetary policy at best can help to
stabilize the market interest rate, which will help to
stabilize the macroeconomy.

e)   The monetarists recommend that the Fed choose a monetary
aggregate as an intermediate target, such as M2. They
propose the monetary aggregate target for several reasons.
First, they do not believe that nominal shocks are an

important source of instability in the economy. In the
monetarist view, money demand is reasonably stable. Second,
they believe that the macroeconomy is reasonably stable, is
self-regulating, and normally operates at the full-
employment level of output, consistent with the natural rate
of unemployment. Third, they believe that the money supply
determines the level of aggregate demand, and that aggregate
demand determines the price level; therefore, the money
supply determines the price level. Fourth, in a stable
economy operating at full-employment, the ultimate target of
monetary policy should be to maintain price level stability
(i.e., zero inflation). Fifth, to hit the price level
target, we need to achieve a constant rate of money supply
growth (i.e., a constant rate of growth in some monetary
aggregate).

4.   **Ultimate targets and monetary policy approaches**

a)   Keynesians recommend that monetary policymakers attempt to
      maintain a low, stable market interest rate as its ultimate
      policy target in the short run. Keynesians believe that
      nominal shocks are a major source of economic stability, and
      that monetary policy can help to reduce the economic effects
      of nominal shocks. However, the real interest rate cannot
      be a long-run target, because money is neutral in the long
      run. In the long run, money has no real economic effects.
      In the long run, monetary policy cannot lower the real
      interest rate, and has only nominal effects.

b)   All economists agree that the ultimate long-run target of
      monetary policy is price level stability, which means a zero
      rate of inflation. Some economists believe that the best we
      can achieve is a very low rate of inflation (e.g., 3%). In
      the Keynesian model, the price level is fixed (i.e.,
      perfectly stable) in the short run; therefore, monetary
      policy does not have to stabilize it.

c)   According to the basic classical model, money is neutral;
      this means that changes in the money supply have no real
      economic effects. In the basic classical model, the only
      policy goal that monetary policy can achieve and, therefore
      the best goal, is long-run price level stability. In the
      extended classical model, only unanticipated monetary
      policies could have short-run real economic effects.
      Although these real economic effects are relatively small
      and short lived in the extended classical model, they are
      undesirable effects. Therefore, the extended classical model
      supports the basic classical model conclusion that monetary
      stabilization policy cannot produce significant, desirable
      economic effects, even in the short run. The monetarists,
      however, conclude that monetary stabilization policies can
      have very large real economic effects in the short run;
      money is nonneutral in the short run. The monetarists

reject the use of short-run monetary stabilization policies
because they believe these attempts to stabilize the economy
have been and will be mostly destabilizing. For example,
monetarists believe that monetary policy caused the Great
Depression. Monetarists and classicals agree that the
economy is stable and self-regulating. They also agree that
monetary policy is not likely to have any significant
stabilizing effect. Unlike the classicals, however,
monetarists believe that monetary policy attempts to
stabilize are very destabilizing. Monetarists conclude that
the best way to reduce business cycle fluctuations is to
prohibit the use of monetary stabilization policies.

d)   Monetarists believe that business cycle fluctuations will be
small in the absence of the destabilizing effects of
monetary stabilization policies. Monetarists propose that
the money supply be increased at 3% per year, without
variation. If monetary policymakers adopted this constant
money growth rule (CMGR), the output would grow along the
potential output growth path at about 3% per year.
According to the quantity theory of money, the inflation
rate will be zero when the money supply grows at the same
rate as output grows. At zero inflation, the price level is
stable.

e)   Keynesians do not believe that the economy is stable and
self-regulating. Consequently, the economy does not quickly
recover from recessions. In the Keynesian view, recessions
may be severe and persistent, as was the Great Depression.
Keynesians do not accept the monetarist view that only a
decline in the money supply could reduce aggregate demand
and, thereby, create a recession. Keynesians emphasize that
a decline in any type of spending (i.e., C, I, G, or $(X-M)$
will reduce aggregate demand and thereby create a recession.
In the Keynesian view, the Great Depression was initially
caused by a decline in investment spending. Unlike the
monetarists, Keynesians believe that the Fed is reasonably
efficient and can use monetary stabilization policy
efficiently to stabilize aggregate demand at the full-
employment level of output. Keynesians contend that using
monetary policy to greatly reduce the duration and severity
of recessions is very economically beneficial.

5.   **Game theory, credibility, and monetary policy effects**

a)   In a game theory analysis of the game between firms and the
Fed, the self-interest of the firms conflicts with the self-
interest of the Fed. Firms believe that the Fed will choose
the outcome that it prefers, and firms know the preferences
of the Fed. If the Fed pursues monetary stabilization
policy, it may promise to choose a monetary policy that
maximizes the interest of firms, but such a policy is not
credible. Firms will choose the set of possible outcomes

that provide them with the best outcome when the Fed acts in its own self-interest, under the constraint created by the firms decision. In brief, firms prevent the Fed from achieving its announced stabilization policy goal (i.e., outcome) because they don't believe the Fed will act against its own self-interest to do what it has promised do.

b)   Under a policy rule approach, the Fed does not adjust monetary policy in response to the decisions made by market actors. Under a policy rule, an announced policy is the actual policy that the Fed will execute—no matter what. If the Fed announces that it will only increase the money supply at a rate consistent with zero inflation (e.g.,3% per year), firms know that the Fed is totally committed to do exactly that. In effect, the Fed's policy is credible, so firms believe the Fed's policy announcement. Under a policy rule, the firms must respond to the Fed's policy because the Fed decides first; whereas under discretionary stabilization policy, the Fed responds to the firms' decision, since the firms effectively choose first.

c)   Keynesians contend that in general, monetary stabilization policy does not depend on the Fed making hollow threats. In the Keynesian analysis, firms unintentionally create recessions by individually deciding to reduce their investment spending. By their individual, profit-maximizing actions, they do not intend to create a recession, but that is the aggregate effect of a decline in investment spending by many individual firms. Contrary to the credibility argument, the interests of the Fed and the firms are not in conflict. The Fed can use expansionary monetary stabilization policy to reduce the real interest rate, which lowers firms' cost of financing investments which causes firms to increase investment spending, which increases aggregate spending, which helps return the economy to the full-employment level of output. Keynesians emphasize that monetary stabilization is needed at times, and generally is efficient in reducing the severity and persistence of recessions. Thus, monetary policy should be flexible rather than fixed. Skilled, educated, informed policymakers should be able to use their discretion in employing the monetary policy that they believe is best for the economy under various economic conditions.

d)   At some time during the late 1970s and early 1980s, the central banks of West Germany, Japan, and the United States followed a monetary policy rule of slow money supply growth per year for several years. In all cases, reducing money supply growth reduced the rate of inflation but, with the exception of Japan, unemployment increased significantly and remained high for several years.

e)   The monetarists believe that wages and prices quickly
     adjust to economic shocks, but expectations are slow to
     adjust to unanticipated shocks. This suggests that an
     anticipated reduction in money supply growth would simply
     move the economy down the vertical long-run Phillips curve,
     as both inflation and expected inflation decline. To reduce
     expected inflation quickly, however, monetary policy must be
     credible. Game theory suggests that a policy rule approach
     will be credible. The empirical evidence cited here does
     not strongly support the monetarist argument for a policy
     rule, nor does it strongly support the credibility argument.
     The increase in unemployment that accompanied the decline in
     inflation suggests that the West German and U.S. economies
     were moving down fixed short-run Phillips curves for
     sustained periods of time, because wages, prices, and
     expectations adjust slowly to changes in monetary policy.
     Following a credible policy rule, therefore, did not prevent
     the short-run real economic costs of a disinflationary
     monetary policy. In Japan, however, the decline in
     inflation did not produce any significant increase in
     unemployment; the empirical evidence for Japan supports the
     monetarist views and supports the credibility argument.
     Although the failure of unemployment to rise in Japan may be
     explained by other institutional conditions (e.g., long-term
     employer-employee relationship commitments), the overall
     empirical evidence is mixed. It is noteworthy that
     worsening economic conditions (e.g., trade deficits) caused
     each country to abandon their policy rules. This suggests
     that none of these monetary policymakers were willing to
     follow a policy rule once economic conditions worsened.
     They all acted as if they believed that using discretionary
     monetary stabilization policies would improve the
     performance of their respective economies.

CHAPTER 16

GOVERNMENT SPENDING AND ITS FINANCING

A Review of Chapter Highlights

For a given fiscal year, the **primary government budget deficit** is the amount by which current government spending (i.e., outlays) on current programs exceeds current tax revenue. The primary budget deficit equation is: $[(G + TR) - T]$. The actual budget deficit (i.e., $(G + TR + INT) - T$) is the primary budget deficit plus net interest payments on outstanding government debt. If the government has outstanding debt and the primary budget is balanced, interest payments on the debt create a budget deficit.

In a recession, **automatic stabilizers** increase the budget deficit and the primary budget deficit. Two examples of automatic stabilizers are a progressive income tax system and transfer programs. Automatic stabilizers are fiscal policy stabilizers, but they are not discretionary fiscal policy stabilizers. The **full-employment deficit** is calculated by subtracting the deficit created by automatic stabilizers from the budget deficit. A full-employment deficit measures the amount of the budget deficit created by discretionary fiscal policy.

One instrument of discretionary fiscal policy is the tax rate. During a recession, Keynesians may propose that fiscal policymakers reduce the tax rate to help the economy quickly return to the full-employment level of output. During inflationary periods, at the full-employment level of output, Keynesians may propose that fiscal policymakers increase the tax rate to reduce the rate of inflation. In practice, however, there are many different kinds of tax programs (e.g., personal income tax, sales tax, corporate profits tax).

A tax on any economic activity reduces the after-tax relative rate of return to that activity. Market actors tend to substitute away from activities that are taxed at relatively high rates. These tax-induced changes in the behavior of market actors are called **distortions**. Critics of tax-based changes in fiscal stabilization policy argue that the economic costs of the distortions, created by fiscal stabilization policies, are high. These critics favor annually balanced budgets, but annually balanced budgets do not allow for **tax rate smoothing** when government spending fluctuates. Frequent changes in tax rates required to finance changes in government spending also may create high economic costs.

Government debt is the sum of all unpaid government budget deficits plus unpaid accrued interest on these deficits. The **debt-GNP ratio** is one useful measure of the relative size of the government debt. In 1980, the debt-GNP ratio for the federal debt of the U.S. government was approximately 34%; in 1990, it was approximately 60%. The significant increase in the debt-GNP ratio during the 1980s highlights the effect on the ratio of **rolling over the debt**, which means issuing new debt to pay off maturing debt. Other factors that caused the debt-GNP ratio to increase in the 1980s included ongoing budget deficits, a high real interest rate, and a low growth rate of output.

In addition to selling government securities to the public to finance its deficits and debt, a government could also finance its deficits and debt by selling some of its securities to the central bank, which prints money to buy them. The government revenue raised by printing money is called **seignorage**. Assuming that output remains unchanged, printing money to finance excess government spending is purely inflationary. Inflation is a (hidden) tax on money, because it reduces the real purchasing power of money. In calculating the real seignorage revenue from printing money, the inflation rate is the tax rate and the real money supply is the tax base. The real seignorage revenue collected by government equals the inflation rate times the real money supply. Using unanticipated increases in inflation to finance excess government spending is an inefficient financing method, in part because the **inflation tax** is hidden. However, economic analysis shows that governments can raise revenue by this method, and history shows that, on occasion, they have done so.

Questions

These questions test your understanding of the **key terms**, **key relationships**, and **key diagrams** highlighted in your text.

Multiple Choice Questions

1.   The budget deficit will exceed the primary budget deficit in a given fiscal year, if:

     a.   government spending exceeds tax revenue.
     b.   the economy is in a recession.
     c.   the rate of inflation exceeds zero.
     d.   net interest payments on outstanding debt exceed zero.
     e.   fiscal policy is expansionary.

2.   An example of an automatic stabilizer is:

    a.   consumer spending.
    b.   inflation.
    c.   unemployment insurance.
    d.   discretionary fiscal policy.
    e.   investment spending.

3.   During a recession, discretionary fiscal policy is
    expansionary if:

    a.   tax revenue falls.
    b.   government spending increases.
    c.   money supply growth increases.
    d.   there is a full-employment deficit.
    e.   transfer payments increase.

4.   Assuming that market prices are efficient, taxing different
    activities at different rates creates:

    a.   inflation.
    b.   a budget surplus.
    c.   an efficient tax system.
    d.   tax rate smoothing.
    e.   distortions.

5.   If a government is highly committed to tax rate smoothing,
    it will:

    a.   require annually balanced fiscal budgets.
    b.   reduce tax rates during a temporary recession.
    c.   tax every activity and every source of income at the
        same tax rate.
    d.   balance the budget over the business cycle.
    e.   not change tax rates frequently to finance fluctuations
        in government spending.

6.   According to the Ricardian equivalence proposition, a
    government budget deficit:

    a.   increases government debt.
    b.   increases the real interest rate.
    c.   increases aggregate demand.
    d.   reduces saving.
    e.   reduces output.

7.   Since the end of the Great Depression, the U.S. had the
    highest debt-GNP ratios in the:

    a.   1940s.
    b.   1950s.
    c.   1960s.

      d.   1970s.
      e.   1980s.

8.   Partly because of rolling over the debt, the nominal value of U.S. government debt in 1990 was approximately:

      a. $5000 trillion.
      b. $5000 billion.
      c. $5000 million.
      d. $3000 billion.
      e. $2000 billion.

9.   Assuming that output is fixed, the real revenue raised by government from printing money is:

      a. M/P.
      b.   the inflation rate times the real money supply.
      c.   the real interest rate times the real money supply.
      d.   the tax rate times the increase in the growth rate of output.
      e.   always zero, because money is neutral.

10.   The inflation tax is primarily a tax on:

      a.   government bonds.
      b.   Social Security recipients.
      c.   money.
      d.   real income.
      e.   foreigners.

11.   If the government budget is initially balanced and the economy is operating at the full-employment level of output, a temporary tax cut will most likely:

      a.   reduce labor supply.
      b.   reduce investment spending.
      c.   reduce government purchases.
      d.   create a nominal deficit.
      e.   create tax rate smoothing.

12.   The equation for calculating the growth rate of debt-GNP ratio shows that the growth rate of this ratio will increase when the:

      a.   growth rate of nominal GNP increases.
      b.   growth rate of real GNP increases.
      c.   growth rate of money supply increases.
      d.   inflation rate increases.
      e.   interest rate increases.

13.   If government outlays exceed current tax revenue, the government could best finance its deficit by:

a. eliminating student loan guarantees.
b. reducing its spending on human capital investments.
c. privatizing its infrastructure investments.
d. using "smoke and mirrors."
e. selling government securities.

14. Real seignorage revenue is most likely to be a significant source of revenue for:

a. international development organizations.
b. developing countries during times of war.
c. developed countries during periods of slow output growth.
d. periods of disinflation.
e. state and local governments in the United States.

15. In the 1985-1990 period, after the Gramm-Rudman-Hollings bill was signed into law in the United States:

a. Federal budget deficits and debt increased.
b. the debt-GNP ratio declined.
c. the debt held by the public-GNP ratio declined.
d. the government significantly increased tax rates.
e. the government increased its seignorage revenue.

Short-Answer Essay Questions

1. **Government Budgets**: a) Identify the two largest sources of tax revenue and the two largest outlays in the U.S. Federal government budget. b) Identify the two largest sources of tax revenue and the two largest outlays in the combined state and local government budget. c) State the primary budget deficit equation, the actual budget deficit equation, and the difference between them. d) In comparing Federal government budget deficits of various years, how do nominal deficit comparisons differ from real deficit comparisons? e) Identify and briefly explain one argument for and one argument against removing the Social Security surplus from the Federal government budget deficit calculations.

2. **Fiscal policy**: a) Compare and contrast automatic stabilizers and discretionary fiscal stabilization policy in terms of flexibility and policy lags. b) Compare and contrast the effects of automatic stabilizers during recessions on the budget deficit and the full-employment deficit. c) Compare and contrast the Keynesian and classical models in terms of the incentive effects of a marginal tax rate cut on labor supply and output. d) Why do economists endorse tax rate smoothing?   e) State the log-rolling critique of fiscal policy, and explain how this affected the Tax Reform Act of 1986.

3. **Government budget deficits and debt**: a) Define the terms deficit and debt, and explain how they are related. b) State the growth rate of debt-GNP ratio equation and define the variables. c) Identify and briefly explain two constraints of the government's ability to roll over the debt forever. d) Identify and briefly explain two reasons why a large government debt may not be a major burden on the future generation asked to pay it off. e) State one argument in favor of a balanced budget amendment to the U.S. Constitution, and state one argument against a balanced budget amendment.

4. **Ricardian equivalence proposition**: a) State the Ricardian equivalence proposition.   b) Does Barro's theoretical research support the Ricardian equivalence proposition? Briefly explain. c) Identify two conditions under which the Ricardian equivalence proposition may not hold. d) Does the empirical evidence strongly support the Ricardian equivalence proposition? Briefly explain. e) Compare and contrast the short-run effects of a tax cut on unemployment and output in classical and Keynesian models.

5. **Deficits and inflation**: a) Define seignorage. b) State the nominal and real seignorage equations, and explain why they are equivalent. c) Use *AD-AS* analysis to explain what causes inflation. d) Explain how governments could use seignorage to finance deficits or debt. e) Draw a real seignorage revenue diagram in terms of inflation, and use the diagram to show why government policymakers might prefer an intermediate rate of inflation over a high rate of inflation.

Answers to Multiple Choice Questions

1.	d	8.	d	15.	a
2.	c	9.	b		
3.	d	10.	c		
4.	e	11.	d		
5.	e	12.	e		
6.	a	13.	e		
7.	a	14.	b		

Answers to Short-Answer Essay Questions

1. **Government budgets**

a) In the U.S. Federal government budget for 1990, the two largest sources of tax revenue were: 1) personal taxes (e.g., Federal income taxes), and 2) Social Security (FICA) taxes.   The two largest outlays were: 1) transfer payments, and 2) purchases of goods and services (e.g., national defense).

b)   In the combined state and local government budget for 1990, the two largest sources of tax revenue were: 1) indirect business taxes (e.g., sales and excise taxes), and 2) personal taxes (e.g., state income taxes and local property taxes).   The two largest outlays were: 1) purchases of goods and services (e.g., education and highways), and 2) transfer payments (e.g., welfare assistance).

c)   The primary budget deficit = $[(G + TR) - T]$.   The actual budget deficit = $[(G + TR + INT) - T]$.   The budget deficit exceeds the primary budget deficit by the value of interest payments on government debt.   Note that budget deficits may be positive, negative, or zero; a negative budget deficit is a budget surplus.

d)   Nominal deficits are government budget deficits measured in current dollars at the time they are incurred.   Real deficits are government budget deficits measured in constant dollars, which means for a given value of the dollar. Nominal deficit figures can be converted to real deficit figures by using a price level index to deflate the nominal values.   Comparisons of nominal deficits are distorted by changes in the price level over time (i.e., by inflation). For example, budget deficits under the Reagan Administration were higher in nominal terms than budget deficits under the Carter Administration because the price level rose each year, over the 1977–1988 period.   Unlike comparisons of nominal deficits, comparisons of the real deficits in 1982 dollars are not distorted by inflation.

e)   In recent years and for the next couple of decades, the financial managers of the Social Security program must accumulate a surplus in order to finance the increased Social Security payments out of a declining tax base when the baby boomers retire.   The current Social Security surplus is now considered to be part of general tax revenue, which is all spent on general government outlays.   One argument against including the surplus in the government budget is that all the surplus is now being spent, leaving no money for future retirees.   An argument in favor of leaving the Social Security surplus in the government budget is that the Social Security fund is receiving an equivalent value of government bonds that can be cashed in the future to pay future retirees.   However, to cash these bonds in the future, the government will either have to achieve a primary budget surplus or roll over this huge amount of debt, thereby substantially increasing the amount of outstanding debt.

2.   **Fiscal policy**

a)   Automatic stabilizers have virtually no policy lags and they
     are very flexible in creating changes in government spending
     and taxes, because these adjustments are automatic. In
     contrast, discretionary fiscal stabilization policy changes
     in government spending and taxes have long policy lags
     (e.g., eighteen months) and are not very flexible.

b)   During a recession, automatic stabilizers increase
     government spending in the form of transfer payments and
     reduced taxes, thereby creating a budget deficit. In
     contrast, automatic stabilizers do not create a full-
     employment deficit, because automatic stabilizers do not
     create a deficit at the full-employment level of output.
     The full-employment deficit is the amount of the budget
     deficit created by discretionary fiscal stabilization
     policy. The difference between the budget deficit and the
     full-employment deficit is the deficit created by automatic
     stabilizers.

c)   In economic analysis, the real after-tax wage provides an
     income incentive to supply labor in the market economy. A
     temporary decline in the marginal tax rate increases the
     market incentive to supply labor by increasing the after-tax
     real wage. In both the classical and Keynesian models, this
     increases the supply of labor, assuming that the
     substitution effect exceeds the income effect on labor
     supply. In the classical model, an increase in labor supply
     increases output. In the Keynesian efficiency-wage model,
     an increase in labor supply does not affect employment or
     output; an increase in labor supply simply increases the
     excess supply of labor at the efficiency wage.

d)   The output cost of an increase in a tax distortion is
     proportional to the square of the increase in the tax rate.
     For example, if a 20% tax rate reduces output by $100, a 40%
     tax rate (i.e., 20% × 2) would reduce output by $400 = $100
     × 2^2. Likewise, a 60% tax rate would reduce output by $900.
     Tax rate smoothing reduces the output cost per year of
     raising a given amount of tax revenue over a number of
     years.

e)   The log-rolling critique of fiscal policy is that many
     policymakers in the U.S. Congress will only agree to approve
     a budget if it includes special programs or special-interest
     legislation (e.g., pork-barrel projects) that particularly
     benefit their constituencies. As a result, any budget that
     has enough votes to get it passed contains many special-
     interest programs. This implies that much of government
     spending is economically inefficient. However, the 1986 Tax
     Reform Act budget agreement did not include many special-

interest programs, and it was passed by a wide margin of votes in both houses of the U.S. Congress.

3. Government budget deficits and debt

a) A budget deficit is the amount by which government spending (i.e., $G + TR + INT$) exceeds tax revenue in some fiscal year. In the absence of inflation, budget deficits are financed by borrowing from the public. As a result of borrowing from the public to finance a budget deficit, the government now owes debt. Each deficit adds to the outstanding (i.e., unpaid) debt. The government debt is the sum of accumulated, unpaid budget deficits.

b) The growth rate of debt-GNP ratio is:

primary deficit/$B + r$ - growth rate of real GNP

The variables are defined as:

primary deficit (for the current fiscal year) = $(G + TR) - T$

B = outstanding debt at the beginning of the fiscal year

r = real interest rate

growth rate of real GNP = the growth rate of output

c) One constraint on the government's ability to roll over a given amount of debt forever is a high interest rate; another constraint is a low growth rate of output. If the real interest rate remains sufficiently low and the growth rate of real GNP remains sufficiently high forever, the government might be able to roll over a fixed amount of outstanding debt forever, thus obtaining a "free lunch." If the real GNP growth rate is the growth rate of real wealth, and the interest rate is the growth rate of debt, this implies that a country could roll over its debt forever if the debt-wealth ratio did not become unacceptably high to debtors and/or creditors.

d) Two reasons why a large government debt might not be a large burden on the future generation asked to pay it are:

1) This generation might have received bequests to cover the debt payments from the generation that incurred the debt.

2) If the debt is "internal debt," then the future generation owes the debt to itself. Although some

people are harmed by having to pay it off, others gain by receiving the debt payments.

e)   A balanced budget amendment to the U.S. constitution would force fiscal policymakers to balance the government budget each fiscal year. One potentially positive effect, cited by proponents of the amendment, is that it would prevent the government from incurring huge deficits. One potentially negative effect cited by opponents of the amendment is that the government would have to stop using discretionary fiscal stabilization policy and would have to eliminate its automatic stabilizers.

4.   Ricardian equivalence proposition

a)   The Ricardian equivalence proposition states that a tax cut financed by the sale of bonds is not expansionary, because the effect of bond financing on the present value of lifetime resources of the public is equivalent to tax financing. The Ricardian equivalence proposition assumes that the public does not face binding borrowing constraints and that future taxes will increase enough to pay off the bonds and the interest earned on the bonds.

b)   Yes, Robert Barro's theoretical research fully supports the Ricardian equivalence theory. David Ricardo and Robert Barro reach the same conclusion, which is that reducing current taxes and selling bonds to offset the decline in tax revenue is not expansionary. One theoretical argument made against the Ricardian equivalence proposition is that the current taxpayers may not incur higher taxes in the future as a result of the deficit if the government continues to roll over the debt forever. Robert Barro answered this objection by showing that the current generation will save all the income they receive from any temporary tax cut and bequeath this accumulated tax savings plus interest to the future generation that is asked to pay off the debt. Barro recognizes that the current generation could burden the future generation by borrowing against its future income, but he contends that the current generation does not choose to do that, since it values the well-being of its offspring. Since the current generation prefers to transfer income and wealth to the future generation, it will not take the opportunity provided by a budget deficit to reverse this transfer. A budget deficit will not change the preferences of the current generation.

c)   The Ricardian equivalence proposition may not hold when either of its two principal assumptions is violated. If a significant percentage of taxpayers face binding borrowing constraints, they will spend some of the extra after-tax income they receive from the tax cut. Likewise, if people are shortsighted and, consequently, do not believe that their future taxes or their children's future taxes will be increased by enough to pay off the government debt, they will spend some of the extra after-tax income they receive from the tax cut. If the Ricardian equivalence proposition fails to hold, a temporary tax cut will increase aggregate spending, which is expansionary.

d)   The empirical evidence is mixed. For example, the decline in aggregate saving that followed the Reagan tax cuts in the U.S. in the early 1980s does not support the Ricardian equivalence proposition. However, temporary tax cuts in some foreign countries in recent years did not significantly reduce aggregate saving; this empirical evidence is consistent with the Ricardian equivalence proposition.

e)   The Ricardian equivalence proposition holds in the classical model, but not in the Keynesian model. Given the Ricardian equivalence proposition, a temporary tax cut does not change saving in the classical model; because it does not change saving, it has no output or employment effect. In the Keynesian model, a temporary tax cut reduces saving, which causes aggregate demand to increase, which causes output to increase, which causes unemployment to decline.

5.   **Deficits and inflation**

a)   Seignorage is the government revenue raised by printing money.

b)   The nominal value of seignorage revenue equation is:

$$\Delta M = \pi M$$

The real revenue value of seignorage equation is:

$$R = \frac{\Delta M}{P} = \frac{\pi M}{P}$$

In converting the nominal equation to real terms, we simply divide both sides of the equation by the price level, which does not change the equality. Therefore, the equations are equivalent, meaning that they express the same relationship. At a given price level, the nominal value of seignorage revenue equals the real value of seignorage revenue.

c)   In terms of aggregate demand-aggregate supply (AD-AS) analysis, any economic event (e.g., an increase in the money supply) that causes AD to increase relative to AS causes inflation. Since inflation is the percentage increase in the price level, anything that causes the price level to increase creates inflation. For example, an increase in AD shifts the AD curve up to the right along a given AS curve, which increases the price level, which creates inflation.

d)   Excess money supply growth creates inflation, which reduces
      the real value of outstanding government nominal debt,
      thereby reducing the amount of real tax revenue needed to
      pay off a fixed amount of nominal debt. More importantly,
      and more directly, the government uses newly printed money
      to pay for some of its expenditures.

e)   The real seignorage revenue diagram, in terms of inflation,
      shows that government policymakers might prefer an
      intermediate rate of
      inflation (e.g., 8%)
      because it raises more
      seignorage revenue than
      would be raised by a high
      rate of inflation (e.g.,
      20%).

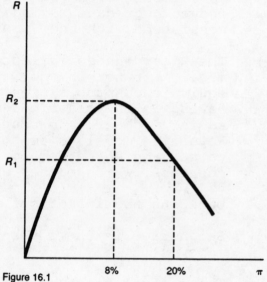

Figure 16.1

CHAPTER 17

FINANCIAL MARKETS AND THE MACROECONOMY

A Review of Chapter Highlights

Financial markets provide **diversification** of financial investments. Diversification reduces risk, which raises the risk-adjusted expected rate of return on financial investments. Financial markets also transfer risk from **hedgers**, who expect to profit by reducing their financial risk, to **speculators**, who expect to profit by increasing their financial risk.

Debt and **equity** are the two principal types of financial instruments. Debt instruments, such as corporate bonds, provide loans to borrowers; lenders buy debt to earn interest income. Equity instruments, such as corporate stocks, provide ownership of firms; equity investments earn profits. Profits on corporate stocks are paid to stockholders as **dividends** plus capital gains. Dividends represent the annual payments on the equity investments; capital gains represent the appreciation of the stock over the holding period, received when the holder sells the stock (i.e., liquidates the investment).

Financial instruments are traded in various kinds of markets. Newly issued instruments are traded in **primary markets**; existing instruments are traded in **secondary markets**. Short-term instruments, which mature in less than a year, are traded in **money markets**; long-term assets are traded in **capital markets**. In **auction markets**, such as the New York Stock Exchange, financial instruments are sold to the highest bidders at a central location. In **over-the-counter markets**, such as through brokers and dealers, financial instruments are traded in many locations, using a computerized exchange network. In **spot markets**, financial instruments are traded at current market (spot) prices and delivered immediately. In **financial futures markets**, buyers and sellers agree today to trade financial instruments at some specified future date and price. In the **options markets**, people buy and sell the right to trade financial instruments without having the obligation to trade them at some specified future date and price. Options and futures are **derivative securities**, which means that their asset values depend on the values of other assets.

Savers and investors may trade financial instruments directly. For example, you may make a loan to one of your friends. However, most savers and investors trade indirectly through **financial intermediaries**. For example, you deposit some of your savings in a bank, which makes a loan to one of your friends. Financial intermediaries include banks, thrifts, insurance companies, pension funds, mutual funds, and finance companies.

The saving-investment diagram provides a supply and demand model of the **credit market**. In the credit market, savers supply funds and investors demand funds.

Borrowing and lending generally takes place under conditions of **asymmetric information**, where some borrowers may not disclose all the information needed to determine their creditworthiness. The existence of asymmetric information is one reason for trading indirectly through financial intermediaries, since these financial firms are more efficient at gathering and analyzing the information needed to determine the creditworthiness of potential borrowers properly. Given a symmetric information, if the demand for funds exceeds the supply of funds at the prevailing interest rate, banks may engage in **credit rationing**. With credit rationing, banks generally will lend to the relatively low-risk borrowers within the group of potential borrowers; some firms and consumers will not receive credit even though they are willing to pay the prevailing interest rate.

Government intervention in financial markets also may restrict the availability of credit significantly. In 1980 for example, the U.S. government imposed selective **credit controls** to reduce the availability of credit card lending by banks. In response, the economy quickly entered a recession. This caused the government to remove the credit controls quickly. Consequently, the recession was brief. Other government policies, such as the ceiling interest rates on deposits imposed by Regulation Q, may create a **credit crunch**, in which the amount of bank lending significantly declines. In recent U.S. history, credit crunches caused the growth rate of output to fall in 1966, 1969, 1973-1974, and 1990. Until Regulation Q was phased out in the early 1980s, the availability of bank loans declined whenever market interest rates rose above the ceiling interest rates that banks could pay on deposits. Rising market interest rates on nonbank assets caused depositors to withdraw some of their deposits to make investments elsewhere. This withdrawal of funds from banks is called **disintermediation**. When bank deposits decline, bank lending declines. A sufficiently large decline in bank lending creates a credit crunch.

Firms may use **internal funds**, as well as **external funds** to finance their investments. Undistributed profits provide a source of internal funds to supplement or replace the external funds received from financial intermediaries. Large firms tend to rely more on internal funds; small firms are more dependent on bank lending. Economic analysis shows that the heavy reliance on internal funds by large firms can explain why investment spending declines in a recession, and can also explain why a tax cut may be expansionary.

At times, financial markets have been unstable. **Financial panics** and **bank panics** highlight this instability. In a typical financial panic, stock prices decline dramatically, bank runs occur, and some large financial firms go bankrupt. The United States experienced its worst financial panics during the Great Depression. In a **banking panic**, bank runs affect many banks in the banking system, causing some banks to fail. By establishing the Federal Reserve System in 1914, and giving it the right to act as a **lender of last resort**, the U.S. government expected to eliminate banking panics. As a lender of last resort, the Fed could provide banks with enough liquidity (i.e., money) to cover any unexpected deposit withdrawal demands, especially at the onset of a bank run. Yet the Fed failed to use this authority efficiently during the Great Depression when over 10,000 banks failed. The government responded by creating federal deposit insurance (FDIC) on bank deposits; this appears to have eliminated bank runs.

During the 1950-1980 period, the rate of bank failure was very low. Since the early 1980s, however, bank failures have increased dramatically. One explanation is that **bank capital** requirements were very low in the 1980s, so that the capital-asset ratios of some banks are low. Given low capital-asset ratios and the relaxed regulatory restrictions created by banking deregulation, some banks have increased the riskiness of their assets. Short-term losses on high-risk assets during periods of slow economic growth have been sufficient to cause an increasing number of bank failures, because losses further reduce bank capital.

Although large financial market fluctuations suggest that financial markets are inefficient, **efficient markets theory** suggest that they are efficient. Efficient markets theory is the most widely accepted theory of financial market performance. Economic analysis shows that efficient stock market prices may fluctuate substantially, without deviating from their **fundamental values**, in response to some economic events. The fundamental value of a share of corporate stock is the present value of its future income. The stock price is the market estimate of this fundamental value, based on a market forecast of the stock's future income.

Efficient markets theory does suggest that very similar assets will earn a similar nominal rate of return. However, assets with different characteristics will earn different nominal rates of return. Differences in risk, liquidity, maturity, and tax liability will cause the rate of return on assets to differ. Corporate stocks have higher risk than corporate bonds. To compensate financial investors for assuming this higher risk, the average rate of return on corporate stocks exceeds the average rate of return on corporate bonds by a **risk premium**. The risk premium helps to make the risk-adjusted rate of return on stocks equal to the risk-adjusted rate of return on bonds.

Under various imperfections in financial markets, stock prices could deviate from their fundamental values. **Bubbles** and **fads** provide two examples of excessive fluctuations in stock prices. A bubble exists when stock prices rise above their fundamental values, because the market expects them to keep rising. A bubble may be a **rational bubble** because within certain limits, stock prices could keep rising if market participants continue to believe they will rise forever. A bubble may also be an **irrational bubble**, because some buyers could irrationally overestimate the value of some stocks temporarily. Irrational bubbles still can be very profitable for those who sell their stocks before the bubble bursts. **Fads** are temporary periods of excessive stock price fluctuations, caused by excessive enthusiasm or pessimism in response to changes in market conditions.

The stock market crash of 1987 has caused some market analysts and policymakers to propose a number of regulatory changes in an attempt to reduce such large stock price fluctuations. One proposal is for the Federal Reserve to increase its **margin requirement** on stock purchases. A margin requirement is the portion of the stock price that has to be paid at the time of purchase with the investor's own money (e.g., 50%). Other proposals include: instituting a trading halt rule, eliminating program trading, and imposing a transactions tax on stock purchases. To date, however, neither theoretical economic analysis nor empirical economic evidence has clearly shown that any of these proposals would efficiently reduce stock price volatility.

Questions

These questions test your understanding of the **key terms**, **key relationships**, and **key diagrams** highlighted in your text.

Multiple Choice Questions: Circle the letter corresponding to the correct answer to each question.

1. The principal benefit of diversification of investments is that it:

    a. eliminates losses.
    b. reduces stock prices.
    c. reduces portfolio risk.
    d. eliminates the cost of financial intermediation.
    e. reduces liquidity.

2. Hedgers buy financial assets:

    a. to bet against the market.
    b. to hold as long-term investments.

c. to sell in the future at a lower price.
d. in one market to sell in a different market at a higher price, at the same time, without risk.
e. to reduce their exposure to risk.

3. To make an equity investment, a market participant could buy:

a. government bonds.
b. Treasury bills.
c. commercial paper.
d. corporate stocks.
e. certificates of deposit.

4. If two different corporate stocks have the same expected capital gains, the one paying smaller dividends will:

a. depreciate.
b. pay a higher interest rate.
c. not be sold in primary markets.
d. have a longer maturity.
e. have a smaller price per share.

5. Secondary markets for financial instruments:

a. are not regulated by government.
b. do not include trading of investment-grade stocks.
c. include trading of existing assets.
d. are illegal in the United States.
e. include trading in only highly illiquid assets.

6. Which of the following assets would be bought and sold in the capital market?

a. investment goods.
b. real capital stock.
c. money market deposit accounts.
d. corporate bonds.
e. commercial paper.

7. Unlike over-the-counter markets, trading in an auction market:

a. occurs at one central location.
b. is done secretly, behind closed doors.
c. often involves resale of existing assets.
d. occurs in financial centers throughout the world.
e. involves the use of computers.

8. One characteristic that spot markets have in common with futures markets and options markets is that:

a.   delivery is immediate.
b.   the prices of assets traded depend on the fundamental values of these assets.
c.   buyers pay the full cost of their purchases immediately; payments are not made in the future.
d.   in the United States, all these markets have been large markets for many decades.
e.   trading in these markets is very similar to buying and selling apples at a farmers' market.

9.   One function not performed by financial intermediaries in a credit market is to:

a.   help smooth consumption across time periods.
b.   reduce liquidity.
c.   allocate savings to its highest-valued uses.
d.   reduce the transactions costs of trading financial assets.
e.   help gather and analyze information.

10.   Given asymmetric information, banks may engage in credit rationing if demand for loans:

a.   exceeds supply at the prevailing interest rate.
b.   is less than supply at the prevailing interest rate.
c.   equals supply at the prevailing interest rate.
d.   is relatively low.
e.   is based on fundamental values.

11.   According to economic theory and recent U.S. macroeconomic performance, credit controls and credit crunches can significantly:

a.   increase inflation.
b.   increase the real wage.
c.   increase bank profits.
d.   reduce output.
e.   reduce the real interest rate.

12.   If a significant share of large firms rely heavily on internal funds to finance investments:

a.   an economic slowdown could not reduce output below the full-employment level of output.
b.   investment spending will be procyclical.
c.   expansionary fiscal policy will be ineffective.
d.   the Ricardian equivalence proposition will hold.
e.   credit crunches will be inflationary.

13.   The macroeconomic effects of stock market crises:

a.   are relatively small, compared to the effects of banking panics.

b.   are typically very large, as illustrated by the Great Depression.

c.   are usually underestimated by economists and other market experts.

d.   include a much greater output effect than price level effect in the classical model.

e.   include a much greater price level effect than output effect in the Keynesian model.

14. One possible problem with the Fed acting aggressively as a lender of last resort during a financial crisis is that:

a.   this could create a credit crunch.

b.   the Fed could run out of money quickly .

c.   the U.S. President and Congress would stop this misuse of tax revenue quickly.

d.   the money multiplier would increase dramatically.

e.   some banks may default on these central bank loans.

15. One reason why banking regulators may impose some minimum bank capital-asset ratio is that banks operating with very low capital-asset ratios:

a.   are too profitable.

b.   are too conservative in their lending practices.

c.   are more likely to fail during economic slowdowns.

d.   are illiquid.

e.   cannot diversify their assets.

16. According to the efficient markets theory:

a.   insurance policy premiums typically exploit investors.

b.   mutual funds are often overvalued.

c.   the rate of return on pension funds is not competitive with the rate of return on mutual funds.

d.   most financial assets earn the same nominal rate of return, even though their characteristics differ.

e.   financial asset prices usually equal the fundamental values of their respective assets.

17. One reason why "junk bonds" are high-yield assets is that:

a.   they are worthless.

b.   they have no maturity date.

c.   selective credit controls keep the interest rate high.

d.   the yield includes a high risk premium.

e.   margin requirements are too low.

18. Bubbles and fads explain why:

a.   markets are efficient.

b.   futures and options instruments are not needed.

c.   hedgers dominate financial markets.

    d.   financial panics create severe depressions.
    e.   stock prices may temporarily deviate from the
          fundamental values of their respective assets.

19. Margin requirements for stock market purchases are set by:

    a.   the New York Stock Exchange.
    b.   the National Association of Securities Dealers.
    c.   the Fed.
    d.   individual brokers.
    e.   the President of the United States.

Short-Answer Essay Questions

1. **The financial system:** a) Identify the four types of market
    participants who supply and demand funds through financial
    intermediaries. b) Identify the two general types of
    financial instruments traded in the financial system. c)
    Identify and briefly describe the four fundamental functions
    of the financial system. d) Identify four industries that
    compete for savings and investments in the financial
    markets. e) Compare and contrast hedgers and speculators in
    terms of their orientation toward risk.

2. **Saving, investment, and financial intermediation:** a) Why do
    savers supply funds to financial intermediaries rather than
    make their own financial investments? b) Why do investors
    demand funds from financial intermediaries, rather than use
    internal funds exclusively to finance their investments? c)
    Identify a financial instrument issued by banks and a
    financial instrument issued by insurance companies, identify
    a financial asset each buys, and explain how firms in these
    industries compete in terms of these instruments. d) Define
    the term asymmetric information, and explain why this market
    imperfection may cause banks to engage in credit rationing.
    e) Define the term credit crunch, and explain how a credit
    crunch can create a recession.

3. **Instability in banking:** a) Briefly describe the economic
    events that would identify instability in banking. b) Is
    the Great Depression the only period in which the banking
    system appears to be unstable? Briefly explain. c) Briefly
    explain how the Fed, as a regulator of banks and as a
    "lender of last resort" can help prevent banking panics. d)
    Briefly explain how federal deposit insurance (FDIC) acts to
    reduce banking panics. e) Does it appear that deregulation
    of banking in the 1980s has helped to stabilize the banking
    system, and does this appear to be a good time to institute
    additional banking reforms? Briefly explain.

4. **Instability in the stock market:** a) Briefly describe the
    economic events that identify a financial crisis. b) State
    the efficient markets hypothesis. c) Does the efficient

markets hypothesis explain past financial crises and predict future financial crises? Briefly explain. d) State the "bubbles" and "fads" explanations of stock price instability. e) Identify two proposals for reforming the stock market and briefly explain how they might reduce instability.

5. **The Savings and Loan crisis**: a) Was (is) the S&L crisis really a "crisis" or just an efficient market adjustment to some change in market conditions? Briefly discuss. b) Identify and briefly explain two principal causes of the S&L crisis. c) Does either the efficient markets hypothesis or "bubbles and fads" clearly explain this instability in the S&L industry? Briefly explain. d) Identify and briefly describe two proposed solutions for the S&L crisis. e) Evaluate the two policy proposals in terms of their expected effects on financial markets. Consider any tradeoffs (i.e., offsetting negative effects).

Answers to Multiple Choice Questions

1.	c	8.	b	15.	c
2.	e	9.	b	16.	e
3.	d	10.	a	17.	d
4.	e	11.	d	18.	e
5.	c	12.	b	19.	c
6.	d	13.	a		
7.	a	14.	e		

Answers to Short-Answer Essay Questions

1.   The financial system

a) The four types of market participants who supply and demand funds through financial intermediaries are: households, firms, governments, and foreigners.

b) The two general types of financial instruments traded in the financial system are: debt instruments and equity instruments.

c) There are four fundamental functions of the financial system.

   1) consumption smoothing: Income earners do not generally wish to consume all of their earnings and wealth in one year. Generally, individuals want to consume at a reasonably stable standard of living over some planned time horizon. This generally requires that they borrow money as young adults, repay their loans and save

during their middle-age years, and live off their
wealth (i.e., accumulated savings plus interest) during
their retirement years. An efficient financial system
provides credit for borrowers at relatively low cost,
while providing a relatively high rate of return on
savings.

2)   reducing and sharing risk: The financial system
     reduces risk through diversification of financial
     investments made with pooled funds. The financial
     system also reduces risk by creating markets in which
     instruments of various degrees of risk can be bought
     from and sold to market participants with various
     degrees of risk preference. For example, futures and
     options are very useful financial instruments for
     transferring risk among hedgers and speculators.

3)   allocating savings to its highest valued uses: In
     financial markets, those buyers who most highly value
     obtaining financing purchase savings through financial
     intermediaries at the market interest rate (i.e., the
     price of credit) from those sellers who least value it.
     Therefore, financial markets facilitate the allocation
     of savings to its highest valued uses.

4)   providing liquidity: Money is the most liquid asset.
     Using money significantly reduces the costs of trading
     other assets and the costs of saving income for future
     use. The financial system creates a market in many
     different financial debt and equity instruments.
     Increases in the number of market participants and in
     the volume of trade increases the liquidity of these
     instruments, which means the transaction costs of
     trading them quickly for money is significantly
     reduced. This effectively creates income. For
     example, a decline in the transaction costs of buying a
     diversified portfolio of money market assets enables
     more people to buy these assets for a given holding
     period; by buying them, they earn a higher risk-
     adjusted return than they would earn with money,
     thereby increasing their income.

d)   Four industries that compete in financial markets are:
     banks, thrifts, insurance companies, and mutual funds.
     Others include: pension funds and finance companies.

e)   Hedgers and speculators differ in their risk-orientation.
     Hedgers want to reduce risk, whereas speculators want to
     increase risk. Although hedgers have to pay something to buy
     an instrument that effectively reduces their risk, and
     speculators have to pay something to buy an instrument that
     effectively increases their risk, both market participants
     expect to profit by these financial transactions.

2.   **Saving, investment, and financial intermediation**

a)   Savers supply funds to financial intermediaries to smooth
consumption, reduce risk, obtain higher interest income, and
hold their accumulated savings in some portfolio assets with
varying degrees of liquidity. In brief, savers use
financial intermediaries as an income-maximizing strategy
for managing their savings.

b)   Investors demand funds from financial intermediaries to
smooth consumption, reduce risk, obtain credit at relatively
low interest rates, and increase the liquidity of their ebt.
In brief, it is an income-maximizing strategy; they borrow
from financial intermediaries to obtain the credit they want
at the lowest possible risk-adjusted cost.

c)   Banks issue deposits and insurance companies issue insurance
policies. Deposits and insurance policies are liabilities
of these financial firms. Firms in these industries sell
these instruments to attract savings from households, firms,
governments, and foreigners. Banks use deposits to buy
loans. Insurance companies use insurance premiums to buy
corporate stocks. Loans and corporate stocks are examples
of assets these firms buy with their available funds. Both
firms bid for those assets that earn the highest expected
risk-adjusted, real, after-tax rate of return over some
holding period, and for those that satisfy their liquidity
needs. In brief, firms in all financial industries are
bidding for the available savings and assets in the market.
However, this competition among firms is not perfect
competition for all instruments; this means that they cannot
issue the same set of liabilities and cannot buy the same
set of assets. Banks cannot sell insurance and they cannot
buy corporate stocks. Insurance companies cannot sell
deposits and cannot make bank loans.

d)   Asymmetric information is the absence of symmetry in
information among parties to a transaction. Under
conditions of asymmetric information, borrowers have more
information than do lenders about how they intend to use the
funds loaned, how creditworthy they are as borrowers, and
how likely it is that they will repay the loan fully on
time. Financial intermediaries help to reduce this
difference in information between ultimate savers and
ultimate borrowers because they are experts at gathering and
analyzing information regarding these lending criteria.
Despite their skills, banks may be unable to eliminate all
asymmetric information efficiently; this suggests that there
is an economically efficient residual degree of asymmetric
information in financial markets. Under conditions of
asymmetric information and excess demand for funds at the
prevailing interest rate, banks will ration credit. Banks

ration credit in order to pick the relatively low-risk borrowers from its pool of potential borrowers.

e)   A credit crunch is a decline in the availability of bank lending and, therefore, lending in general. There are many potential causes of credit crunches; they may arise from some nonpolicy shock or from some policy shock. For example, the Federal Reserve's Regulation Q interest rate ceilings on bank deposits created several credit crunches in the 1960s and 1970s before it was dropped. A credit crunch can create a recession by reducing the availability of credit to investors, causing desired investment spending to decline, which causes the demand for goods to decline, which causes output to decline in the Keynesian model and extended classical model. A significant decline in output is a recession.

3.   **Instability in banking**

a)   Widespread operating losses, a high rate of bank failure, bank runs, and banking panics all identify instability in banking.

b)   No. The economy has suffered short-run periods of instability throughout its history. The Federal Reserve was created by the Federal Reserve Act of 1913 to eliminate instability in banking. Unfortunately, the greatest banking crisis in U.S. history occurred in the Great Depression in the early 1930s.

c)   The Fed can help to reduce banking panics. As a regulator, it attempts to issue regulations that promote the efficiency and stability of the banking system. To the extent that the regulations achieve their desired goals, they will have prevented the onset of banking panics. Prevention may be the best cure. As a lender of last resort, the Fed can provide liquidity to banks that face bank runs. This will enable the banks to satisfy depositors' demands for withdrawals. As long as depositors are confident that they can withdraw their deposits on demand, they will choose not to withdraw an unexpectedly high amount. Indirectly, the lender of last resort function of the Fed ensures depositors that banks will be able to meet their withdrawal demands. Therefore, it reduces the need for bank runs, and reduces bank runs. Without bank runs, there are no banking panics.

d)   FDIC is Federal government insurance on bank deposits. Currently, it insures up to $100,000 per account. Deposit insurance guarantees depositors that they will be able to get their deposits back from a bank even if if fails. By eliminating the fear that banks will lose their money, deposit insurance eliminates the reason for bank runs, eliminates bank runs, and eliminates banking panics.

e) Without offering a substantial two-handed argument (i.e.,
    on the one hand, but on the other hand), we cannot conclude
    that banking deregulation in the early 1980s, which followed
    significant regulatory changes in previous decades, directly
    caused the very high rate of bank failure that began in the
    mid-1980s and that has been increasing since then. However,
    the high correlation of the two events suggests the
    possibility of causality. Therefore, it is useful to
    consider reversing some of the earlier reforms or offsetting
    the effects of earlier reforms with new reforms. It is
    worth noting that the existence of instability suggests a
    need for action to correct the causes, before losses lead to
    runs, which lead to panics. On the other hand, many
    economists believe that there are too many banks; this
    suggests that a high rate of bank failure is desirable at
    this time. The inability of the FDIC to cover increasing
    losses in 1991 does suggest, however, that these bank
    failures are costly.

4. Instability in the stock market

a) A financial crisis is characterized by a significant decline
    in stock prices. It is also characterized by a banking
    crisis, as described previously. Usually, many firms fail
    in the economy.

b) The efficient markets hypothesis is that market prices,
    including stock prices, are unbiased estimates of the
    fundamental values of assets. In part, this means that the
    price of a share of stock equals the expected present value
    of the future income that stock will generate in the form of
    dividends and capital gains.

c) No. The efficient markets hypothesis cannot predict
    nor explain financial crises, because these events are not
    efficient. In efficient financial markets, only small
    continuous changes in market prices occur; no opportunities
    exist for incurring large, unexpected losses or profits.

d) The bubbles explanation is that stock prices rise because
    market participants expect them to rise, even though there
    is no rational explanation for this expectation, except
    possibly that everyone seems to have the same expectation.
    The fads explanation is that investors' expectations swing
    wildly from optimism to pessimism and that investors'
    expectations are mutually interdependent, so that they
    change their expectations in herdlike fashion, and create
    large swings in stock prices.

e) Two proposals for reforming the stock market are: raise
    margin requirements and eliminate program trading. The
    proposal to raise margin requirements is an old proposal
    that is already in force. The only question is whether it

would be useful to raise the margin requirement further than
it has already been raised. It would reduce borrowing in
the stock market, but those who want to borrow could borrow
in other markets and bring the borrowed funds to the stock
market to buy their stocks. The proposal to eliminate
program trading has been accepted by some Wall Street firms.
The idea here is to reduce the linkages of different kinds
of trading. However, computers only make the trading
faster, which is usually efficient. Computers do not devise
trading strategies of financial firms.

5.   **The S&L Crisis**

a)   Economists disagree in evaluating the costs and benefits of
the S&L crisis, which leads them to disagree about whether
or not to call it a crisis. The event meets the criteria we
have defined above as conditions indicating a crisis. In
addition, the general public and government policymakers
have responded to this event as if it were a crisis; this
response further suggests that it is a crisis. In addition,
as of January 1992 it is not yet over.

b)   Two causes of the S&L crisis are deregulation in the early
1980s for banking and thrifts, and deposit insurance.
Deregulation significantly increased competition among
thrifts and between banks and thrifts. Although an increase
in competition has net economic benefits in the long run, it
creates a short-run adjustment period in which the
relatively high-cost firms are forced out of the market
(e.g., fail). Deposit insurance enabled nearly insolvent
S&Ls to increase the riskiness of their portfolio of assets,
and a slowdown in economic growth led to high losses. These
losses were sufficient to cause many S&Ls to fail,
especially because their capital-asset ratios were initially
low.

c)   The efficient markets hypothesis cannot explain this crisis,
because crises are not efficient. Bubbles and fads may
partially explain it, but the particular institutional
conditions and regulatory provisions constraining S&Ls
(e.g., low capital-asset ratios, flat-rate deposit
insurance, relaxed regulatory supervision, relaxed
accounting standards) and changes in these regulations also
contributed to this crisis.

d)   Two proposed solutions include: letting S&Ls establish
branches in diversified geographic markets and raise capital
requirements.

e)   Diversification reduces risk, but allowing other financial
institutions to enter each other's local market also creates
short-run adjustment problems, including an increased
failure rate. Higher capital requirements makes S&L

managers less risk oriented, but regulators could create a credit crunch if they demand that capital requirements be raised too quickly.